A Practical Guide to Delivering Personalisation

of related interest

Mental Health, Service User Involvement and Recovery
Edited by Jenny Weinstein
ISBN 978 1 84310 688 3
eISBN 978 0 85700 212 9

Person Centred Planning and Care Management with People with Learning Disabilities
Edited by Paul Cambridge and Steven Carnaby
ISBN 978 1 84310 131 4
eISBN 978 1 84642 140 2

Person-Centred Dementia Care
Making Services Better
Dawn Brooker
ISBN 978 1 84310 337 0
eISBN 978 1 84642 588 2
Bradford Dementia Group Good Practice Guides series

Enriched Care Planning for People with Dementia
A Good Practice Guide to Delivering Person-Centred Care
Hazel May, Paul Edwards and Dawn Brooker
ISBN 978 1 84310 405 6
eISBN 978 1 84642 960 6
Bradford Dementia Group Good Practice Guides series

Hearing the Person with Dementia
Person-Centred Approaches to Communication for Families and Caregivers
Bernie McCarthy
ISBN 978 1 84905 186 6
eISBN 978 0 85700 499 4

Rights, Risk and Restraint-Free Care of Older People
Person-Centred Approaches in Health and Social Care
Edited by Rhidian Hughes
Foreword by Baroness Greengross
ISBN 978 1 84310 958 7
eISBN 978 0 85700 222 8

Co-Production and Personalisation in Social Care
Changing Relationships in the Provision of Social Care
Edited by Susan Hunter and Pete Ritchie
ISBN 978 1 84310 558 9
eISBN 978 1 84642 721 3
Service User Involvement series

Reaching the Hard to Reach in Supported Housing
Helen Brafield and Terry Eckersley
ISBN 978 1 84310 343 1
eISBN 978 1 84642 745 9

A Practical Guide to Delivering Personalisation

Person-Centred Practice in Health and Social Care

HELEN SANDERSON AND JAIMEE LEWIS

Jessica Kingsley *Publishers*
London and Philadelphia

Extract from Lovett 1996 on p.93 is reproduced by permission of Herb Lovett.

Quotation from Marianne Selby-Boothroyd on p.119 is reproduced by permission of Marianne Selby-Boothroyd.

The 'Chance of Positive Change' diagram from O'Brien, Pearpoint and Kahn 2010 on p.127 is adapted by permission of John O'Brien and Jack Pearpoint – www.inclusion.com.

Extract from Social Care Institute for Excellence 2010 on p.222 is reproduced by permission of the Social Care Institute for Excellence.

First published in 2012
by Jessica Kingsley Publishers
73 Collier Street
London N1 9BE, UK
and
400 Market Street, Suite 400
Philadelphia, PA 19106, USA

www.jkp.com

Copyright © Helen Sanderson and Jaimee Lewis 2012

Library of Congress Cataloging in Publication Data
Sanderson, Helen, 1965-
  A practical guide to delivering personalisation : person-centred practice in
health and social care / Helen Sanderson and Jaimee Lewis.
      p. cm.
  Includes bibliographical references and index.
  ISBN 978-1-84905-194-1 (alk. paper)
  1. Integrative medicine. 2. Patients--Care. 3. Medical social work--
Administration. I. Lewis, Jaimee, 1979- II. Title.
  R733.S56 2011
  610--dc23
                              2011024046
British Library Cataloguing in Publication Data
A CIP catalogue record for this book is available from the British Library

ISBN 978 1 84905 194 1
eISBN 978 0 85700 422 2

Printed and bound in Great Britain

Contents

Acknowledgements

The learning shared in this book has been developed in partnership with an international community around person-centred practices. We are particularly grateful to: Michael Smull and the Learning Community for Person-Centred Practices, who developed many of the person-centred thinking tools shared in this book; Jenny Pitts for her work with us on the New Reablement Journey; Max Neill for his work with us on risk; Helen Bowers and Gill Bailey for their work with us on person-centred thinking and older people; and John O'Brien for his reflections and insights.

Thank you to Gill Bailey, Michelle Livesley, Jane Bayley, Amanda George, Julie Malette, Deb Watson, Alison Short, Charlotte Sweeney, Julie Lunt, Jo Harvey, Suzie Franklin, Tricia Nicholl, Ruth Gorman, Julia Winter, Sally Percival, David and Wendy Blundell, Jo Francis, Tracy Meyerhoff, Laura Wigley, Neil Woodhead, David Coyle, Ian and Elizabeth Hart, Ben and Charlotte Morse, Marianne Selby-Boothroyd and everyone who shared stories and examples.

For their help in reviewing earlier drafts and support we are grateful to Martin Routledge, Zoe Porter, Shahana Ramsden, Catherine Wilton, Kerry Buckley, Sue Soper, Julie Barclay, Natalie Valios, Andy Gitsham and Damian Walne.

The diagrams in this book were developed by Julie Barclay.

Introduction

> Personalisation to me is about enabling me to do the things that I took for granted for so long. It's only recognising something essential in human life – which is that everyone is an individual, like it or lump it.
>
> *Stephen, an individual receiving support[1]*

> When I first trained as a psychiatric nurse, we would dictate what somebody would require from their morning medication right the way through to what time they went to bed... And we couldn't understand why people weren't responding (well) to that... That's one of the reasons why personalisation is so important and that it's led by the individual. All we are is somebody to help facilitate that, rather than somebody who's dictating what should happen.
>
> *Tracey, a social worker[2]*

This book will show you what true 'personalisation' is and will explore and describe the contribution person-centred practice can make to delivering it.

Personalisation means more than just personal budgets – it means people having real choice and control over their support on a day-to-day basis. Handing over financial control – as required by current national policy[3] – is crucial, but so, too, is social workers, support workers, health professionals and others working in a way that sees people as individuals and equal partners; treats people, their families and carers with respect; and does not make assumptions about who people are or what they might want to do, based on labels or lifestyles.

To deliver personalised services, we need to know what is important to a person; how to best support them; the way they communicate and make decisions; and how we are doing in delivering personalised services – what is working and not working?

This book will show you how to deliver personalisation and self-directed support through person-centred practice. It recognises that staff have a key contribution to make in changing people's lives by adapting and improving the way support is provided. This enables people to take greater control in developing arrangements that make sense to them, their families and carers – the reason most social workers and other professionals enter the profession in the first place.

We are doing this not because the government says we should (though it does help, as we'll explore in Chapter 1) but because, from a human perspective, we would argue it is the right thing to do. Delivering personalisation through person-centred practice supports the work of the disabled people's movement, which has fought – and continues to fight – for the right to lead the full and independent lives that others can sometimes take for granted.

We passionately believe that person-centred practice has a strong role to play in helping people be heard, finding solutions and changing people's lives, while also changing the culture of the organisations that provide care and support services.

Simple, effective and evidence-based practice – including person-centred thinking, person-centred reviews, person-centred planning and support planning – are proven ways to do this.[4]

'Person-centred thinking' refers to a range of practical tools and skills that staff can use on a day-to-day basis to deliver more personalised services. 'Person-centred reviews' are a way to transform and replace the statutory required reviews in services, to create person-centred actions. 'Person-centred planning' refers to processes for planning around an individual, which focus on creating a positive future and being part of a community. 'Support planning' is a way for individuals to describe what they want to change about their life and how they will use their personal budget to do so.

We show how these practices help people achieve the outcomes they want, and potentially avoid unnecessary dependence on support in the future.

The current vision for health and adult social care requires that person-centred practice and self-directed support become mainstream activities in order to deliver personalisation.[5, 6] But there is a risk of being distracted from this goal in the context of the difficult economic climate. We have written this book to show that it can be done, even at a time when the sector faces arguably its greatest financial and resource challenge in a generation.

The journey towards personalisation of support for disabled and older people – and people with complex needs or long-term health conditions – must continue for the sake of their independence. It is part of a wider shift in our society towards fully including all people as equal citizens. This is long overdue, has had to be fought for, and is far from complete.[7]

We want to show that personalisation can happen across all types of service or support, regardless of the financial resources available, because it focuses more on changing the way people think about 'power' and acknowledges the contributions that both individuals and communities make to supporting people.

This book is divided into four parts, based on the building blocks required to deliver personalisation through person-centred practice.

Part I, 'Person-Centred Practice: Why This, Why Now?', is a detailed introduction. Chapter 1 looks at the current context for delivering personalisation and why person-centred practice can make a contribution. It briefly describes the challenges faced by the sector, the current policy landscape and recent activity in support of the agenda. Chapter 2 provides a historic overview of person-centred thinking and planning, while Chapter 3 discusses the values and principles on which they are based.

Part II, 'Person-Centred Thinking', demonstrates how to learn and understand the balance between what is important to and for a person (Chapter 4) and describes the foundation of person-centred thinking and planning as a range of simple and practical person-centred thinking tools (Chapters 5–8). These can be used to create day-to-day change for people using services, as well as building a person-centred plan or support plan. Each tool is described with examples. Chapter 9 describes how to decide which person-centred thinking tool to use and what is involved in growing a detailed person-centred description.

Part III, 'Person-Centred Reviews and Person-Centred Planning', explains the review process (Chapter 10) and how it is different to traditional reviews in different settings, including the care programme approach (CPA) in mental health services (Chapter 11). Person-centred planning and support planning are described in Chapters 12 and 13.

Part IV, 'Person-Centred Thinking from Prevention to End of Life', looks at the important contribution of person-centred practice to the journey of support through adulthood: from prevention and well-being (Chapter 14), helping people self-manage long-term health conditions (Chapter 15) and recovery (Chapter 16), to reablement (Chapter 17), domiciliary and residential care (Chapter 18) and end-of-life care (Chapter 19). Using a person-centred approach to risk is the focus of Chapter 20.

This book builds on the work of an international learning community, and specifically brings together and updates previous work developed by Helen Sanderson with Michael Smull, Pete Ritchie and colleagues in their books:

- *People, Plans and Possibilities: Exploring Person Centred Planning* (1997)[8]

- *People, Plans and Practicalities: Achieving Change Through Person-Centred Planning* (2003)[9]

- *Essential Lifestyle Planning for Everyone* (2005)[10]

- *Personalisation Through Person-Centred Planning* (2010),[11] guidance published for the Department of Health's 'Putting people first' programme.

A note about how this book was written

This book focuses on how person-centred practice can be used across all services – including mental health and other services for people with long-term conditions or those approaching the end of their lives – by staff (in whatever role) supporting people in health and social care (and 'prevention'). We use the term 'staff' to include any paid staff or professional role that helps disabled and older people, their families and carers. In this book the use of 'he' and 'she' is alternated by chapter when referring to an unspecified person. This is done for ease of reference only, and is not intended to reflect any gender bias.

When writing, we have tried to include quotes and stories to bring person-centred practice to life and show what good practice looks like. The examples we share are from a wide range of people in different situations, with people telling their own story, or staff talking about how they have used different approaches. Earlier writing on person-centred planning (for example, *People, Plans and Possibilities*[12]) shared stories from the lives of people with learning disabilities. We have intentionally tried to balance this with stories and examples from people with long-term conditions, older people and people who use mental health services. Some people you will meet several times: James, who is managing a long-term condition; Jennie, a young woman with a personal budget who has autism, and her mum, Suzie; Madge, who is thinking about the end of her life; and Sandra who describes herself as being in recovery. Although the focus of this book is on delivering personalised services through using person-centred practice, person-centred thinking and planning are for everyone, regardless of whether you are currently receiving a service or not, so the examples also include people who don't receive services, families and carers. So you will meet Michelle, who planned with her dad around his future; Helen, who is part of a circle of support; and Jaimee, who has used person-centred thinking to improve her well-being.

This book does not cover how person-centred practice is used by managers or throughout organisations (this is covered by the companion book *Creating Person-Centred Organisations*). Nor do we describe an implementation strategy for person-centred practice. This is explored in the 2010 Department of Health guidance on person-centred practice.[13]

A final message before you get started

Why should you make the effort with person-centred practice? There are a number of reasons. Teaching and supporting the use of person-centred thinking skills will mean that it is more likely that people's person-centred plans and support plans will be used and acted on and that their lives will improve. This is especially important when people have been given a personal budget, as great support planning is rooted in person-centred practice. We will spend the rest of the book explaining what this means, starting with our understanding of the current policy context, history of person-centred practice, and the underpinning values and principles.

Ultimately, by the end of this book, you will know how you can use person-centred practice to help people:

- have more positive control over their lives

- have more of what is important to them

- have a better balance between what is 'important to' and what is 'important for' them

- become more connected with their communities

- develop and move towards their own dreams.

Part I

Person-Centred Practice

Why This, Why Now?

Never doubt that a small group of thoughtful citizens can change the world. Indeed, it is the only thing that ever has.

Margaret Mead

Personalisation means, for me, that I stay living in my own home. I want to be able to access every kind of public transport. I guess it's really about the ordinary, to be honest. It's about what people choose to do and what I choose to do is not very different from other people.

Anne, an older person living at home[14]

This part is an introduction to person-centred practice and looks at the current context for delivering personalisation and why person-centred practice can make a contribution (Chapter 1), with a brief description of the current policy landscape and some of the challenges faced by the social care sector. Chapter 2 provides a brief history of how person-centred thinking and planning have developed and evolved over time, while Chapters 3 discusses the values and principles on which they are based.

Chapter 1

Context

Why Person-Centred Practice Is Important Now

> We live in challenging times, but we also have real opportunities to design and co-produce care and support services which are fit for the 21st century.
>
> *Dame Philippa Russell, veteran disability rights activist and chair of the UK government's Standing Commission on Carers*[15]

This chapter briefly outlines how personalisation started with the disability movement and moved to the mainstream health and social care policy agenda. It provides an abridged policy timeline; highlights some of the recent challenges and positive developments; and introduces the contribution person-centred practice can make in delivering personalisation.

Why this? Why now?

The current vision for health and adult social care in England requires 'individuals, not institutions' to take control of their support. It calls for all eligible disabled and older people[16] as well as people with long-term health conditions or who are approaching the end of their life[17] to have access to direct payments or personal budgets. This hands financial control of the support available over to people, their families and carers so that they have maximum flexibility in deciding how they can achieve their desired life outcomes. So that people are truly empowered to do this, person-centred practice and self-directed support should become mainstream activities[18,19] in personalising health and social care.

But how did this become mainstream government policy and why do we think person-centred practice is central to its delivery? Let's start by considering Anita and Trevor's story:[20]

Anita and Trevor's story

Anita, 56, has Huntingdon's Disease and is cared for by her husband Trevor. Life changed dramatically for both of them with Anita's diagnosis. According to Trevor, the effects were hard to imagine. 'We used to go all over – theatre, go out to the cinema and really enjoy life. Then when the Huntingdon's came on it was misdiagnosed for years. It was just so bad. I had to give my job up five years ago because she...couldn't eat, couldn't swallow. She was a skeleton. I was physically and mentally exhausted. I was ready to end it all.'

Trevor was committed to caring for Anita at home, but he struggled to cope. Living only on savings and his carer's allowance and without significant outside help, something had to change.

'...It was terrifying. Later on in the Huntingdon's she was bedbound; she was laid in bed and wouldn't get up, she wouldn't speak. All she ever said from morning to night was one sentence: "Can I have a nap?" Nothing else; nobody seemed to care. Nobody bothered and she was in hospital twice with pneumonia.'

At that time, Anita was also suffering from a form of mood disorder; she was quite depressed and anxious.

Debbie, the community matron within the long-term conditions team in Hull, started working with Anita and Trevor about three years ago. 'Previous support had been offered... traditional things like day centres and all that type of thing, but had not really been suitable... I think it had been suggested at one time that Anita may need to go into a nursing home, which she absolutely didn't want to and neither did Trevor.'

Debbie spoke to them both about what kind of support would make a difference for them. 'Anita and Trevor said that they would like to get a couple of people to help Anita go out and do activities such as swimming and go to the theatre.'

Trevor said it was important that they had help from regular people who Anita knows and trusts: 'She can be quite aggressive, so you (need to) know her moods and when they're going to change. It's just nice, thinking it's more comfortable for her knowing the same person, certainly for the likes of personal care...if she sees a familiar face it's a bit more soothing for her.'

Debbie discussed the idea of a personal health budget with Anita and Trevor. They were able to choose the best support in terms of Anita's quality of life. 'Care at home is the right choice for us because it actually gives my wife a quality of life and something to focus on. How can I put it? It's a far cheaper treatment than expensive drugs that would do no good whatsoever.'

Over the past couple of years, they have got to know two carers really well, so it means that they don't have lots of different people coming into their lives and into the house and then disappearing. One of the carers, Lizzie, takes Anita out regularly to the theatre and helps with activities such as painting her nails and going swimming.

Debbie says supporting Anita in this way has made a massive change to the couple's life. 'Anita's like a different person. She initiates conversation more, she's very bright, and she's much more orientated than she was. Trevor is much less stressed; he's more relaxed and happy... It gives him a mental break, so he can go out...and have a bit of freedom to do what he wants to do.'

The push for 'personalisation' has come from disabled people, their families and their progressive allies in public services. For decades now, they have been fighting for independent living and full citizenship. People increasingly want to use the resources available for their support – whether they are publicly or privately funded – in a way that is most meaningful for them, rather than the state or the organisation providing a 'one size fits all' approach. Anita and Trevor's story demonstrates this and the crucial need to listen to what people want. They are their own best experts in how to be supported and recognising this is a key trait of person-centred practice.

Organisations and individuals working with people who need support are starting to understand that to deliver personalisation, there must be root and branch changes to policies, practice and culture. This increased awareness has been supported by the disabled people's movement – the introduction of direct payments legislation in the mid-1990s was one of their key achievements – but also by the work of successive UK governments from both sides of the political spectrum. Some of the recent key policies have included:

- *Our Health, Our Care, Our Say* (2005)[21] – a Department of Health response to consultation with disabled and older people, their families and carers who called for more choice and control over their support. The White Paper announced that individual budgets would be piloted in 13 councils across England from 2006–08, building on the pioneering work of the charity In Control.

- The cross-government concordat *Putting People First: A Shared Vision and Commitment to the Transformation of Adult Social Care* (2007).[22] Councils in England received a share of the £520 million transformation reform grant over three years (2008–11) to start making the necessary changes to their systems, service, practice and cultures. This heralded the start of personalisation's journey to mainstream government policy. Key elements like prevention, choice and control, universal services and social capital increasingly became part of the narrative of social care.

- The NHS *Next Stage Review High Quality Care for All* (2008),[23] which made the commitment for everyone with a long-term condition to have a personalised care plan. It also announced the pilot of personal health budgets.

- *The Coalition: Our Programme for Government* (2010)[24] which included a specific commitment to put patients in charge of making decisions about their care, including control of their health records, as well as extending the greater roll-out of personal budgets to give people and their carers more control and purchasing power. The Comprehensive Spending Review[25] that same year also committed to extending personal budgets for long-term health conditions.

- The new vision for adult social care, *Capable Communities and Active Citizens* (2010),[26] with its renewed focus on personalisation.

- the sector-wide agreement *Think Local, Act Personal* (2011)[27] which brought together over 30 health and social care organisations to set out their continued commitment to transforming adult social care, following on from the conclusion of the 'Putting people first' programme.

- The *Right to Control* pilot (2010)[28] where seven 'trailblazer' councils are working with the Office for Disability Issues and Jobcentre Plus for up to two years to give disabled adults the right to combine the support they receive from six different sources and to decide how best to spend the funding to meet their needs.

This list is by no means comprehensive, but demonstrates building momentum and strong, current political consensus.

> The overall aim is to secure a shift to a position where as many people as possible are enabled to stay healthy and actively involved in their communities for longer and delaying or avoiding the need for targeted services. Those who do need such help, however, should have maximum control over this, with the information, means (financial and practical) and confidence to make it a reality.[29]

Despite the political consensus, there have been many challenges to the implementation of personalisation, particularly around winning the hearts and minds of those involved in the sector. On the one hand, there is confidence that full-scale transformation is worth the effort and energy required because the agenda is based on what disabled and older people increasingly say they want, and is part of a wider societal shift towards full inclusion of disabled and older people in society. But on the flip side – and despite the good will and efforts of many people working in public services – there are still many services that have struggled to escape their institutional roots. 'Combining person-centred approaches with the power of flexible self-directed services through individual budgets could be a potent force for empowerment'.[30] Various reports relating to personalisation in health and social care have highlighted some of the positive developments in implementing personalisation.

The final report of the individual budgets pilot (2008)[31] showed that overall, in comparison with traditional services, individual budgets not only had the potential to be more cost effective than standard care and support arrangements, but that those with individual budgets were more likely to report they felt in control of their daily lives and the support they accessed as well as better overall social care outcomes. There were significant improvements in outcomes for people with mental health problems – they reported a higher quality of life – and younger physically disabled people who reported a higher quality of care and greater opportunity to build support networks. People with learning disabilities were more likely to feel a greater degree of choice and control in their lives. And while the initial findings for older people were less positive, it was generally recognised that it would take more time and support for older people to develop the confidence to assume greater control.

> Almost half of those who accepted the offer of an individual budget…described how their aspirations had changed as a result, in terms of living a fuller life, being 'less of a burden' on their families, and having greater control and independence. They were also more likely than other holders to report satisfaction with the support planning process and financial arrangements.[32]

This was reinforced by the positive results of the carers' study undertaken in parallel – which showed encouraging results relating to older people and their family carers, including the finding that individual budgets were significantly associated with positive impacts on carers' reported quality of life.[33] Evidence collected in the three years since that report suggests that disabled and older people have said personal budgets offer them more independence, choice and control[34] and improve the quality of care they receive or of enabling them to stay living in their own homes.[35] 'As well as providing care, personal budgets can also help older people regain independence, feel less socially isolated, and address the impact on the caring relationship with a partner or family member.'[36]

Within health services, Vidhya Alakeson argued in her report *Putting Patients in Control: The Case for Extending Self-Direction into the NHS*[37] that for personal health budgets to succeed there needs to be a shift in the way in which care is planned:

> The most effective spending plans tend to be the outcome of a person-centred planning process. This is different from most care planning processes in two important respects. First, it is driven by the patient and, therefore, engages his or her experience, expertise and creativity in health improvement far more than professionally dominated processes. Second, it looks at a patient's wider health and life goals rather than focusing exclusively on a diagnosis. Many of the causes of poor health or barriers to effective treatment are not clinical or even health-related and are, therefore, more likely to be captured by starting with the person rather than their care.[38]

Alakeson says that when a person experiences a long-term health condition, there are four dimensions to the care they would receive: clinical condition, educational need, psychological and behavioural issues and lifestyle and social issues.[39] In the example of someone with diabetes, Alakeson argues that they would be able to self-direct their own care and take control of the non-clinical areas because they can express personal preferences about how to achieve goals like weight loss. She cites an example where a person could prefer to join Weight Watchers or purchase a gym membership, rather than being sent to a hospital-based nutritionist, with progress monitored through regular visits to the GP.

Meanwhile, the second interim report into the progress of the personal health budgets pilot, which is scheduled to roll out from October 2012, described the 'overwhelming view that personal health budgets would have a positive impact on both budget holders and carers'.[40] This was attributed to people's perceptions of increased choice and control over, and flexible and creative use of, services; increased self-confidence, self-esteem and sense of purpose and improved relations between them and their health practitioners because they felt that their views were being listened to.

Many working at the centre of the personalisation agenda feel the momentum has reached a 'tipping point'. Modest numbers of people receiving direct payments are becoming big numbers of people getting a personal budget (many as direct payments), and there is a clear, driving idea that person-centred practice is central to how things need to be. At a leadership level, decision makers are recognising that we have to move away from the institutional roots of public services. Places on the ground are recognising that people have a contribution to make, while people themselves are just starting to find their own power.

There are, however, constant reminders about the scale of the challenges still to be faced and the cultural shift required in delivering personalised supports.

There are many practical and technical obstacles to real personalisation, especially given the pace of change required, as well as understandable challenges from professional and other groups who are sceptical about change associated with government policy. On the health side, work on personalisation in the NHS is at a relatively early stage and has a long way to go to be recognised as a vital part of the way the health service supports people to live well with their health conditions.

There is also the sudden reality of serious budget cuts with which to contend. At the time of writing, there are increasing concerns raised by professionals and service users alike that personalisation is at risk of derailment by the debate on the use of public resources. The strong financial pressure on councils, government bodies, charities and private sector providers, and proposed reforms set out in *Liberating the NHS: Legislative Framework and Next Steps*,[41] means that there is a risk that personalisation will be pushed to one side under the guise of 'cuts', or that it is implemented in a way that isn't true to the core principles of increasing choice and control for people.

How person-centred practice can help

So we need to ask, what is the strategy to get to a future where millions of people can benefit from personalisation? In social care, yet more needs to be done to avoid a situation where disabled and older people and their families feel that after so much progress, there is a risk that control over their support will diminish. More also needs to be done to support frontline staff in making the changes required. In the health service, there is the need to have a wider discussion with clinicians about the value that their expertise can play in helping someone to design their health support, and also the kind of skills that they can further develop to help people take more control and come up with solutions themselves.

This is where person-centred practice has a strong contribution to make – it is the 'how' to deliver choice and control for people and can make a genuine impact on improving and meeting people's desired outcomes. Person-centred practice enables staff to learn what matters to an individual; what good support looks like; and how an individual communicates their choices and makes decisions. It also helps staff think about their role in the person's life, and what they need to do on a day-by-day basis, to support people in the life which they want to lead. We'll explain more about person-centred practice – the simple, practical tools and processes that can unlock energy and creativity to start making these changes – in Part II. Meanwhile, in the next chapter, we set out a brief history of the disabled people's movement and the development of person-centred practice.

What is the problem person-centred planning is designed to solve? Person-centred planning is designed to overcome inertia – the tendency for things to continue in a straight line. For many disabled people the status quo is isolation, invisibility, and dependence. Their identity is defined by others, they live to other people's clocks, and their life is restricted by the absence of their own power or by the misuse of other people's power.

Pete Ritchie[42]

Chapter 2

The History of Person-Centred Planning and Thinking

> When people not used to speaking out are heard by people not used to listening then real change is made.
>
> *John O'Brien*[43]

This chapter looks at the key elements of the history of person-centred planning, which is one element of person-centred practice, as well as the continued emergence of person-centred thinking and person-centred reviews. We also share some of the evidence to support the idea that person-centred practice can make a significant contribution to the implementation of personalisation.

Person-centred planning has emerged from a continuing search by disabled people and their allies for better ways to include disabled people in society, resulting in new ways of thinking about the relationship between disabled people, society and services. Chapter 1 focused on some of the positive changes over recent years, but the truth remains that the culture of services still has some way to go to deliver support that meets people's wishes and aspirations for an independent life as equal citizens.

Person-centred thinking and planning is a way to connect fundamental beliefs about what people want with practical ways of making things happen for individuals. Here we describe the key ideas and practices that have contributed to the development of person-centred thinking and planning over the past three decades.[44] These developments have been the result of the work of an international learning community, with leadership from John O'Brien, Michael Smull, Suzie Burke-Harrison, Herb Lovett, Jack Pearpoint, Marsha Forest, Connie Lyle O'Brien, Beth Mount, Judith Snow, Lynda Khan and Jack Yates.

The social model of disability and the disability movement

Disability activists and people in the mental health survivor movement have consistently argued for a shift in the balance of power between disabled people and the services on which they rely. People have campaigned for 'choice and control': a shift in the focus of decision making to the person, from the professionals. Person-centred planning also seeks to shift the power to make decisions back to the person.

Disabled people in the USA and the UK developed their own theoretical framework for understanding disability and the role of disabled people in society. John Swain, Vic Finkelstein, Sally French and Mike Oliver[45] described disability as:

> Not a condition of the individual. The experiences of disabled people are of social restrictions in the world around them, not of being a person with a 'disabling condition'. This is not to say that individuals do not experience 'disability'; rather it is to assert that the individual's experience of disability is created in interaction with a physical and social world designed for non-disabled people.

The social model of disability locates disability in the interaction between the individual and the social and physical world. The job of services is not to fix the individual but to reduce the restrictions she faces and to support her in leading her own life. Person-centred planning works from the social model of disability because it places the emphasis on transforming the options available to the person, rather than on fixing or changing that person.

The introduction of direct payments as legislation, and the government's drive to ensure all eligible people have personal budgets, responds to this legitimate demand by allowing councils to give people money to buy their own services instead of providing services directly or arranging services on a person's behalf. Person-centred thinking and planning start with what is important to the person, and how she wants to use her personal budget to achieve this, rather than what services are available.

Normalisation and the five accomplishments

The principle of normalisation was developed initially by Bengt Nirje[46] and then by Wolf Wolfensberger[47] to argue that disabled people should have a position in society which is equal to – and valued by – non-disabled people. John O'Brien was one of Wolf Wolfensberger's early collaborators. In 1987, he and Connie Lyle O'Brien embarked on research in Seattle on what makes a good quality of life. Their Framework for Accomplishment[48] proposed five areas which are widely agreed to be important in shaping everyone's quality of life and where disabled people are likely to be disadvantaged by society. The framework argues that services should be judged by the extent to which, as a result of the service's work, people are:

- sharing ordinary places

- making choices

- developing abilities

- being treated with respect and having a valued social role

- growing in relationships.

Personal futures planning, developed by Beth Mount and John O'Brien and described in Chapter 12, is based explicitly on this framework.

The inclusion movement and institutional closure

Jack Pearpoint, Marsha Forest and Judith Snow built on the work of John O'Brien, John McKnight, Bob Perske and others to develop the theory and practice of inclusion. They developed the concept of 'gifts' to describe how difference and diversity create opportunities for interaction. They went further than the concepts of citizen advocacy and natural supports to shift attention from services to people, and from formal systems to intentional community building. Rather than settle for integrated education, they pioneered the notion of inclusive education – 'schools where all kids belong' – and inspired thousands of families around the world to dream.

Their work created and developed new ways for people to work together. Their own experience of friendship was the foundation for the idea of 'circles of support',[49] now an international movement supporting people's presence and participation in their community. MAPs (Making Action Plans) and PATH, the person-centred planning styles they developed with John O'Brien, and which we explain in Chapter 12, are processes for bringing people together to make change around a common cause.

Fundamental to inclusion is people living and being part of their communities. 'Essential lifestyle planning' began at the University of Maryland in 1989, where Michael Smull and Susan Burke-Harrison were asked to help people to return to their home communities from institutions and residential schools. In supporting people to move back into their communities, they recognised that the records kept on people gave no indication of who they really were and what was most important to them. All of the people involved had 'developmental disabilities' and because of 'challenging behaviours' had been labelled as 'not ready' for life in the community. It was discovered that these were people who could live successfully in their communities but who had been trapped by their labels and the 'reputations' they had acquired. The approach that was then developed was called 'essential lifestyle planning' (ELP).[50]

By 1995, the term 'person-centred planning' was commonly used to describe these efforts. Beth Mount[51] characterised the 'family resemblance' of these different methods and approaches into four themes:

- seeing people first rather than relating to diagnostic labels

- using ordinary language and images rather than professional jargon

- actively searching for a person's gifts and capacities in the context of community life

- strengthening the voice of the person and those who know the person best in accounting for her history, evaluating her present conditions in terms of valued experiences, and defining desirable changes in her life.

People, Plans and Possibilities (1997),[52] described how person-centred planning was starting to be used in the UK. At that time, the four main approaches to person-centred planning were ELP, 'personal futures planning', PATH and MAPs. Michael Smull, one of the originators of ELP, saw that change was most powerful when all staff were using person-centred thinking tools in their roles, rather than only relying on person-centred planning facilitators to create plans. Since then, the contribution of ELP has changed as it has been de-constructed into a range of person-centred thinking tools (described in Part II) and a person-centred review process (described in Part III). To really make a difference in someone's life – and to ensure that she has more choice and control – staff supporting her need to participate in an ongoing loop of listening, learning and action. The person-centred thinking tools are a way to do this – to keep learning and acting on what they learn. This information is recorded as a person-centred description of what is important to the person and how she wants to be supported. To deliver personalised services requires that people have a person-centred description of how they want to live, that staff act on every day. Person-centred reviews are a way to build person-centred descriptions; to analyse together what is working and not working; and to make decisions about how to change what is not working, and what else we need to learn.

Person-centred planning is evidence-based practice

By the turn of the century, person-centred thinking and planning was part of UK policy, initially in *Valuing People* (2001),[53] for people who have learning disabilities, and later for everyone, in *Putting People First*.[54] As John O'Brien and Connie Lyle O'Brien[55] said, this marked a turning point for the development of person-centred planning.

> It positions person-centred planning as one key tool for achieving a deep shift in a nation's culture and practice of services and defines a long term organisational change strategy to create a context in which person-centred planning can make sense...it is the best effort

that we know to think through the strategic implications of implementing person-centred planning.

At the same time as person-centred planning became embedded in policy, the Department of Health commissioned research into its effectiveness and implementation. In 2005, the Institute for Health Research, at Lancaster University, published the results of this research, detailing the impact of person-centred planning on the life experiences of people with learning disabilities, the associated costs and what factors impede or facilitate its introduction and effectiveness.[56] This demonstrated person-centred planning to be evidence-based practice:

> Very little change was apparent in people's lives prior to the introduction of person-centred planning. After the introduction of person-centred planning, significant positive changes were found in the areas of: social networks; contact with family; contact with friends; community based activities; scheduled day activities; and levels of choice.[57]

The research supports the current emphasis within health and social care policy on using person-centred thinking and planning to improve the life chances of people.

> Self-directed support should be available wherever people live, including in residential and nursing homes. Simple but powerful person-centred approaches to practice have been shown to work within such settings – without additional costs – helping people retain their dignity and stay connected to their families, friends and communities.[58]

This chapter has shown that person-centred thinking and planning is not just the latest 'fad'. It has emerged naturally from the most progressive movements in the field of disability in the last 30 years, bringing together important strands of policy and practice, particularly around the personalisation agenda. Person-centred planning has also evolved, with ELP changing to become a range of person-centred thinking tools and a person-centred review process. The next chapter looks at the values that underpin all person-centred practice.

Chapter 3

The Values and Principles Underpinning a Person-Centred Approach

Everybody in this world today needs support of one kind or another. People need support to go ahead and do things whether this support comes from a good friend, parents, a social worker, or guardian. There is no person so independent in the world that they don't need anybody. We all need support, but with that support, we don't want somebody coming in and taking over our lives.

Michael J. Kennedy[59]

All person-centred practices share a common set of values. This chapter briefly explains these beliefs and values, which are:

- independence and rights

- co-production, choice and control

- inclusive and competent communities.

Independence and rights

Independence is about disabled people, including older disabled people, having the same level of choice, control and freedom in their daily lives as any other person. It does not mean people doing things for themselves or living on their own, but having choice and control over the assistance needed to go about daily life and having equal access to housing, transport, mobility, health, employment, education and training opportunities:[60] 'It is important to recognise that anyone, whatever their level of impairment, can express preferences and therefore express choices about how these needs should be met.'

Current national policy says that everyone needs assistance or equipment of some kind. However, many people with physical and/or sensory impairments, learning disabilities, mental health support needs, long-term health conditions or who experience frailty associated with old age, have additional needs for assistance.

Professional effort has traditionally focused on people's impairments. The assessment process then analyses and quantifies the impairment and its impact on the person's ability to undertake a range of tasks, resulting in a description of the person in terms of what he cannot do – his deficits – rather than addressing disabling barriers like being unable to use public transport or to find employment, or finding the right support for a specific impairment or condition.

Disabled and older people are then channelled into different services depending on the category of their impairment – for example, by learning difficulty, sensory impairment or loss of mobility. The Independent Living Strategy[61] says that too often, these additional needs for assistance or equipment have been met in ways which do not give people choice and control. Instead, others decide on behalf of disabled people how assistance should be provided, leading to segregation and social exclusion.

Everyone, regardless of their level of impairment, can express preferences and choices about what is important to them (see Chapter 4 for more information). Person-centred thinking and planning ask, 'How do you want to live your life? What would make sense for you?' before looking at, 'How could we work with you to make this possible, given your particular situation and the things with which you need help?' It extends the range and depth of choice and control, both in the planning processes and the way services and supports are planned and organised.

Person-centred practice assumes that disabled people are ready to do whatever they want as long as they are adequately supported. The 'rehabilitation' approach tended to lock people into a 'readiness' trap: they could have more freedom only if they could master a set of skills and behaviours which professionals decided were essential for living and working 'in the community'. Through personalisation, this 'readiness model' is replaced with the 'support model' which acknowledges that everyone needs support and some people need more support than others.

> Real independence is nothing to do with cooking, cleaning and dressing oneself. If you ask me what is my experience of being independent, I would not automatically think about self-help skills but of being able to use my imagination to create fantasy, of enjoying music and drama, of relishing sensual pleasures and absorbing the natural life around me.
>
> John Corbett[62]

Co-production, choice and control

Choice and control are crucial because many disabled and older people are powerless: others control their lives, and they do not have direct ways of saying how to spend their time, what they eat, how they behave or even what they say. Person-centred practice works to redress this balance of power by processes that are designed to shift control towards the person. This means sharing power differently and moving away from the 'professional gift model'[63] where the power and the resources are held by professionals. This shift of power is seen in co-production.

> Co-production means delivering public services in an equal and reciprocal relationship between professionals, people using services, their families and their neighbours. Where activities are co-produced in this way, both services and neighbourhoods became far more effective agents of change.[64]

FOCUS ON CAPACITY

> Co-production is an assets-based approach which starts first and foremost with people's energy, skills, interests, knowledge and life experience.
>
> Lucie Stevens[65]

Co-production begins with an appreciation and respect for people's capacities, gifts and skills. Co-production and person-centred practice start from the position that people are assets who are equal and essential partners in their own support, treatment and recovery, as well as in designing and delivering services. This is different to the deficiency-based perspective of people, where people are seen in terms of their labels, disability or illness first, with a focus on what they cannot do and how to fix that.

> The deficiency-led assessment is so deeply entrenched in policies, procedures and resource allocating models in health and social care that it can both diminish the humanity of its 'clients' and undermine their ability to make a contribution both to their own welfare and to the wider community. Often families and individuals feel 'assessed to death', yet discover that this leads to no practical help at all or to the allocation of a service which at best approximates the help required. This can be profoundly disempowering.[66]

Person-centred planning focuses immediately on the positive aspects of a person's life rather than assessing what they cannot do. Focusing on the person's strengths, passions, interests and the things that others like and admire about them provides a tremendous starting point for a co-productive relationship.[67] 'Focusing on the things people can do and teasing out their passions and interests is often the key to unlocking the potential for effective recovery.'[68]

Identifying people's assets is also known as 'social capital', and in mental health and drug services, it is described as an important part of 'recovery capital'. Effective treatment and recovery is reliant on the process of self-directed support – working with people to identify what it is they want and need to do to live the lives they want – while utilising all the relationships and networks of support they have available to them. This includes the strengths, knowledge, talents and resilience that people bring to bear on their own situations, and using these to help shift their lives to a more positive place. Focusing on capacities and helping to draw out characteristics and talents is central to person-centred philosophy and approaches. 'People are best understood in terms of their contributions, personal interests, and gifts. The way a community regards people with disabilities typically inhibits the discovery and expression of a person's contributions to the common good.'[69]

Co-production is underpinned by a belief that disabled people, older people and their families are in the best position to determine their own needs and goals, and to plan for the future, to whatever extent they want to.

> *Each of us has our own ideas about our health and how we would like to be looked after. These ideas may not be the same as the doctor or nurse's agenda. We all need a chance to share these thoughts with the healthcare team looking after us. Being told what to do feels uncomfortable for most people! Care should be agreed not imposed.*
>
> *Respondent to 'Diabetes Dialogue'*[70]

The Picker Institute found that 75 per cent of people believed that the appropriate course of treatment should be their decision, or a decision they make with their doctor.[71]

Co-production in practice has six components:[72]

1. Building on people's existing capabilities: altering the delivery model of public services from a deficit approach to one that provides opportunities to recognise and grow people's capabilities and actively supports them to put these to use at an individual and community level.

2. Reciprocity and mutuality: offering people a range of incentives to engage, which enable them to work in reciprocal relationships with professionals and with each other, where there are mutual responsibilities and expectations.

3. Building support networks: engaging peer and personal networks alongside professionals as the best way of transferring knowledge and supporting change.

4. Blurring distinctions: removing the distinction between professionals and recipients, and between producers and consumers of services, by reconfiguring the way services are developed and delivered.

5. Facilitating rather than delivering: enabling public service agencies to become catalysts and facilitators rather than central providers themselves.

6. Recognising people as assets: transforming the perception of people from passive recipients of services and burdens on the system into one where they are equal and essential partners in designing and delivering services.[73]

There is evidence that co-production increases people's well-being and stops people from getting ill. In health services,[74] co-production is reflected in the thinking behind patient engagement and expert patient models. Sue Roberts talks about patient engagement and self-management for people with diabetes, and how this changes the power in relationships: 'This new emphasis on skills training is designed to give people a personal understanding of diabetes and the confidence to control it efficiently and effectively. That inevitably leads to a very different relationship with healthcare professionals.'[75]

Working as equal partners with individuals and families rather than on their behalf will be a challenge for many healthcare professionals who have not been trained in this way. For example, where there is a conflict between individual preferences and clinical judgement, an individual's behaviour is often described as 'non-compliant' rather than being perceived as the exercise of individual choice and preference.[76]

Choice, control and co-production lie at the heart of person-centred practices because they are based on partnerships between people who rely on care and support services and the people and agencies providing those services working together to improve the quality and well-being of someone's life.

As explained in Chapter 1, this is becoming increasingly important for councils and service providers given current national policy, which encourages councils and their partners to 'actively involve people, carers, families and communities in the design, development, delivery and review of innovative care and support arrangements to maximise choice and independence.'[77]

Co-production can take place at an individual, service or system level. Person-centred thinking and planning is an example of co-production in action at an individual level: co-designing and co-delivering a person-centred plan for a life that makes sense to the person. Person-centred planning takes into account and reflects the person's capacities, community resources and networks.

> Person-centred planning has given us hope and a vision for a better future for Mohammed. We feel now we can have a say in how and what service support he receives. We no longer believe that only professionals know best for our son. Mohammed's faith and cultural needs are recognised and responded to.
>
> Joynab, Mohammed's mother[78]

At a service and system level, co-production can mean obtaining information from groups of people, and then through a facilitation process, using their points of view and expertise to help make changes to the way services are designed and delivered, and ultimately, the way individuals can experience the care and support system. This process is called Working Together for Change, which directly links person-centred information to strategic change.[79]

For some disabled or older people, choice, control and co-production are relatively new concepts. They have been used to being done to, rather than done with. We must move away from the idea of people being passive recipients of services to active citizens taking control of the decisions about the right care and support choices. Personalisation requires changes both to the role of people using services, and professionals.

> Dependent users become consumers and commissioners, and eventually co-producers and co-designers. Their participation, commitment, knowledge and responsibility increases. As the role of the service user fills out, so too the role of the professional must change in tandem.[80]

Gerry Smale and colleagues[81] describe the changes for professionals in their description of three models of assessment: the questioning model, the procedural model and the exchange model.

In the questioning model, professionals apply their expertise, built up from their training and previous experience, to determine the correct 'diagnosis'. They can then make the correct 'prescription' of services. The questions they ask reflect what the professional sees as important, rather than individual priorities.

It is based on a clinical understanding of 'need'. The person's individual impairment or disability and how this impacts on his social situation becomes the focus of enquiry, and the person's universal needs – for friendship, freedom and meaning – move into the background. It may be more or less effective (depending on the skills of the assessor) in producing an accurate account of the situation from the perspective of the professional and in generating a package of care which addresses the person's clinical needs. It is not an effective way to engage or empower the person, his family and friends, because the assessment process so clearly belongs to the professional.

The procedural model is a variation on the questioning model. The professional is still in control of the situation, but her authority derives not from her clinical expertise but from her administrative responsibility for the allocation of resources. The key task is 'people-sorting' – finding out enough about the person and his situation to allocate him to a particular category of need and services.

The person's situation is analysed against a set of criteria laid down by the agency – for example, the degree of physical mobility, the availability of informal support, the ability to prepare a hot meal – and this then determines his eligibility for particular types of service at a particular level.

Helpful workers may exaggerate people's dependency and attach extra 'neediness' labels so that they become eligible for particular services. These good intentions can seriously damage people's social identity and autonomy.

Personalisation requires that staff operate from the exchange model. The exchange model assumes that all people are expert in their own problems and that there is no reason that staff will or should ever know more about people and their problems than they do themselves, and certainly not before they do.[82] The assessor's expertise is in negotiation and problem solving: engaging the person and the other people in the situation to achieve a common understanding of 'the problem', and negotiating an agreement about who will do what within the constraints of available formal and informal resources.

Smale was focusing on the professional's role in assessment; however, the power issues are the same for treatment and support. Staff, whether a doctor, nurse or a social worker, still have important professional knowledge, but any treatment or service has to be negotiated with the person, to enable him to meet his personal outcomes. Personalisation means that it is no longer the professional who solely defines needs and treatment; professionals are, as Mike Lawson puts it, 'on tap, rather than on top'.[83] As Vidhya Alakeson suggests:

Healthcare is a technically complex field in which technological and pharmaceutical innovation is rapid. The skills and knowledge of professionals will remain important, even if individuals choose to take greater control. However, healthcare professionals have tended to neglect the views of patients, despite general agreement that patient-centredness is a feature of a high quality healthcare system and clear evidence that patients want to make decisions about their own care.[84]

In person-centred practice, we therefore assume that the person is the first authority on their life and that a dialogue with other people – family, friends or service workers – can build on this. Jonathan Glover[85] describes this dialogue:

This talk, when we share what we have been doing and our responses to things that have happened, is not just an exchange of information. When we talk together, I learn from your way of seeing things, which will often be different from mine. And, when I tell you about my way of seeing things, I am not just describing responses that are already complete. They may only emerge clearly as I try to express them, and as I compare them with yours. In this way, we can share in the telling of each other's inner story, and so share in creating ourselves and each other.

Inclusive and competent communities

> The overwhelming evidence is that what people do for themselves and with others – not services – delivers the bulk of social outcomes.
> *Martin Routledge and Catherine Witton*[86]

Communities that are more diverse and create more opportunities for people to help each other directly are better places for everyone to live. This is sometimes described as a 'competent community'.[87, 88] People with dementia and their supporters were asked about communities and said that they wanted communities where they would be able to:

- pursue hobbies and interests
- simply 'go out' more
- make more use of local facilities
- help others in their community by volunteering.

This led to identifying characteristics of a 'dementia-capable community'. Many of these characteristics reflect what all of us would like to see – inclusive, capable communities. This is what is could mean for people:[89]

It is really clear what the community has to offer people and what people have to offer their community and we see people leading ordinary, fulfilled lives in their own homes, work, leisure and personal relationships. Disabled and older people are connecting with and involved in building their local communities. They are central to and valued and respected by all parts of their communities because they are seen as community leaders and participants. Public services, businesses and community organisations and groups know the value of disabled and older people because of the positive impact their leadership has made on all parts of the community. Community initiatives are led by disabled and older people and the wider community knows and trusts that the initiatives will make a positive difference to the community.

People who use person-centred practice have a bias towards actively building communities which are competent in including everyone, and which do not just provide better services. They will assume that the person wants to have friends, prefers freedom to captivity, wants somewhere decent to live, would like the chance to contribute, and would rather be included in a community than excluded from it – unless the person clearly tells or shows them differently.

For most of us, relationships are the basis of our lives. We fear rejection and isolation more than anything. We need to belong, to be a part of other people's lives and have them be a part of ours. Person-centred practice seeks to help people create and maintain meaningful connections with people who are not paid to help them.

Staff who want to help people make these connections need to look outside the confines of services. Person-centred planning asks 'how could we find someone who knows about this?' and recognises that the service world cannot meet, and should not seek to meet, a person's every need. It looks for respectful ways to strengthen people's connections with family, friends and community members.

In mental health and substance misuse, some people may have partners, friends and family willing to help them address their substance misuse, as well resources available locally, many of which can be used to help people strengthen their community connections and improve their longer-term prospects. These resources should be regarded as an individual's 'recovery capital', and as many different resources as possible should be used alongside personal budgets, to help people live the lives they want in their local communities.

It was the support of Joanna's friend Sally and the willingness of the nuns at the local Buddhist monastery in her local community that helped Joanna in her recovery.

Joanna's story

Joanna, 24, has a personality disorder which can lead to extreme behaviours like self-harming. She has hypersensitive hearing and an autistic spectrum condition. She lived in a ground-floor supported-living flat, but began having 'major meltdowns' after a new tenant moved in above and played music around the clock. Eventually, Joanna threatened to commit suicide, but with the help of police and her friend Sally, she was found and taken to hospital. The psychiatrist visited her and asked what she dreamed of. Joanna said that all she wanted was to live somewhere quiet.

Joanna was finally discharged, but she still lived in a noisy environment, meaning the meltdowns started again. Sally used the person-centred thinking to discover what was working and not working for Joanna, and what she wanted for the future. Through asking the right questions and listening closely, she found that it was clear that Joanna needed a calm, quiet and supportive environment in which to live. They agreed that Joanna should have two weeks away at a local Buddhist monastery to give them both time to relax.

While Joanna was at the monastery, her self-harming stopped, she became calm and there were no more 'meltdowns'. She was welcomed by the nuns and took the decision to stay. Joanna and Sally then organised her housing benefit to be paid to the monastery and it was agreed that she could move in. She thrived, and in 2007 Joanna was ordained as a

Buddhist nun and has a new name, Genyin. She volunteers in the local charity shop twice a week and sings in the local choir. The police, psychiatrist, psychiatric nurses and key workers are a distant memory.

Conclusion to Part I

Joanna's story shows that delivering personalisation is more than just handing over financial control – it is about working creatively to find solutions that suited her on a day-to-day basis. In Part I we have set out how the historical development of person-centred planning and thinking has led to the emergence of practice which is based on the values of independence, choice and control and inclusive communities. This has made it possible for people like Joanna to experience improved outcomes in their lives. In the following parts, we will explain how you can use person-centred thinking, person-centred reviews and person-centred plans to deliver the personalisation agenda, based on the values and principles we have just explained.

Part II

Person-Centred Thinking

Social care as a sector, talks extensively of values, but values are worthless unless they are reflected in the behaviours of the people working to those values every day, in every interaction. People don't experience our values, they experience our behaviour.

Bill Mumford[90]

Support professional development and equip staff so they can play their part in the shift to personalisation. Ensuring all interactions are respectful and encourage the increasing choice and control of the person's support is at the heart of all personalised service provision.

Think Local, Act Personal Partnership[91]

So that we can demonstrate personalisation in action, we need to understand person-centred thinking, its origins and how the various person-centred thinking tools can enable staff to demonstrate the skills essential to creating personalised support including:

1. learning and understanding the balance between what is important to and for a person (Chapter 4)

2. enhancing a person's voice, choice and control (Chapter 5)

3. clarifying roles and responsibilities in providing support (Chapter 6)

4. achieving change through analysis and action (Chapter 7)

5. learning more deeply about a person (Chapter 8).

Chapter 9 explains how to decide which person-centred thinking tool to use and about moving from person-centred thinking to a person-centred description.

This will help us to live the values described in the previous chapter, which are demonstrated by the following beliefs:

*   We believe that disabled people are entitled to whatever support they need to live their life independently and therefore person-centred practice is based on understanding and acting on what matters to people and how they want to be supported.

*   We believe that everyone has gifts and capacities and therefore person-centred practice involves describing and building on people's assets, rather than on labels and stereotypes.

- We believe that disabled people are entitled to be in control of their own lives and choices, and therefore person-centred practice ensures that people have as much choice and control as possible and that solutions are co-produced.

- We believe that inclusive communities benefit everyone and therefore person-centred approaches seek solutions that enable people to be full members of their communities.

An introduction to person-centred thinking

> Our quality of life everyday is determined by the presence or absence of things that are important to us – our choices, our rituals.
>
> *Michael Smull*[92]

The Joseph Rowntree Foundation's study into person-centred care at the front line[93] found that the relationship between individuals and staff is pivotal to their experience of good person-centred support and therefore how much choice and control people experienced on a day-to-day basis. However, they also found that frontline workers often feel that they receive little support from managers in their day-to-day work. Often staff and managers simply don't know what they can do to deliver personalised support beyond just listening to people. Person-centred thinking tools are structured, practical ways for staff and managers to listen, learn and act to deliver personalised services.

'Ping! They got it, wow it works.' This was the response from a manager two weeks after they had attended a person-centred thinking workshop. He had just used the important to and important for person-centred thinking tool with staff to help them focus on the support they provide to people. He said 'I have been trying for the past year to get support staff to think differently – what I achieved today was amazing.'[94]

For people to have real choice and control over their lives and services, the people who provide support need to know:

- what is important to people, so that services and supports are built around what matters to them as individuals – instead of people being seen as a label, condition or stereotype

- how, when and where people want support or services delivered – rather than a standard 'one size fits all' approach

- how people communicate the way in which they want their services to be personalised. If the person does not use words, there needs to be clear ways to make these decisions and judgements and to record them.

We will show how person-centred thinking tools provide practical ways to achieve this. Let's start by considering Pat's story and how she manages long-term health conditions using person-centred thinking.

Pat's story

Pat is an outgoing, confident, independent and stylish woman, but she has suffered with Raynaud's in her feet since her early thirties. It affects her mobility and while she managed without the need of walking aids for a long time, she recently purchased a mobility scooter.

Pat also has Chronic Obstructive Pulmonary Disease (COPD) and Diabetes Type 2, which she has controlled by a combination of her diet and medication since 2002, but her condition can vary daily. Sometimes she is unable to leave her home; she may need oxygen and/or nebulisers and will need help with almost everything. During these times she is looked after by her daughter, Su, or is hospitalised.

When Pat moved into her new house, Su arranged all the practical alterations to ensure safe and easy access in, out and around the home. Grab rails and bathroom equipment such as a hoist, shower attachment and non-slip mats were purchased and fitted.

Pat didn't receive homecare or other formal services because she felt that she had lots of support from her daughter, neighbours, friends, the gardener and occasionally the district nurse. Su, however, thought her mum's care had room to improve. She had the opportunity to do person-centred thinking training through her job, so became excited about how she could better understand her mum's perspective on the support she needed.

'I wanted to apply the approach at home, and look at whether there were any changes we could make that would make a difference to Mum in her life. Over a couple of glasses of wine, we talked about it and looked at some stories of how the approach had made a difference to different people, and the tools which we could use.'

By developing a one page profile together, Pat and Su were able to work out the things that Pat needed for 'peace of mind' and other things to help her be 'content' and 'happy'.

'Mum's condition is exacerbated by stress, so we talked things through to pin-point what was causing it. The one-page profile gave Mum the opportunity to tell me about these things without it feeling like she was "bothering me". Mum thought that I would think these were silly little things, but when put into the context of her life, they were in fact incredibly important to her.

'To give Mum a break from her own house, she now regularly comes and stays with me. In the past, I had been reluctant to arrange this because I thought Mum would find the stairs difficult. However, she loves coming to stay and feels that the risk is worthwhile. Sleepovers are now a regular arrangement: Mum brings her medications, and I respect her decision to take that risk.'

Pat and Su also used the 'working and not working' tool to find ways of easily improving her home as well as things which they needed to buy that could help Pat on a daily basis.

'We re-arranged Mum's bedroom so that she can move about easier. We made sure she can reach the mattress variator controls to help her get in and out of bed, and extended the pull cords for the curtains that she previously couldn't reach,' Su said.

'Mum was feeling very stressed and worried (which affected her physically) about being left in the house without any food. Previously I had done the shopping for her, but Mum told me that she wanted to go to the supermarket herself and pick her own food. Her diet had changed dramatically since her diabetes so she wanted to be more creative with her diet. We bought a freezer so she can stock up on the basics. It relieves her anxiety about having no food in the house. She now feels so much more in control and this eases the stress and therefore helps manage her health conditions.'

The 'decision making agreement' tool helped Pat explain to her daughter that she sometimes felt Su made too many decisions.

'We agreed that Mum will go to all her medical appointments on her own. She's feeling a lot better in herself now, so she can take on more information and she's been attending a lot of hospital clinics and programmes, especially about her diabetes. Previously, I had always accompanied her but Mum is confident about going on her own and actually enjoys organising her own transport to and fro. I also found out that when Mum was talking, which could take a long time due to her getting breathless, I would end up speaking for her. Mum now has a memory board where she writes any questions down that she would like to ask, a diary of her appointments, a list of her medications and feels much more in control of her medical care.'

Su said that the tools have helped her mum be more informed and more in control, allowing her to step back. 'Mum recently had to go into hospital. Before she used to fight it as she felt other people were making the decisions for her, but now she's more informed about her condition and recognised that she needed the extra help to get her better and the whole hospital experience was less stressful.'

Su even took her mum's one page profile into the hospital and stuck it over Pat's bed so that the nurses could see it.

'Using the person-centred thinking tools helps you think outside the box to find simple and cost effective solutions for providing personalised care. Mum's emotional and physical well-being has improved dramatically since these changes. Even her GP is recognising that she is managing her condition more, as she is now more independent and has more control over her health and the life that she leads.'

Pat's experience illustrates how simple person-centred thinking tools can contribute to providing personalised, responsive and holistic support that treats her illnesses in a way which suits her and how she wants to live her life.

THE ORIGINS OF PERSON-CENTRED THINKING TOOLS

The foundation for person-centred thinking is being able to understand what is important to and for someone, and the balance between them. This foundation was the ELP,[95] from which most of the person-centred thinking tools were developed.

Other tools have been adapted from management practice. For example, the 'doughnut' is taken directly from Charles Handy's work on organisational behaviour and management.[96] Person-centred thinking tools have been developed from the contributions of leaders in the inclusion movement – for example, Beth Mount's[97] 'relationship circle' and John O'Brien's[98] work. Finally, some tools have been developed from professional practice; for example, the work of speech and language therapists has inspired the development of various communication tools (which we outline below) and Simon Duffy's[99] work on self-directed support resulted in the 'decision making' tool.

Person-centred thinking tools enable staff to deliver personalised services by helping to answer the following questions:

- How does the person want to live and be supported?

- How can people have more choice and control in their lives?

- What is our role in delivering what is important to people and how they want to be supported? How are we doing in supporting people in the way they want to live? How can we work together to keep what is working and change what is not working?

- How can we keep learning about the person and what we need to do to provide the best support?

Table II.1 lists the person-centred thinking tools that can contribute to answering these questions.

Each person-centred thinking tool does two things. It is the basis for actions and it provides further information about what is important to people and how they want to be supported. This information is recorded as a person-centred description and may start with information on just one page (a 'one page profile'). In the following chapters, we introduce each of the person-centred thinking tools and illustrate how they have been used with people in different situations to create change.

Table II.1 Person-centred thinking tools

Questions for staff and services in delivering personalised services	Person-centred thinking tool that can help
• How does the person want to live and be supported?	**Learning and understanding the balance between what is important to and for the person** Good days, bad days and routines. Top tips. Relationship circle. Synthesising and recording this information on a person-centred description.
• How can people have more choice and control in their lives?	**Enhancing voice, choice and control** Communication charts. Decision making profiles.
• What is our role in delivering what is important to people and how they want to be supported?	**Clarifying roles and responsibilities** Doughnut. Matching support.
• How are we doing in supporting people in the way they want to live? How can we work together to keep what is working and change what is not working?	**Analysis and action** Working/not working from different perspectives. 4 plus 1.
• How can we keep learning about the person and what we need to do to provide the best support?	**Learn more deeply** Generally: learning log. About the future: hopes and dreams. Learning from the past: histories and stories. In specific areas of the person's life – for example, deeper learning about how people can be a part of their community: • gifts to contribution • community map • presence to contribution or about work and careers, or health.

Chapter 4

Learning and Understanding the Balance Between What Is Important To and For the Person

> The idea of the balance between what is *important to* and what is *important for* a person is rooted in the human condition where none of us has a life where we have everything that is *important to* us and none of us pay perfect attention to everything that is *important for* us. All of us strive for a balance between them. A balance that accounts for issues of health and safety but recognises that perfect health and perfect safety are rarely achieved and all of us address what is *important for* us in the context of what is *important to* us. This is a human issue, not just a disability issue.
>
> *Michael Smull[100]*

The first and fundamental person-centred thinking skill is to be able to learn what is important to someone, what is important for her and the balance between the two. This is a principle that underpins person-centred change.

Independence means that we are all competent and that we all have areas in our lives where we need support. Historically, we have come from a culture where 'professionals know best' and it was easy for people's lives to reflect more of what was important for them, with the greatest emphasis on developing skills and being safe. The focus was on 'fixing people' and addressing any 'deficits' found through assessment. Developing skills and being safe for most of us are still necessary, but need to be addressed in the context of what is important to us, so we learn the skills that fit with what we want to do or who we want to be, not skills for their own sake.

There have also been times in services where the emphasis has been too strongly on what is important to the person, and in these situations choice was king. People were 'allowed' to stay in bed for much of the day, or to do what they wanted, and this was justified as their 'choice' and therefore completely acceptable. The waste of lives and contributions makes this unacceptable. Our challenge is to find the best balance together. This person-centred thinking skill is a way to separate what matters to the person (what is important *to* them) with the support that they want and need (what is important *for* the person).

As Michael Smull says,[101] learning what is 'important to' and what is 'important for' has to be done before you can help find the balance. Everyone finds that what is 'important to' them and what is 'important for' them are in conflict from time to time. For example, a way to illustrate this is to ask 'When you have a bad day, do you eat or drink something fattening?' The answer from many people is 'yes'. The next question is 'What would happen if you had not had a bad day but a bad year? Would you become a bigger person?' Again the answer from many people is that they would gain weight. Finally ask 'What if we were tracking your weight and after it had gone up we came to you and said that we were putting you on a 1200 calorie diet because of the weight gain. How would you feel – better or worse? Would you follow the diet?' Most people answer that they would feel worse and would not follow the diet.

In this story, people are using something fattening to comfort them after a bad day, day after day. The bad days are occurring because something that is 'important to' them is not present (or things that need to be absent are occurring). Helping this person lose weight has to start with understanding why she is having bad days. Then, after helping the person look at what can be done to decrease the bad days, you can look at alternative ways for the person to comfort herself. What works for us and for those with whom we plan is to look at both and then try to account for what is 'important for', using what is 'important to' people as the context.

Any therapeutic intervention or programme designed to address what is 'important for' someone without taking into account what is 'important to' that person is not adequate and will often fail. Conversely, simply saying that we support choice and without paying any attention to what is 'important for' people creates an environment where choice is used as an excuse for doing nothing and as a result people may be hurt. Every programme and intervention must take both into account and strive to find a balance between them that works for the person.

Part of why those who work with people with significant disabilities must apply this skill in their day-to-day work is not just the presence of a disability, but also the absence of control in critical areas. We should all be trying to help people maximise the positive control they have over their lives. This means that you are helping people find the balance between 'important to' and 'important for' that works for them. A balance must account for issues of health and safety, while at the same time recognising that perfect health and perfect safety are rarely achieved and all of us address what is 'important for' us in the context of what is 'important to' us. Again this is a human issue, not just a disability issue.

What is important *to* a person is what she says through her own words and behaviours about what really matters to her. What is important *for* a person are the things that help her become or stay healthy and safe, whether it is important to her or not.

The balance between the two is the compromise that all of us experience in life: between wanting to eat chocolate and maintaining weight and between having lazy evenings and wanting to get fitter at the gym. We all need to find a balance so that our lives are not just about what we choose, but also what we know needs to happen for us to be safe and healthy. These are the judgements that parents make for children all the time.

To find the balance we need to know:

'What is important to a person?'

'What is important for a person?'

'What else do we need to learn?'

These three questions look deceptively simple; however, experience tells us that asking these directly rarely works. We have learned that people need structured practice and specific feedback to be able to answer the 'to' and 'for' questions. This chapter looks at the person-centred tools and conversations we can use to draw this information out, like asking about morning routines, good days and bad days, and top tips for support at short notice. Then once we have that information, we go on to explain how it can be recorded on a one page profile and developed into a more detailed person-centred description to share with others.

Good days, bad days and routines

Good day?

Bad day?

What will it take to have more good days and fewer bad days?

Figure 4.1 Good days, bad days

'Good days, bad days' is a person-centred thinking tool (see Figure 4.1) that simply asks the person to describe what a typical day is like, starting with when she wakes up and continuing until she goes to bed. Then you can ask for the same detailed information about what an especially good day is like and a particularly bad day. This tells you what needs to be present for her in her day-to-day life and what needs to be absent.

In reality, the conversation is likely to meander. Some people cannot describe a good day or a bad day, but can tell you about the last week in great detail, so that you can gently ask which bits of the day were good and which not so good. If the person has not had good days for some time, she may be able to tell you about a good day from her past.

When the person cannot tell you directly herself, then family or support staff can help. You could ask:

'If you had a magic wand and were going to create a really good day for the person
– what would happen? What would she be doing? Who else would be there?'

And then ask a similar question about a bad day:

'What would you do if you wanted to ruin someone's day?'

This teases out what is important *to* and *for* a person and it can then be used to make changes by asking 'What would it take for you to have more good days and fewer bad days?'

Jane used 'good days, bad days' to take more control of her life and her long-term condition:

When I was first diagnosed with ulcerative colitis I had no idea of the impact it was going to have on my life. I thought, OK, now it has a name, give me the medication that'll clear it up and I'll be on my way, thank you very much. But I soon realised it wasn't going to be that easy. I've spent the last nine years having regular colonoscopies, short- and long-term hospital stays, constant medication changes, and as for the enema department, then don't even go there! I think I've tried them all! I was so full of steroids when I got married that I went up three dress sizes!

Back then, I presumed that you get poorly, get a diagnosis and then get on with it. I honestly thought that if I struggled on each day, did what the consultant, GPs and specialist nurses told me, then that was a good way of dealing with the colitis that attacked my body far too frequently.

Jane used the template on www.thinkaboutyourlife.org and filled in her good day and bad day information. From this she thought about what she could do to have more good days (see Figure 4.2).

Her good days included being able to eat what she liked, suggesting that food and eating out are very important to her. Her bad days meant no energy for running and being alone or isolated, suggesting that running and certain people were also important to her. She was able to make decisions about changes in her life, and used this information to build her one page profile, which we explain in more detail towards the end of this chapter.

Sandra also used the 'good days, bad days' tool:

Sandra's good and bad days

Sandra has just turned 47 and those who know her describe her as someone who is honest, passionate, insightful, courageous and committed to helping others. Sandra has struggled with her mental health and staying well since she was a teenager. She has been in and out of hospital on countless occasions over the past 25 years and has repeatedly attempted suicide.

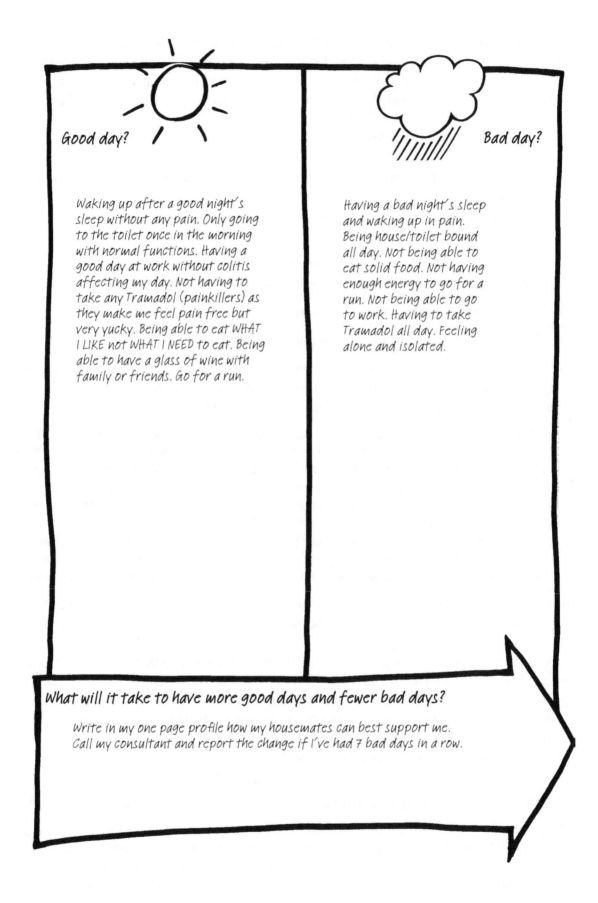

Good day?

Waking up after a good night's sleep without any pain. Only going to the toilet once in the morning with normal functions. Having a good day at work without colitis affecting my day. Not having to take any Tramadol (painkillers) as they make me feel pain free but very yucky. Being able to eat WHAT I LIKE not WHAT I NEED to eat. Being able to have a glass of wine with family or friends. Go for a run.

Bad day?

Having a bad night's sleep and waking up in pain. Being house/toilet bound all day. Not being able to eat solid food. Not having enough energy to go for a run. Not being able to go to work. Having to take Tramadol all day. Feeling alone and isolated.

What will it take to have more good days and fewer bad days?

Write in my one page profile how my housemates can best support me.
Call my consultant and report the change if I've had 7 bad days in a row.

Figure 4.2 Jane: good days, bad days

Sandra is now at a stage where she feels she is in recovery. She has lots of good days and fewer bad days where she feels down and is hearing voices. Sandra was born in Lancashire and moved with her mother, brothers and sister to the Caribbean when she was three, and then moved back to England when she was 14. In 2000, there was a turning point in Sandra's life when she was allocated a black social worker. For the first time she felt listened to – particularly in relation to her cultural needs.

Table 4.1 shows what a good day and a bad day look like for Sandra.

Table 4.1 Sandra's good days, bad days

Good day	Bad day
• I have had a good night's sleep and wake feeling like I can cope with the world. • I wake up without hearing voices. If I can hear them, then at least feel like they are not controlling me. • I want to get up, have a wash and get dressed – I am excited about what I want to wear. • I take my medicine. • I feel good about myself. • I know what I am doing with my day – I have a plan and am happy to get out either walking or using public transport. • I go to a group or college – at the moment I am really enjoying my woodwork group, I have made a CD cabinet and am now making a cat house. • I initiate conversations and am able to ring a friend for a chat and catch up. • I eat well and have three meals throughout the day – go to Take Two to get a nice Caribbean dish or cook myself something. • I listen to music in the evening (I really like instrumental jazz) or watch TV (I like programmes like *Grand Designs* and rom-com films). • I spend some quality time with my cat giving her lots of attention and playing games with her.	• I haven't slept well and wake up tired. • I can't hear my voice – just the ones in my head. • I feel paranoid and can't trust my decisions because I feel like everyone is out to get me. • I have a flashback triggered by something on TV or somebody saying something like 'you're selfish' to me. • I won't take my medication. • I have to wash and clean myself and the flat repeatedly – I cannot leave my flat in case I contaminate other people. • I won't get out of bed, answer my phone or watch the TV in case people come out of it. I will just sit or lie in the dark. • I won't cook or eat because I think all food is contaminated. • I can't pull myself back and need to be admitted to hospital.

Looking at Sandra's 'good days, bad days' provides rich, detailed information about what is important to her, and clues about what support she wants and needs. Like Jane's example, it is also a way to have conversations that lead to action about what Sandra and the people supporting her can do to help her have more good days than bad.

Routines

Routines are a way to ease ourselves through the day. Finding out about someone's routines is a great way to learn about what matters and what support the person needs in order to have good days.

Here are some routines to have conversations about:

- What is your *morning routine*? How do you wake up in the morning? What happens next? Tell me about breakfast.

- What is your *evening routine*? What do you do to get ready for bed? What do you do next?

- *Routines for comfort*: What do you do when you have had a bad day? How do you try and cheer yourself up?

- *Routines of celebration*: What is your favourite way to celebrate? What would you do after a particularly good day? What would you do to celebrate good news or achievements? How do you like to celebrate your birthday? What else would you always celebrate? What religious or cultural festivals do you celebrate? How do you celebrate?

- *Transition routines*: What do you do when you first get to work? What do you do as soon as you get home?

- *Weekly routines*: What do you do almost without fail every week? Are there any TV programmes that you just have to see? What are they? Are there people that you see every week? What else do you do each week?

One of Sandra's important routines is taking her medication: 'The medicine I am taking at the moment is good for keeping the voices under control, and giving me a sense of normality. The weight gain that comes with the medicine is a small price to pay'. Every morning Sandra plays with Molly, her cat. She says that she loves playing with Molly and will spend ages throwing balls for her to chase and stroking her: 'Molly gives me a reason to get up in the morning.' Sandra has a plan of what she wants to do every day and likes to set herself targets. She watches TV and listens to music every day. One of her weekly routines is going to church every Sunday: 'My faith is really important to me and it is helpful if people around me understand this and don't think it's my illness when I say that God is talking to me!'

Top tips

Another way to learn what matters to someone is to ask them and the people who know them well, their 'top tips' for providing great support. This person-centred thinking tool is sometimes called 'the two minute drill' and asks the question:

> 'If you only had two minutes to share what you know about supporting [name of individual] well, what would you say?'

This is what Suzie said about her daughter Jennie, when she was asked that question:

If I only had two minutes to share information, I would tell the person who was going to support her to be smiley and happy with Jennie and have fun with her, and do all this in a way with which Jennie can cope. This means that you would need to do all this knowing how Jennie communicates and how she would communicate with you. You need to communicate with Jennie using clear, short sentences most of the time. When she gets anxious, you need to use as little language as possible. You need to support this with visual prompts – for example, her visual diary and flash cards.

Keep your language positive at all times – tell her what you want her to do instead of what you don't want her to do. The main thing is to have fun. You need to understand the things that she likes doing and the people she likes to be around, and then you are half way there. I would be planning to take her horse riding, going to the pictures or going out for a meal. Let Jennie know in advance that that is what she is going to do, with pictures of what she is doing and of yourself, so that she knows that you are going to support her. She needs to clearly see what she is going to be doing, and with whom she is going to do this.

This gives lots of information about what is important to Jennie and what is important for her so that people can support her well.

WHAT THIS TELLS US ABOUT WHAT IS IMPORTANT TO JENNIE

- To have fun – for example, by going horse riding, out to the cinema or for a meal.

- To know what is going to happen in advance, and whom she will be with.

- To be supported by people who know her well, and have fun with her.

WHAT THIS TELLS US ABOUT HOW TO SUPPORT JENNIE WELL

- Use clear, short sentences with Jennie, and if Jennie is anxious use as little language as possible.

- Use pictures with Jennie of what she is going to do next and with whom she will be – for example, through a visual diary or flash cards.

Relationship circle

What is important to someone will almost always include who is important to her. We can learn and record the important people in someone's life by having conversations and using the 'relationship circle' person-centred thinking tool. It is common practice in social work with children and young people to record information about relationships and this is another way to capture this information with the person whom you are supporting.

A relationship circle is particularly useful for exploring:

- whom a person knows

- how they know them

- who knows whom

- how these networks can help the person find opportunities and support to live the life she wants.

These relationships can be represented as a circle, or in columns, or as a spider diagram with the person at the centre. However it is represented, it is vital to be clear not just about who is in the person's life, but how important they are to her. Typically this is done by putting her name or photo in the middle and the names of the people who are most important in her life closest to her.

If you are doing this using the rings of a 'relationship circle' (see Figure 4.3), then the people in the closest ring would be people that the person loves; the second ring would be people the person likes; the third ring would be people the person knows; and the final ring would be people who are paid to be in that person's life, like support staff, hairdressers or GPs.

This process not only identifies who is important in the person's life, but can suggest how she can stay in contact with them and whether there is any support she may need in keeping and developing those relationships. It can also show if there are other people with whom the person could share ideas, support or resources.

If people find that their circle is not as full as they would like, then it can become a focus for action by asking: 'What would it take to increase the number and depth of your relationships?'

Elsie's story

Elsie is described by all who know her as 'the salt of the earth'. Her ability to connect with people meant she was very close to her family and had many friends in her life. Elsie first developed dementia six years ago and is now bedbound. Her family felt that it was important that Elsie stays connected with friends and family. Her support staff in the care home developed Elsie's relationship circle with her and her daughter Karen. Not only did it show who was important in her life and of whom she wanted to see more, it gave support staff a starting point in conversations and an at-a-glance guide to the other professionals working with her. The relationship circle was a way of showing all those involved in Elsie's care who is in her life and what role they could play in providing support. This contributed to improving Elsie's quality of life. (See Figure 4.4.)

Ann Marie's story

Ann Marie lives on the south coast of England with five other people whom she has known since her childhood. They are supported by a local learning disability provider who is working to personalise its services. There are 16 people in the staff team which supports Ann Marie and her co-tenants. Naturally, Ann Marie gets on better with some people than others. Carolynn, the manager, used a version of the relationship circle with Ann Marie to find out which staff she liked the most and by whom she wanted to be supported. Ann Marie put three staff members in the circle closest to her, the rest of the staff in the next circle out, and the last staff member in the furthest circle to her. She made it clear that she had three staff members that she really wanted to support her, and one that she did not want to assist her at all. Lynne used this information to develop a personalised rota for Ann Marie based around her favourite three staff and ensuring that the staff member that she did not like was not on the rota at all.

One page profiles and person-centred descriptions

In some service processes, information about what matters to the person is recorded but is 'hidden' within lots of detailed information. In mental health services, it could be in her Wellness Recovery Action Plan (WRAP); in social services, it might be in her care plan; and in the health services, this information could be found in the patient notes.

Pulling out what is most important to someone, and for her to describe this in her own words, is very powerful. It serves as the best quality of life measure as it is her individual reflection on what matters and what needs to be present in her life. This information, together with an awareness of what good, personalised support looks like, enables a service to measure its effectiveness by simply asking whether the person has what is important to her in her life (within the sphere of what a particular service is responsible for) and whether the service is supporting the person in the way that she wants to be supported.

Relationships

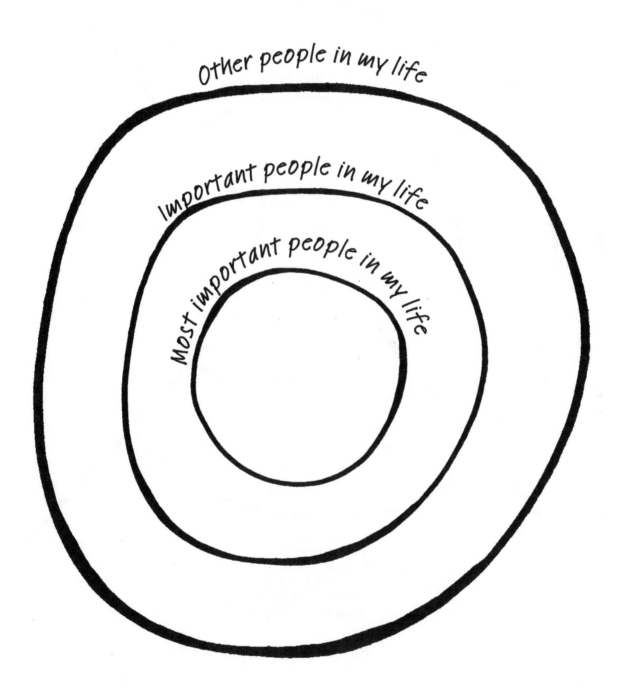

Other people in my life

Important people in my life

Most important people in my life

Figure 4.3 Relationship circle

Elsie's relationship circle

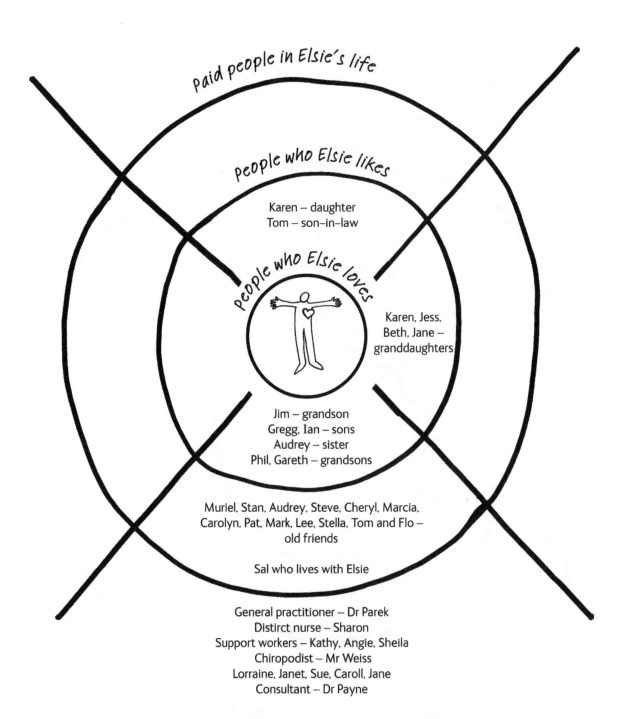

Paid people in Elsie's life

People who Elsie likes

People who Elsie loves

Karen – daughter
Tom – son–in–law

Karen, Jess,
Beth, Jane –
granddaughters

Jim – grandson
Gregg, Ian – sons
Audrey – sister
Phil, Gareth – grandsons

Muriel, Stan, Audrey, Steve, Cheryl, Marcia,
Carolyn, Pat, Mark, Lee, Stella, Tom and Flo –
old friends

Sal who lives with Elsie

General practitioner – Dr Parek
Distirct nurse – Sharon
Support workers – Kathy, Angie, Sheila
Chiropodist – Mr Weiss
Lorraine, Janet, Sue, Caroll, Jane
Consultant – Dr Payne

Figure 4.4 Elsie's relationship circle

Learning what is important *to* and *for* someone can be recorded on one page to begin with. We call this a one page profile. Usually, what is important *for* the person is framed as 'best support' or 'what we need to know or do to support the person'. A one page profile typically has three sections: an appreciation about the person; what is important to that person from her perspective; and how to support her well.

This is what people appreciate about Sandra:

- her honesty and her loyalty

- when Sandra gives her word, she keeps it

- Sandra is unfailingly kind

- she treats everyone equally and does not discriminate

- Sandra is determined and does not give up

- she is willing to share, especially if it will benefit others

- Sandra has a real passion for wanting to help others

- she has a warm sense of humour and is able to laugh at herself

- Sandra has a real curiosity about the world and is always looking to learn something new

- Sandra has great courage.

From talking and learning about Sandra's good days and bad days and what her routines are, her support worker was able to determine what is important to her and how best to support her. This became Sandra's one page profile.

WHAT IS IMPORTANT TO ME?

- Going to church every Sunday. My faith is really important to me and it is helpful if people around me understand this and don't think it's my illness when I say that God is talking to me!

- Spending time with Molly, my cat. I love playing with Molly and will spend ages throwing balls for her to chase and stroking her. Molly gives me a reason to get up in the morning.

- I love having lots of channels to choose from on my TV and use TV and music to relax. I love listening to instrumental jazz like Kenny G.

- Keeping busy! I always have a plan of what I am doing on any given day.

- Keeping the voices under control. The medicine I am taking at the moment is good for doing this and giving me a sense of normality. The weight gain that comes with the medicine is a small price to pay.

- Doing things and going to places that aren't associated with being ill. I like going to college and meeting people who don't know me for having mental health issues and accept me for who I am.

- Setting myself little targets. I like achieving and pushing myself to achieve.

HOW TO BEST SUPPORT ME

- I prefer to have people around me who understand me and my illness so that I don't feel like I have to pretend.

- *I can appear really confident when inside I am really scared. You need to check with me at each stage of doing something.*

- *If you are going to ask me to do something, don't give me too long to think about it as I start to really worry about it and the fear takes over. It's better if I am told about something as close to the event as possible so that I don't think too much and just do it!*

- *I find it really hard to join a group. If possible I will want to arrive early so that I can be the first and be settled before the crowd starts to build.*

- *Change really upsets me. If there are going to be changes in who is supporting me, it is better if this is done gradually. It is important that you tell me that it is not personal and that you give me a chance to talk about how I feel.*

- *I find my CPA meetings really stressful. I find them a waste of time and get angry really quickly. I am told that I behave completely differently in these meetings to anywhere else. I need those supporting me in these meetings to stick up for me and take a stand if they feel something isn't right.*

- *I can get overwhelmed by going to places and meeting people. If I am asked to help out in some way, this is a good distraction for me and I feel more comfortable.*

A one page profile can also be the beginning of a more detailed person-centred description (see Figure 4.5). Once you have a one page profile, each person-centred thinking tool used both leads to actions and further information which can be added, so that the document turns from being a one page profile to being at least a couple of pages long (a person-centred description).

After each person-centred thinking tool is used, ask:

- What does this tell us is important to the person?

- What does it tell us about how to support the person well?

- What clues does it give us about the person's gifts and contributions?

Then add this information to the original one page profile which then starts to become a longer person-centred description. For example, using the relationship circle will lead to action by asking: 'What would it take to increase the number of people in the person's life?' Then: 'What do we need to do to start this?' The relationship circle will also provide information both on who is important to the person, and what staff need to do to support the person around her relationships. The next person-centred thinking tool to use when you have a one page profile is 'working and not working' and we talk about this at the end of this chapter. In Chapter 7, we explain how you can go from 'working and not working' to decide what other person-centred thinking tools could be helpful and discuss how to develop person-centred descriptions.

The most common errors in one page profiles and person-centred descriptions are:

- Assuming that if it is important to others in the person's life (for example, staff or families), it must be important to the person. Among the worst examples was a plan that said that implementing a restrictive behaviour programme (that the person clearly hated) was important to the person.

- Describing what is *important to* the person in brief, telegraphic phrases that give an idea of what is important, but are easily subject to misinterpretation by the reader. A common example is to have the single word 'privacy' listed, without saying more about what privacy means to the person. Since, in the absence of other information, people operate out of their own experiences and perceptions, privacy will be interpreted as meaning what it means to the reader and this is likely to be different from what it means to the individual.

One page profile

Photo

Each one page profile has a current photo of the person.

Appreciations

This section lists the positive qualities, strengths and talents of the person. It can also be called 'like and admire'.

What's important to the person

This is a bullet list of what really matters to the person from their perspective (even if others do not agree). It is detailed and specific. This section needs to have enough detail so that someone who does not know the person can understand what matters to them. It could include:

• Who the important people are in the person's life, and when and how they spend time together.

• Important activities and hobbies, and when, where and how often these take place.

• Any routines that are important to the person.

How to support the person

This is a list of how to support the person, and what is helpful and what is not.

The information in this section includes what people need to know, and what people need to do.

Figure 4.5 One page profile

- The basics should be assumed, unless there is a history of their being absent. A list of things that sound like a recitation of Maslow's hierarchy – for example, food, shelter, clothing – should be avoided unless they have been absent in the person's life. Someone who has been hurt by an individual with whom she lives may want to say that she must not live with people who hurt others. People who have never lived with such a person will take it as a given.

The purpose of a one page profile and a person-centred description is to provide a summary of person-centred information that people in the person's life can use to either get to know her quickly, or ensure that they are providing consistent support in the way that the person wants. They are not the latest way to produce quality records, but by considering what is important to and for a person, and what good support looks like, they are a way to create actions that make a difference.

The one page profile provides the information to use to base conversations about what is working and not working in the person's life. Even where someone is not supported by services, this information can still be important to record and share in this way. This made a significant difference for Dan.

Dan's story

The only services that Dan uses to help control his obsessive compulsive disorder (OCD) is his GP and cognitive behavioural therapy (CBT). He has a one page profile that he uses to help his family understand the best ways to support him. His brother-in-law, Tom, was surprised to see that to support Dan it was important that the family did *not* ask about his OCD. The family thought that they had been helping by asking about it, but the opposite was true (see Figure 4.6).

In Maureen's story, her one page profile possibly saved her life.

Maureen's one page profile

Just before Christmas, Kevin, a service manager for Supported Living, took an urgent call from his local hospital.

'One of the people we support – Maureen – was seriously ill,' he explained. 'Her general health had been suffering for some time, but then she caught a chest infection that became a real problem. She was admitted to a hospital in Bath following a number of visits by GPs and council staff to her home. Health professionals called me to say they were gravely concerned about her condition and that Maureen's next of kin should be called...'

Following this call, Kevin and his team became aware that hospital staff were struggling to communicate with Maureen and this was having a dramatic impact on the way she was responding to her treatment.

'Maureen has a learning disability and mental health problems,' he said. 'She has difficulty communicating with people which is made worse by a hearing impairment. The nurses at the hospital couldn't communicate with her or understand what she was trying to say. Maureen had to wear an oxygen mask but she kept taking it off. The nurses had to do blood tests and take samples...there were lots of medical things going on, and Maureen wasn't dealing well with that.'

Kevin's colleague Rachel went straight down to the hospital and explained to nursing staff the key points about the type of support Maureen needed, especially when it came to communication.

Dan: one page profile

What people like and admire about me

Dan is a practical hands-on guy (DIY and engineering enthusiast), efficient (and best working to deadlines), caring, gentle, loyal, hard working, doer, tall and handsome.

What's important to me

To spend time 1:1 with my wife regularly (at least twice a month or more if possible) going out for a meal, taking a walk together, going to the cinema or watching DVD at home.

Spend quality time with my daughter weekdays before her bedtime (i.e. giving my undivided attention to her – reading books, interactive play such as using building blocks, bath time toys etc).

Have outings with my wife and daughter most weekends.

To have time and space for myself in my garage/workshop (my cave), 1 hour a week.

Get to church at least once a month.

To see family and friends as often as possible (see family at least once a month, and friends every weekend if we can).

To maintain a work/life balance, aiming to bring the maximum of 2 nights a week of work home.

Exercise regularly at least once a week for an hour (e.g. cycling, weights, running).

To manage my Obsessive Compulsive Disorder so that it has little impact on every day life.

I like the house to be organised keeping clutter to a minimum otherwise it leaves me feeling flat and demotivated.

To be debt free.

To have ongoing projects (DIY, kit cars, garden, house).

How best to support me

Challenge odd behaviour such as double checking if locked car, locked the house, whether I've dropped anything or left anything behind etc. (e.g. reassure me that I don't need to check it again).

Only refer to my OCD if you have to.

I may try to lean on other people. I may ask for reassurance (my wife acknowledges this by sticking her tongue out at me!). Remind me I have the power to get through this.

Help me divert my mind. For example by simply asking me to do something which refocuses my mind, or talking about something that would interest me.

Help me not to bring up past memories of my OCD habits.

Plenty of praise and encouragement!

Figure 4.6 Dan's one page profile

'During the transition of wards, Maureen's hearing aid for her right ear went missing, but this information wasn't given to the ward staff,' Kevin said. 'They just saw someone who was ill and decided they must carry on with their treatment without telling her what was happening. This was making Maureen really stressed. Rachel showed the nurses how to speak with her by getting up close to her right ear and speaking very loudly, while at the same time, using gestures that Maureen was used to.'

Kevin said this was the first step in helping Maureen's health take a turn for the better. 'Maureen started to understand what was going on. Once the nurses could communicate with her, she felt a lot happier and realised the important work they were doing to help her.'

Rachel wrote up a one page profile for Maureen. This helped hospital staff understand who Maureen was, what was important to her and the kind of support she needed. When there was a change of shift, the new nurses would be able to communicate with Maureen and continue with her treatment.

'After that, Maureen's condition improved dramatically,' Kevin said. 'She made a full recovery and was able to return home early in the New Year. We helped our health colleagues provide support to Maureen in a person-centred way, including showing how to talk to her differently, recognise what was important to her, and how best to support her. It may seem like a small change, but it made a massive difference to her life, and probably saved it.'

Kevin said the Wiltshire team were now working more closely with other health professionals in their area to introduce person-centred thinking tools – like one page profiles – into all areas of their work.

'Supporting your staff to work in a person-centred way can make such a difference to someone's life. For Maureen, one small change – sharing her one page profile – was crucial.'

A good one page profile provides specific detailed information about how to support the person – on her terms. This can be expanded into more detailed support information where this is needed into a person-centred description. For some people, it can also be developed to inform future support – for example, for people whose support needs will vary at different times. This can simply be described as 'what to do when I become unwell.'

Fiona has bi-polar disorder and found it useful to also have a written description of how people would know when she started to become unwell and what they needed to do about it (see Figure 4.7).

Tools like 'good days, bad days', 'top tips' and 'relationship circles' help us know what is important to and for a person, and the balance between the two and this information is recorded and summarised on one page, or in a more detailed person-centred description.

But what if people aren't always able to be heard? What if they don't use words to communicate? The next chapter describes the importance of enhancing people's voices and also takes us on to the next step of making decisions – with the person we're supporting – about actions that are needed to bring more choice and control into that person's life.

How to spot when I am becoming unwell and what to do

When I do this

First signs

Denial. I refuse to accept that there is anything wrong. If you ask me how I am I will say that I am 'fine'. I am very scared to stop or to take time out. I am likely to appear cross or frustrated if people show that they are worried about me.

Sleep. Sleep patterns deteriorate – almost always towards less or sometimes even no sleep. This can be difficult to identify, as I am not always able to be completely honest and I have a capacity to go for a long time on very little sleep, without too much problem. There are usually some clues – emails at 2.00 a.m. being the most obvious.

Eating. My diet will deteriorate. My fridge may be empty and I will noticeably drink more coffee and/or diet coke. I will refuse invitations that involve food and you will realise that you don't see me eating. At these times, food becomes something I can control and even if I do eat you will realise that you never see me eat.

Disengagement. I disengage from everyone around me. I will refuse invitations to go out and might seem distant. I may make quite plausible excuses for why I cannot join in.

More serious signs

Rocking and pacing. I find it difficult to rest or even to sit still. My body can manifest manic symptoms and I may noticeably rock (although this is a sign that things are extremely bad).

Perceived 'absences'. I appear not to be concentrating or to lose the thread of what is going on. I may 'drift off' for a few seconds or even longer.

Feeling of pressure in my head. My own thoughts and people talking can feel overwhelming. This can be particularly obvious if I am involved in a conversation with more than one person. Telephone conversations may be difficult for me to deal with.

I want you to

The most important thing for me, when I start to get ill, is that something happens to stop the downward spiral sooner, rather than later. I do, however, recognise that at the times when action needs to be taken, I am often most likely to be obstructive.

Everyone involved should therefore

Be honest and direct with me about what they observe to be happening – however worried you are about my reaction. Talk to each other and compare notes – I know that I sometimes play people off against each other and the sooner that this is pointed out to me the better.

Stopping things from getting too bad

At the early stages of my becoming unwell, there are several options that might help me to step off the 'rollercoaster' and prevent things from getting worse.

A change in medication. Sleep is usually a particular problem and, if I can be persuaded, sleeping medication (Zopiclone), even if I just take it for a few nights, can help me to break the cycle of sleeplessness and start to feel better.

Time off work. If I can be persuaded to take a few days off work and relax then this, perhaps coupled with sleeping medication, can break the cycle.

A planned holiday or short break. I sometimes get very claustrophobic in Newcastle and persuading me to take some time away from the city can also break the cycle. Sunshine is a great healer and, particularly in the winter, a week away in the sun can do me the power of good.

I know that sometimes a short period in hospital may be necessary. It is difficult to say exactly when this should happen but please talk to each other and reach an agreement collaboratively. This may have to be a tough judgement call. I accept that the element of choice may have to be removed in order to facilitate this. Being honest about the 'no choice' element has avoided the need for me to be sectioned in the past (e.g. remind me that, if I don't go into hospital now, I will undoubtedly be sectioned very soon).

I need to know that people are pulling together; that they are in control (particularly when I don't feel I am) and they do know what to do. There is a clear plan about what is going to happen to me that I will be told about. That people are making sure that my behaviour or actions are not jeopardising my reputation at work.

What to do during office hours If you feel that action needs to be taken during office hours then you should get in touch with Ruth (CPN) or Jane (psychiatrist) (see professional contacts at the beginning of this document). They will take a lead role in organising care and/or involving CATT.

Figure 4.7 How to spot becoming unwell

Chapter 5

Person-Centred Thinking Tools that Enhance Voice, Choice and Control

Individuals not institutions take control of their care.

Department of Health[102]

[Organisations must] actively involve people, carers, families and communities in the design, development, delivery and review of innovative care and support arrangements to maximise choice and independence and utilise the widest range of resources.

Think Local, Act Personal Partnership[103]

Person-centred thinking tools can help describe the amount of choice that a person has by looking at the decisions he makes. They can also uncover the information needed to inform actions that will help a person take more control. This chapter looks at the tools that enhance people's voices so that they can have more choice and control over the decisions being made in their lives. This is central to the vision for adult health and social care and the sector-wide partnership agreement *Think Local, Act Personal.*

For some people in residential care, research suggests that choice and control can also mean the difference between life and death. Researchers from Yale and Harvard studied nursing home residents to find out what happens when people retain the right to making decisions about their life and what happens if it is taken away.

They divided residents into two groups of people similar in age, sex and illness. The first group was actively encouraged to make decisions about their life in the nursing home while the other was explicitly encouraged to let staff members make those decisions on their behalf. After 18 months, the researchers found that even though a number of residents died at the nursing home (which had been expected), those in the group that couldn't make decisions died at the same rate as was usual for the nursing home, while those in the group that could make decisions died at half the usual rate. The researchers interpreted the findings to mean that those who had more control over decisions in their lives were protected from an earlier death.[104]

For people to have as much choice and control in their lives as possible, we need to know how people communicate (especially if they don't use words) and how people make decisions. This is especially important at the end of their lives. We must ensure that everyone involved in the person's life has and uses that information. There are many detailed and sophisticated approaches to communication used by speech and language therapists. Here are two practical and simple tools that are good places to start.

Communication charts

> Everyone who is dependent on others for support has an especially critical need to have his or her communication understood.
>
> *Michael Smull*[105]

The communication chart is a powerful way to record how someone communicates. This is a critical tool to have when people do not communicate with words. It is also important to use when people communicate with their behaviour (also known as 'challenging behaviour') or when what people say and what they mean are different, as you can see from Nora's story.

Nora's story

Nora, 84, is described as a real character. She is 'full of fun' and lives in a care home in Cheshire. The only words Nora uses to speak are 'yes' and the odd swear word. So if Nora is to have the things that matter to her present in her life, we need to know how she is communicating with us to let us know.

Nora has at least four different ways of saying 'yes', each conveying a different meaning. The staff who know Nora really well have worked out what each of these ways of saying 'yes' means by making their best guesses and checking out that they had guessed correctly. They then record their learning on the communication chart. This means that if any of those staff leave, all that rich knowledge in their head doesn't leave with them; it is instead shared with other supporters and new staff.

Nora carries a small A5 file in her handbag which is full of communication charts so those supporting her can quickly learn what she is telling them, without having to get it wrong 20 times first while trying to figure it out.

Staff continually add their new learning around what Nora is telling them. She has plenty to say, and people must also listen to the subtleties of her expression and body language. Lots of different staff support Nora and they have found each person has a different idea of what Nora was saying with her behaviour or words. The communication chart helps them record this more accurately so that all those supporting Nora are clear about what she is saying and how best to respond. (See Figure 5.1.)

Having the power to communicate and be understood is central to people having choice and control in their life. It is easy to assume that older people who don't use words to speak have little to say – Nora is a great example of how inaccurate that belief is.

There are two communication charts:

'What am I communicating to you?'

'What are you communicating to me?'

The first is a clear, powerful description of how the person communicates. In the second, instead of recording what the person does, we record what we are trying to communicate to the person, and then what we are encouraging the person to do. (See Figures 5.2a and b.)

To get started, it is easiest to look at either what the person does, or what we think it means, filling in the second or third column first (see Nora's example in Figure 5.1). Start with easy, clear communications like knowing when the person is angry or sad. How does he demonstrate this? What do you need to do to comfort or support him? How do you know this? When is he most likely to be angry or sad? Getting it started is relatively easy; keeping it alive is the challenge. It needs to be used and revisited on a regular basis.

Nora's communication chart

What is happening where/when	When Nora does this	We think it means	And we should
Anytime.	Nora shouts 'yes'.	She wants to go to the bathroom.	Support her to go to the bathroom.
Nora is being asked to make a choice or answer a question, for example choosing her clothes.	Nora says 'yes' but her facial expression is cross and her tone is sharp.	She doesn't like the item of clothing you are showing her or the answer to the question is no.	Respect the answer to the question is no. Show her more options when choosing her clothes.
Nora is being asked to make a choice or answer a question.	Nora smiles and says 'yes' enthusiastically.	Nora is telling us 'yes'.	Depends on the question or choice but respond accordingly, letting Nora know we understand she has told us 'yes'.
In the evening.	Nora will take her feet off her footstool, remove the rug from her knee and look in an obvious way at the clock.	She wants to get up out of her armchair and go to bed – usually 7.30ish.	Check with Nora if she wants to go to bed. If so, support her (see Nora's going to bed routine).
Anytime.	Nora grimaces and says 'yes' in a cross tone or swears.	She is unhappy – perhaps her routine has not run like clockwork, the nurse is late or early (Nora hasn't finished her breakfast), somebody may have gone in her bedroom or she doesn't like what is on TV.	Sit and talk to her.
Anytime.	Nora holds your hand/smiles at everybody.	She is happy.	Enjoy her company.

Figure 5.1 Nora's communication chart

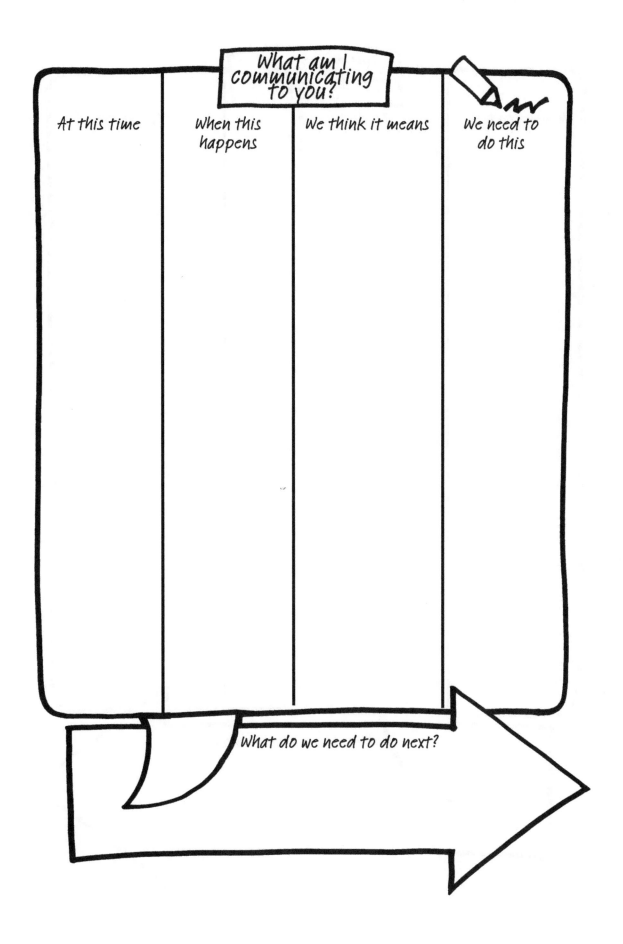

Figure 5.2a What am I communicating to you?

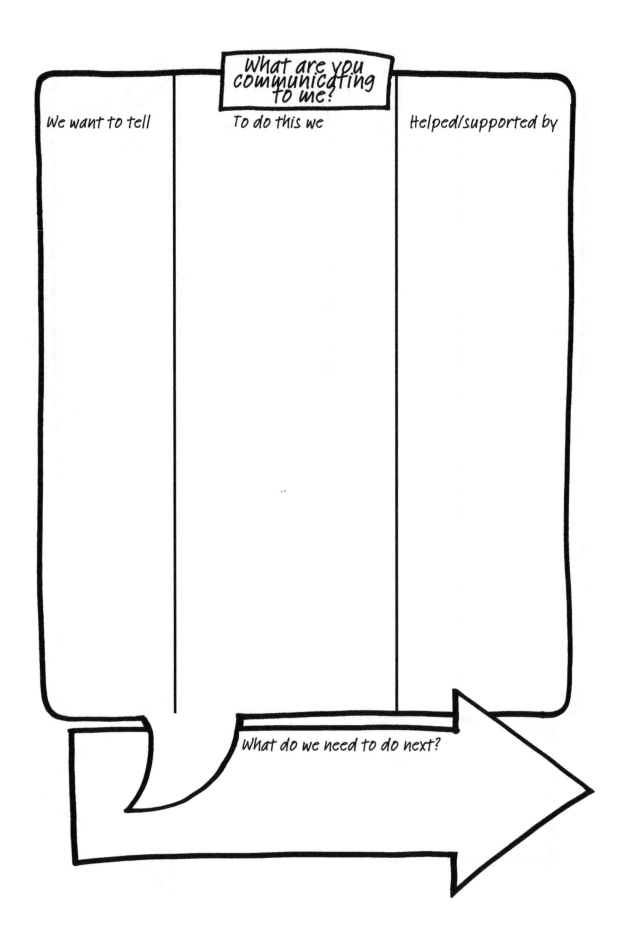

Figure 5.2b What are you communicating to me?

Table 5.1 gives a couple of lines from Sandra's communication chart. Without this communication chart, it would be easy to assume that having different colours on her nails was a sign of feeling confident and taking care of herself. In practice, for Sandra, it means the opposite.

Table 5.1 *From Sandra's communication chart*

At this time	When I do this	It means	You should
When I am depressed.	I stop eating and drinking.	I am feeling really low or I am feeling paranoid that my food is contaminated.	Encouraging me and cooking with me can help.
Anytime.	I pay a lot of attention to my nails – paint them different colours.	My self-esteem is low – I use my nails as a distraction from my face or from what I have to say as I don't think I am worth it.	Listen to me and acknowledge how I am feeling.

The communication charts are just as powerful for people managing a long-term health condition.

Amanda's communication chart

Amanda, 35, works in a busy office. She has a long-term chronic back pain condition. She decided to develop a communication chart to help her manager understand how to support her in different situations. She used the template on www.thinkaboutyourlife.org and printed it out to share with her manager in supervision, who found this helpful and suggested that she share it with her colleagues so they could decide quickly how best to support Amanda. (See Figure 5.3.)

Decision making agreements

> Increasing choice and control of the person's support is at the heart of all personalised service provision.
>
> *Think Local, Act Personal Partnership[106]*

Knowing how someone communicates is essential, yet we need to do more to directly create the amount of choice and control people have in their lives. Self-directed support means making choices and decisions about how people want to be supported, so that they are in control of the services they receive. Two areas to think about in decision making are the person's ability to make decisions, and who else could or should be involved. Personalisation and the development of individual budgets are good examples of how joined-up approaches at all levels are required to support individuals to make the best choices for themselves to improve their own mental health and well-being. Individuals, with the help of friends and family and professionals, consider their own needs and goals and how they want them to be met.[107] This requires us to think differently

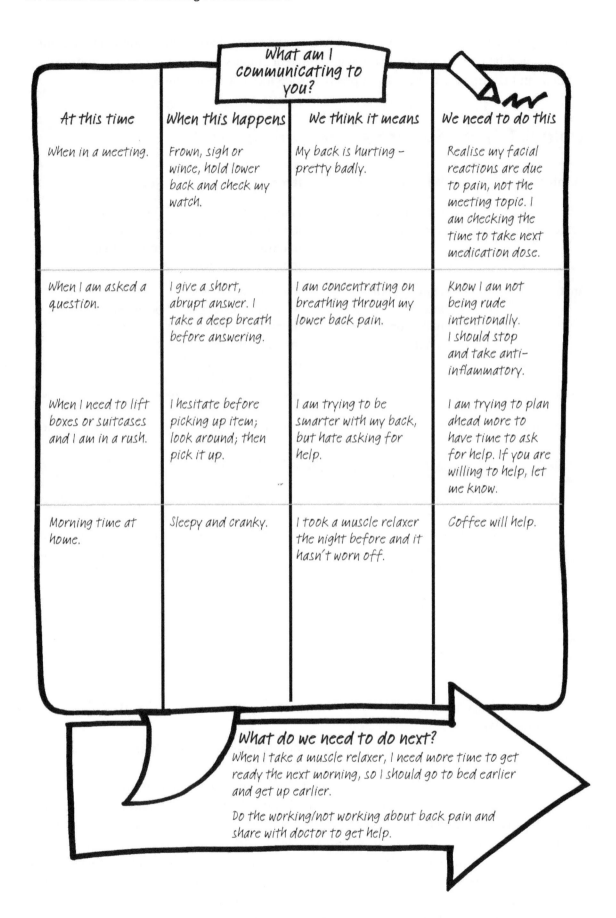

What am I communicating to you?			
At this time	When this happens	We think it means	We need to do this
When in a meeting.	Frown, sigh or wince, hold lower back and check my watch.	My back is hurting – pretty badly.	Realise my facial reactions are due to pain, not the meeting topic. I am checking the time to take next medication dose.
When I am asked a question.	I give a short, abrupt answer. I take a deep breath before answering.	I am concentrating on breathing through my lower back pain.	Know I am not being rude intentionally. I should stop and take anti-inflammatory.
When I need to lift boxes or suitcases and I am in a rush.	I hesitate before picking up item; look around; then pick it up.	I am trying to be smarter with my back, but hate asking for help.	I am trying to plan ahead more to have time to ask for help. If you are willing to help, let me know.
Morning time at home.	Sleepy and cranky.	I took a muscle relaxer the night before and it hasn't worn off.	Coffee will help.

What do we need to do next?
When I take a muscle relaxer, I need more time to get ready the next morning, so I should go to bed earlier and get up earlier.

Do the working/not working about back pain and share with doctor to get help.

Figure 5.3 Amanda's communication chart

about who could contribute to decision making. The quote from the Department of Health's *Vision for Adult Social Care* directly refers to carers, different providers and multidisciplinary team members, but in reality there is a broader range of people who could contribute. A wide range of people will be offering formal and informal support – from family and friends, to peers and self-help groups, to faith communities and employers. The full range of people who support someone are not usually identified or acknowledged in the assessment and care planning process:

> Within a recovery context, mental health support can be accessed from a wide range of sources: from family members and professional mental health teams, through to education providers, employers, community groups and social groups. As a result there is often a range of individuals involved in a service user's daily life that are not identified or acknowledged as part of the network in the assessment and care planning processes.[108]

Doing a 'relationship circle' (see Chapter 4) is a way for the person to think about and describe those people who are important in his life, and what role they could play in planning and decision making. If there are very few people in the person's life, then the relationship circle may be the beginning of developing goals and outcomes in this area, and marking progress. Another person-centred approach called an 'inclusion web'[109] offers another way to track progress in relationships and connections.

Having important people in your life is not an automatic passport to shared decision making. For example, people may have an important relationship with their parents, but may not want them to have a substantial decision making role in their life. People generally want to involve different people in different decisions: friends about what to wear for an important event; a partner and family on where to go on holiday; or a business partner on which options to prioritise in the next three months.

People's ability to make decisions is related to their mental capacity, and the opportunities and choices they have to make decisions. Mental capacity simply means the ability of an individual to make their own decisions. Some people need help making decisions, and the 'decision making agreement' is a way to think about how much control people have over their decisions, and how they can be increased. Needing support to make decisions should not prevent people from having control over their lives and exercising their human rights.

Figure 5.4 shows a person-centred thinking tool that helps staff to know how to support people to make decisions, and for this to be consistent across a team. This supports a culture of 'power with people' by working towards increasing the number and significance of the decisions that people make in their lives.

The Mental Capacity Act (2005) established for the first time that people can no longer make decisions on behalf of other people without going through a process. The decision making agreement is a way to reflect how decisions are made, in the light of this legislation.

When supporting someone in their decision making, here are some important questions to ask:

- Do I fully understand what is important to the person and their communication?

- Am I the best person to support this decision making?

- Is the information that I have and am giving the person relevant to the decision?

- Am I presenting it in a way that the person can understand?

- Am I giving the information in the right place and time?

- Have I given the person the best chance to make the decision themselves?

Figure 5.4 Mental health capacity

Anna has learning disabilities and lives with two other people in the north east of England. Those supporting her wanted to make sure Anna had as much choice and control in her life as possible, and so worked with her to put the chart in Figure 5.5 together.

This information is important to use to assist in decision making. We also need to record the decisions that the person makes. You can use the blank template like the one in Figure 5.6.

Joan's decision making agreement

Joan, 73, lives in a nursing home because of her dementia. When Joan was young, she couldn't afford chocolate, but says that now she can, staff at the residential care home won't let her. Joan has unstable diabetes and staff felt that they had a duty of care to prevent her eating something that may make her ill. However, Joan was frustrated at the lack of choice she had over her life. Chocolate means a lot to her because while she was growing up with 13 siblings in a two-up two-down with weekly visits to the pawnbrokers, it was considered an unaffordable luxury at the time.

The problem was that staff lacked an understanding of mental capacity and didn't recognise that Joan was perfectly capable of making some decisions for herself. By developing a decision making agreement, staff were clear that this was a choice Joan could make herself (see Table 5.2).

Decision making profile				
How I like my information	How to present choice to me	How can you help me understand	When are the best times to ask me to make a decision	When is it not a good time for me to make decisions
• In small amounts; I can read but can't take in the information very well. • Spoken to me is best and picture books with examples can help. • I like information to be factual and not emotional.	• Tell me that I need to make a choice and give me a number of options or pretend one hand means one thing and the other hand another, and then I can point to my choice or tell you the number.	• Use a book with pictures in it describing the choice or relate the choice to TV shows I like. • Help me by giving me facts. Don't use emotional reasons, or other people as reasons, as I don't relate myself to others very well.	• Early in the day after breakfast and my tablets. • When I say "I'm cheered up today". • When I have just shown you something new I've bought. • When I'm out after church and I'm shopping. • Over lunch out.	• From 4.00 p.m. onwards I get very tired. • Before meal times I get very hungry. • When I am biting my fingers or punching my stomach. • When I am repeatedly saying "I'm not in a bother". • Before I've had my tablets.

Figure 5.5 Anna's decision making profile

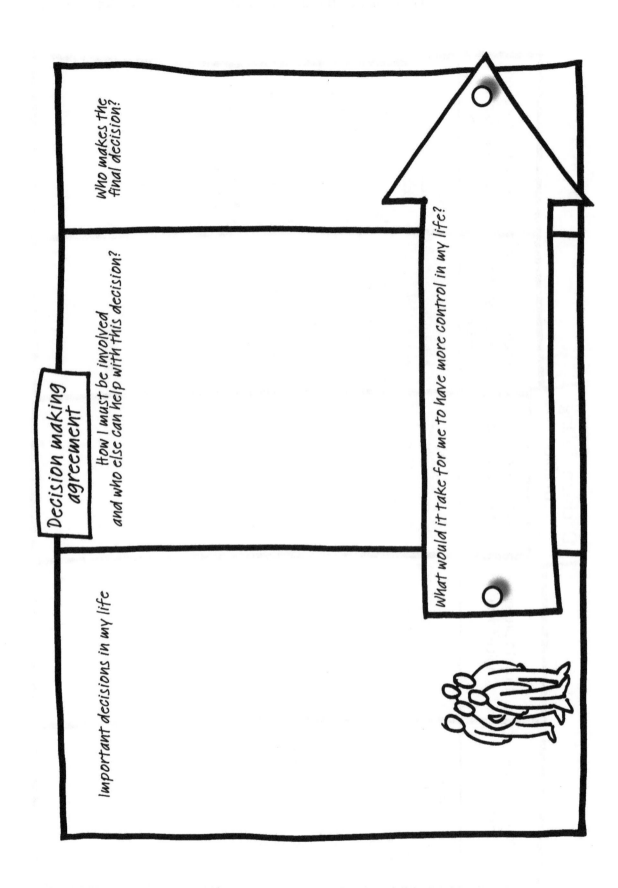

Figure 5.6 Decision making agreement

Table 5.2 *Joan's decision making agreement*

Decision to be made	How I must be involved and who else can help	Who makes the final decision
When I eat chocolate	I can decide if I want some chocolate every now and again. It's my life. I know the consequences and the district nurse checks my blood sugar every day so she can advise me if it's a safer time to eat it.	Joan
Whether I can check my own blood sugar	My diabetes consultant at Manchester Royal Infirmary	My consultant and I together

James is 26 years old, and has a spinal injury. He says:

In the past I was really into sports. With my twin brother, Tom, I was a County Tennis Champion. I also played rugby for my school teams. I have a degree in computing and worked for a large organisation as a software developer. I am proud of my family, particularly my twin brother who qualified as a management accountant.

In June 2007 I had a C5/6 break of my spine as a result of a fall. Initially I couldn't move anything below the break. I have worked really hard and as a result of the physiotherapy I have undertaken, I have regained a lot of movement in my arms. I try to do a lot of exercise to maintain this. I am now able to push a manual wheelchair. I was in hospital for 16 months until I moved to Wheatridge Court in Nov 2008.

Within the next month I will be moving to the bungalow attached to Wheatridge Court before finding my own place to live. I have medication for pain management, and spasm management. I have support from district nurses with skin management/pressure sores and bowel and bladder routines. I have a specialist physiotherapy session with Dave from Physibility once a week. This [see Table 5.3] is how I would like people to assist me when I am making decisions about my life and health.

Table 5.3 *James' decision making chart*

How I like information presented to me	How to present choices to me	How to help me understand information	Best time for me to makes decisions	Worst time for me to make decisions
Written information preferably emailed to me electronically	Comparison information or contrast scenarios	Talking through information and getting advice. I would speak to my dad or my brothers. I would also speak to Gary and Katie as they have had similar experiences.	Morning time	7 p.m. onwards as I will be tired and possibly in pain

Decision making for the future: end-of-life wishes

Person-centred thinking can also be used in decision making for end-of-life wishes and Advance Directives, which set out how a person says they want to be cared for in the future as they come to the end of their life, or if they lose mental capacity.

In the example below, Michelle helped her dad make decisions for the end of his life. She looked at what would and would not work for him from his perspective and also from her own point of view, and together they negotiated the decisions.

When my dad was diagnosed with lung cancer he was determined that life would continue as per usual, only allowing for the inconveniences that having treatment entailed. His quirky sense of humour helped all of us who loved him to deal with what was happening. He would tell me about his group of friends who met two or three times a week in the local pub, each one of them had some kind of serious illness and they would place bets on which one outlasted the other. They would actually collect on these bets too!

After about a year, he stopped responding to treatment and had to come to terms with the fact that he wasn't going to live much longer. His health rapidly deteriorated as the cancer spread and he could no longer do lots of the things he had enjoyed and taken for granted, such as spending time on the computer, reading and writing.

My dad had always been a little unconventional so I was not surprised that he had certain ideas about planning for the end of his life. My dad asked me to ensure that his wishes were honoured and to write these out. This was more difficult than it may first appear as some of his wishes didn't fit with my ideas of giving him a good send off [see Table 5.4].

We considered these wishes along with what I perceived to be the impact of them on me and my children and, together, we agreed a way forward.

I would complete the request to leave my dad's body to medical science. He struggled to write at this point but could just about sign his name.

1. I would follow the contingency plan to the letter and promised not to come to the funeral should there be one.

2. I would leave £100 behind the bar of both of his favourite pubs with the instruction that Tony Noon had bought his last round of drinks and that was enough; there was no way he was paying for a wake that he wouldn't be able to get drunk at!

3. Should there be a cremation, I could have the ashes (this was a hard-fought concession).

4. My dad would leave enough money to pay for me and the kids to spend a day at an amusement park to celebrate his life as this was one of the things he most enjoyed doing with them.

When my Dad passed away Plan B came into effect. He had his cremation exactly how he planned it. I got the ashes and my friend bought me a tree which blossomed during the month he died. His friends raised several glasses to him in the local pub. I used the money he had left to take my three children to Alton Towers for the weekend. We stayed in the chocolate room and had a wonderful time reminiscing about Granddad.

Years later, my kids still talk about this positively. My tree flowers every March and we pour a can of Guinness into the pot on Father's day and Christmas...he wasn't one for birthdays!

Table 5.4 *Michelle's dad: end-of-life wishes*

What would work for Dad (hopes)	What would not work for Dad (fears)	My perspective
To make all decisions about what happened once he died.		I was really pleased that Dad was still able to make decisions and that he was clear about what he wanted to happen. He couldn't really see things from my perspective and thought I was being silly.
Plan A) Leave his body to medical science if they could take him. However, sometimes they are full and cannot!	To pay for a burial he wouldn't be there to enjoy.	Plan A) This was practical and benefits others, but I wanted somewhere to go to remember, and this wouldn't afford this.
Plan B) If he can't leave his body to medical science, then the cheapest possible funeral is to be arranged. No one is to attend this funeral as he really won't be there!		Plan B) At least I would get Dad's ashes and I was appalled at the thought of no one turning up to his funeral. This was really upsetting for me.
That his funeral didn't interrupt anyone's normal routines.	To have a ceremony or wake.	Although Dad was raised a Catholic, he had developed an aversion to anything remotely religious, therefore any kind of service would have been false. A funeral is part of the whole process of grieving, as well as having the opportunity to celebrate life, so how would we say goodbye? How would I support my children to come to terms with the loss of their granddad if they didn't have the opportunity to share stories at the funeral? What about all of his friends? He was a popular man. Would people think I didn't give him a good enough send-off?
That his mates raise a drink to him in his memory.	For this to be formal in any way.	Again, I was conscious of what others might think.

Increasing choice and control

Once we know how much choice and control someone has in their life, as described in his decision making agreement, the next question must be 'What can we do to increase it?'

This can mean looking at the decision making agreement and asking:

'What will it take for you to have more control in the important decisions in your life?'

'Of what other decisions would you like to have more control?'

People having more choice and control requires us to understand why they have so little of it to begin with. Here are some possible reasons (although there are lots more):

- The person has few choices because staff are not giving people opportunities to make decisions themselves.

- The person has few choices because he is not in control of his own services.

- The person has few choices because he does not know what else is possible because his life experiences and opportunities have been limited.

Once we know the possible reason, we can then look at potential solutions. Personal budgets directly address the first two reasons.

If the reason for lack of choice and control is that the person has had limited experiences to choose from, then we need a way systematically to increase his experiences and opportunities. Start with knowing what matters to someone and then intentionally offer more choices.

Derek's story illustrates how person-centred thinking tools like communications charts and decision making agreements provide important information that help professionals find practical solutions to increase the amount of choice in an individual's life.

Derek's story

Derek, 37, lives in Manchester in a shared house with another person, and is described as having 'profound learning disabilities' and 'challenging behaviour'. He is supported by Jane, who leads a team of four staff who are working with Derek to learn about what matters to him and how he wants to be supported.

Derek lived in a children's home with other children with profound disabilities, and had limited opportunities to go outside of the home. Now, as an adult, what matters to Derek is having long walks in the open air, taking his shoes off as soon as he gets in the house, and sitting in 'his' chair when he is in the lounge. The team decided to systematically introduce new experiences to Derek, so that he had the opportunity to develop more interests and to have more to choose from in his life. Jane and the team thought about this in two ways.

The first was: 'if Derek likes this…what else might he also like?' They started with his one page profile (which told them what he already liked) and then mindmapped all possible activities that were similar. Something that is important to Derek is being out in the open. When they listed all the activities that involved being out in the open they came up with being part of a rambling club, taking up golf, kite flying, having a dog and going on long walks with the dog.

The second way that they thought about this was to mindmap: 'what would other 37-year-old men, living in Manchester, be doing in their spare time?' They did this because Derek had not had the same life opportunities as other people and there were lots of activities and experiences that were available to his non-disabled peers that he could enjoy. They thought about family and friends who were in their 30s and lived in Manchester, and what they knew from their own experience and came up with a long list.

Now the team had two lists — one of activities that were based around what they knew Derek already liked, and one that other men of his age may do. Then they took each possibility and 'measured' it against what they already knew was important to Derek and how he wanted to be supported, by asking the question:

'Is there anything in Derek's one page profile that would suggest he may not like this?'

They then decided on two activities to try over the next month: dog walking and going to a pub with live music, and decided how often to try them. They then used the thinking behind the 'matching support' tool to work out who would be the best person in the team to support Derek to try these new experiences.

Lucas has a friendly dog, and the team decided that he was the best match for dog walking, and Jon was 'into the Manchester scene' and had a good knowledge of local pubs and clubs, so he was actioned to support Derek to try the three local pubs that had live music. Finally, Jane juggled the rota to make sure that Jon was supporting Derek in the evenings when the live music was on, and Lucas was put on the roster for at least one weekend afternoon and two other afternoons for dog walking. Jon and Lucas agreed to use 'learning logs' to record how Derek responded, and they decided to review the plan and what they had learned at the team meeting in a month's time.

Person-centred thinking helped Derek try new experiences based on information that was available about what was important to him and how much control he had over decisions in his life. In the next chapter, we look at the importance of matching staff to people and how person-centred thinking can help us be clear about our role and responsibility in delivering what people want from services and increasing that person's choice and control over his support.

Chapter 6

Person-Centred Thinking Tools that Clarify Roles and Responsibilities

However clear the information is about what matters to the person and her opportunities to make decisions, if people are not supported by people that she likes, and who like her, life could still be miserable. Typically when staff from the various services look at the skills required to support someone, they usually limit themselves to the skills needed to address issues of health and safety and the general skills needed for the role. It means that people don't always have the opportunity of working with someone whom they like, and the likelihood of ending up with people who like each other, with interests in common, is then random, at best. Delivering personalisation also requires that staff think about and make decisions, to try new ideas and test out possibilities in a culture that supports learning and creativity.

This chapter looks at the importance of getting a good match between people and the staff that support them and how to make sure staff responsibilities are clear, so that they feel safe in trying new and creative approaches.

Getting a good match

Getting a good match between the person supporting and the person being supported – whether paid or unpaid – is crucial. The *matching tool* is a simple way to record what is needed to give a person the best match between those who use services and those who provide them.

A good match is a win–win. When we take into account a staff member's characteristics and interests, as well as their skills and experience, we are more likely to get a match that is enjoyable for everyone. In the last chapter, we saw how Jane supported Derek to try new experiences by matching the right people in his support team to the right experience. Support worker Lucas loved dogs, and had a friendly dog, so they knew that he'd be a good match to help Derek to go dog walking.

When staff enjoy their work, they are more likely to stay longer in the role; this increases the stability for the individual and decreases the staff turnover for the organisation. It could be argued that we are less likely to see issues of abuse and neglect when we pay good attention to matching people well. This approach is also more likely to help to deliver individualised services rather than 'covering shifts'. 'The quality of the match is one of the most powerful determinants of quality of life for people who are dependent on others for support and the single greatest determinant of turnover among those paid to provide services.'[110]

The 'matching tool' (Figure 6.1) has four boxes. These are the support that the person wants and needs, then the skills required to support them, followed by personality characteristics of the support worker and then shared common interests. The most important part is where personality characteristics are recorded.

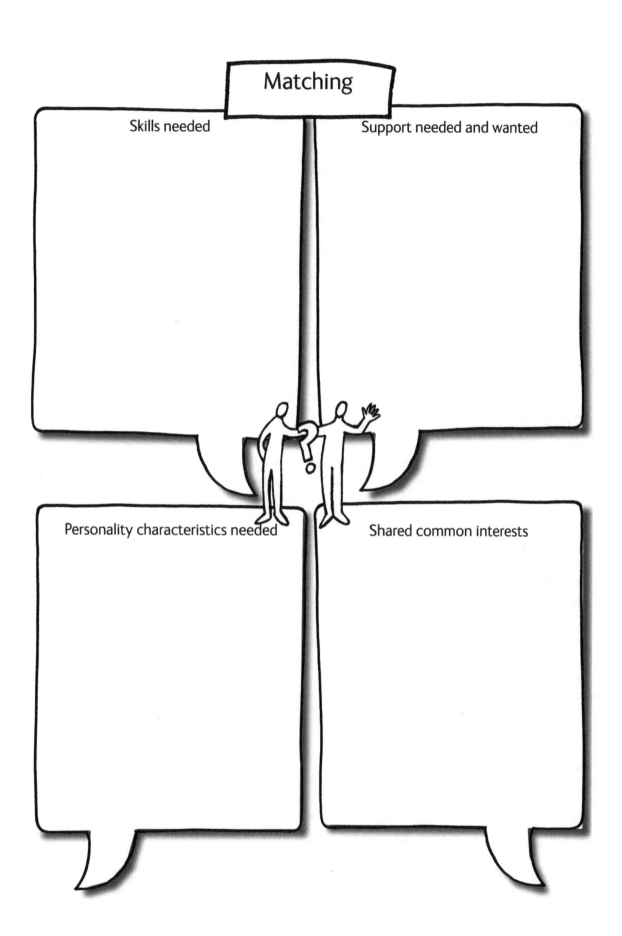

Figure 6.1 Matching tool

Using this person-centred thinking tool should ensure that you list the skills that someone providing support needs in order to meet what is both *important to* them and *important for* the person in need of support. This is a minimum expectation. Matching characteristics is crucial. If the person cannot directly tell you the characteristics of the people with whom she gets on best, here are some questions that are useful:

- Who is the person closest to? What characteristics do they have in common with each other?

- With whom does the person have the most 'good days'?

- Is there anyone whose presence helps create 'bad days'?

- What does this tell you about the characteristics of the support person that work for the person in need of support?

This tool can be used to match existing staff within a team to particular individuals; to recruit new people to a team; or to recruit personal assistants or find volunteers. Table 6.1 is Julia's matching tool for using her personal budget to employ a personal assistant (PA) to support her:

Table 6.1 Julia's matching tool

Support needed and wanted	Skills and knowledge needed	Personality characteristics needed	Shared common interests
Support with the taking of multiple medications – including insulin, nebulisers, tablets and infusion pumps	Competency around the administration of medicines, including injections, nebulisers and infusion pumps	Confident Reliable	
Support to go out shopping and meeting friends	Knowledge of the specifics of health condition so can monitor health and symptoms while out	Outgoing Fun-loving	Crafts and hobbies Shopping Coffee and lunch out
Support with personal care	Moving and handling Training and experience Management of skin integrity Understanding of the impact of lung condition on mobility when dressing etc. Able to apply makeup	As before	Makeup, hair and nails

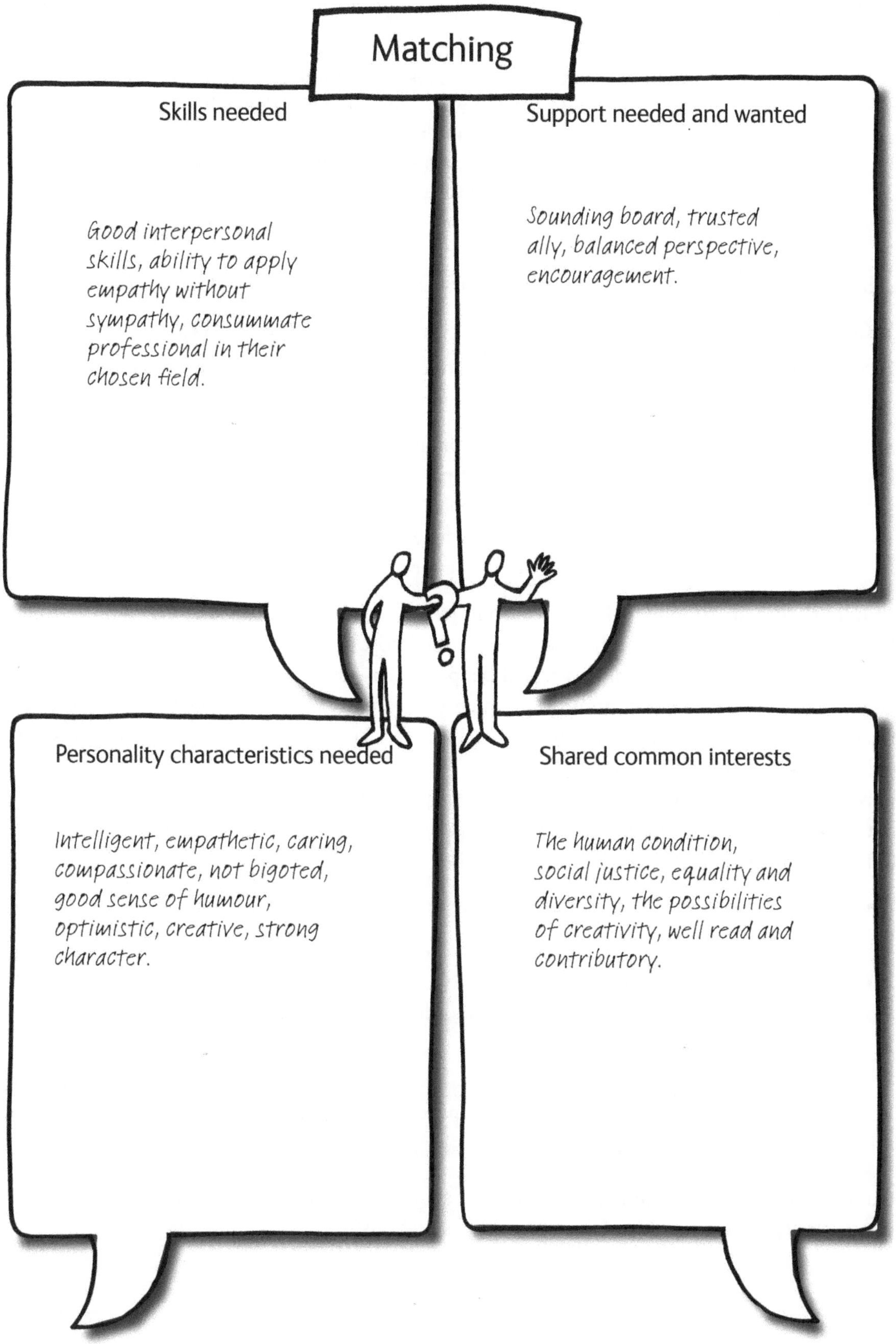

Matching

Skills needed

Good interpersonal skills, ability to apply empathy without sympathy, consummate professional in their chosen field.

Support needed and wanted

Sounding board, trusted ally, balanced perspective, encouragement.

Personality characteristics needed

Intelligent, empathetic, caring, compassionate, not bigoted, good sense of humour, optimistic, creative, strong character.

Shared common interests

The human condition, social justice, equality and diversity, the possibilities of creativity, well read and contributory.

Figure 6.2 Martin's matching tool

Martin's story

Martin is highly intelligent, creative and both well-read and knowledgeable. He wanted to recruit a PA and used the matching tool to begin to think about the sort of person with whom he would want to spend time and who could help him deal with, and monitor, his bi-polar condition. There were very specific interests he would want the person to share with him and also key personality characteristics they would need to have. Martin developed the matching tool to ensure that he was able to get the best possible match. (See Figure 6.2.)

Clarifying the role and responsibilities of others who provide support to the person with the doughnut

Once we know the best person or people to provide support, the next task is to clarify their roles and responsibilities. Charles Handy describes this principle as a 'doughnut':

> The heart of the doughnut – the core – contains all the things which must be done in that job or role if you are to succeed. In a formal job, these are listed as your duties. The next ring is our opportunity to make a difference, to go beyond the bounds of duty, to live up to our full potential. That remains our ultimate responsibility in life, a responsibility always larger than duty, just as the doughnut is larger than its core.[111]

Doughnuts that are 'all cores and no space around them' are all predictable, planned and controlled. Roles that are mainly space, with little 'core', have almost no limit to what can be done. Charles Handy says that some of the most stressed people he has met have been those where their jobs are like that: 'there is no end, no way in which you can look back and say, it was a great year, because it could always have been greater… Without a boundary it is easy to be oppressed by guilt, for enough is never enough.'[112]

Michael Smull developed the doughnut principle to include a third circle, to identify areas that are not the responsibilities of staff (see Figure 6.3). Therefore the person-centred thinking doughnut has three rings:

- The first ring is the inner core, which consists of the core responsibilities of staff or people providing support.

- The next ring is areas where staff need to exercise their own judgement and be creative. These are areas where people must make decisions, problem solve and creatively think about possibilities and potential.

- The final ring is areas beyond the scope of the staff member's role and responsibilities. All roles have limits and boundaries, some of which are formally in place, and some of these are informal – for example, family preferences or respect for cultural differences.

You need to know what is important to and for someone, before you begin to use the doughnut tool to clarify the roles of supporters in specific situations.

Doughnut

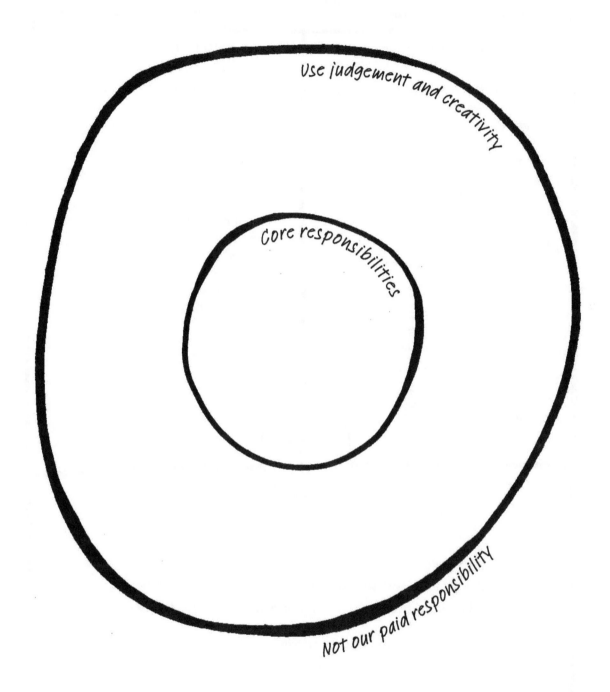

Figure 6.3 Doughnut

Using the doughnut ring is a great way to explain it to people, but hard to use in practice, so we use the same headings in columns (see Figure 6.4).

Responsibilities

Core responsibilities

CPN
Visit every two to three weeks to check he is OK and taking medication.

Psychiatrist
2– to 3-monthly outpatient appointment to review mental health and medication.

Personal supervisor/coach
Weekly assessment of mental health, work on psychological and dependency issues, professional supervision.

PA/domestic helper
Ensure Martin is able to present himself in the best possible light and that his home is fit to invite others into.

Julie: supporting Martin to develop plan
To offer Martin clear instructions and information about developing his person-centred plan.
To answer any questions he may have.
To make sure she has his permission to share any of the information he gives to her.

Use judgement and creativity

Co-create and review care plan. Have a chat to see how he is getting on with things in his life.
Assess his mental well-being and provide advice and support.
Keep him grounded and ensure that he manages financial risk associated with being a social entrepreneur while having a severe and enduring mental health condition.
Provide a secondary source of insight into his mental health presentation and as a source of social support.
How information is given and shared
How to use the plan to share with others. This may be in training on websites etc.
To pace the delivery and content of work in manageable steps.
To comment if she feels the work may be putting Martin under pressure.

Not our responsibility

His unmet needs.

I co-deliver training work with Martin and try to help him get consulting work.

Do not become a business advisor or try to influence the philosophy behind his work. Avoid co-dependency.

Not to become emotionally attached to Martin.

What information Martin chooses to share and what he chooses not to share.

If he decides not to pursue the plan or any statements he makes on the plan.

To become involved with any treatment or therapy.

How Martin chooses to develop and use the plan.

Figure 6.4 Doughnut chart

Charles Handy also talks about two types of errors that staff can make: type 1 and type 2.

Type 1 errors simply mean getting it wrong – an error in the core responsibilities of the doughnut, where someone did not do what they should. Type 2 errors occur when the full possibilities of a situation have not been explored. For example, considering what else could be done to make a difference or achieve an outcome which is better than would be expected by just delivering the core responsibilities.

In tightly planned organisations, with large 'cores' of responsibility, people only have to look out for Type 1 errors, where something that ought to happen is not happening as it should. This is what regulators inspect on. Delivering personalisation requires that staff think and make decisions, to try new ideas and test out possibilities. Without this, we make Type 2 errors – the 'sins of omission' where possibilities haven't been explored and people are just doing the minimum that was expected. Inspectors never look at this, but great managers should be thinking about this with their staff, to keep learning and developing how we support people well.

Using the doughnut also helps to create a culture of learning and accountability, rather than fear and blame, by enabling people to think clearly about responsibilities and possibilities, and clearly delineating who is responsible for what. This enables staff to be creative without anxiety, knowing what would be understood as Type 1 errors, but also aware that not exploring possibilities creatively is a Type 2 error. Research on stress suggests that one of the big stressors in work is lack of clarity of what people expect from an individual. Therefore it is possible and likely that creating this clarity through using the doughnut could have an impact on reducing staff stress and increasing retention.

> A strong blame culture kills creativity, distorts learning, and eventually drives out many of those you want to retain. Some aspects of blame culture are nearly impossible to avoid as looking for someone to blame when something goes wrong is endemic in our culture (just watch the news or read a newspaper). However, the effects of blame culture can be avoided with ongoing work. Part of that work is to create clarity about what is expected of each person in their day-to-day efforts. Where creativity is both safe and encouraged, and where there is clarity regarding where it is and is not expected, you begin to address another critical issue.[113]

In Figure 6.4, Martin records what he sees as the core responsibilities for his community psychiatric nurse (CPN); his coach, David; his PA; and his friend, Julie.

Martin using the doughnut tool

Martin is being supported in his recovery by weekly meetings with a professional job coach called David. They explore how Martin might develop his future and have been using a number of tools to consider what motivates and stimulates him. This has helped Martin to realise that the work he has done in the past is not fulfilling and that earning large sums of money is no longer a motivation. They have also explored together Martin's wish to find someone with whom to spend his life. Martin was quite clear that he felt this was too personal and did not wish to discuss it with David.

At this point, they decided to use the doughnut to clarify what David's core responsibilities were in his coaching role with Martin, and where David could use his own judgement and be creative. Martin also has a PA to help with day-to-day life and is developing a person-centred plan with his friend Julie.

There will never be enough money in the system or in people's personal budgets to do everything that is important in people's lives. This makes it even more important that there is room for creativity when it comes to understanding the roles and responsibilities of different people working together to support a person: from the individuals themselves, from the team supporting them, and from other people in the organisation. Clear boundaries help to create that culture.

Clear boundaries are also very important when people have different roles in a person's life. Jennie has a circle of support, and uses her personal budget to employ a provider to support her in her own home. This decision making agreement makes it clear who is responsible for what in recruiting Jennie's staff, and how the final decision is made (see Table 6.2).

Table 6.2 Jennie's decision making agreement

Area of Jennie's life	How Jennie must be involved	Circle's role in decision making	Provider's role in decision making	When and where the decision is made	How the final decision is made (consensus on who has the final decision making responsibility)
Recruiting staff for Jennie's team.	Meeting people before the formal interview.	Contributing to the job description, person specs, and advert (ensuring that they reflect Jennie's person-centred plan). Contributing to the interview questions to include questions directly relating to Jennie's plan and scenarios from Jennie's life. Circle members being part of the panel and decision making.	Finalising the job description, person specs and adverts to ensure that they fit the requirements of the organisation/law.	Working on job descriptions etc. done through email according to recruitment timetable. Decision on staff made as part of panel process after interview.	Circle needs to sign off the final versions (Suzie and Helen). Circle members have the casting vote in interviews (Suzie).

In the next chapter, we look at moving from 'knowing' information about someone and how they want to be supported, and understanding our role in delivering this, to 'acting' on it.

Chapter 7

Person-Centred Thinking Tools for Analysis and Action

Moving from 'knowing' to acting on information about what is important to and for a person, and how much control they have in their life, is central to person-centred thinking. Otherwise, we simply create what Michael Smull describes as 'good paper' instead of working with people to enable them to have 'good lives'.

So far we have looked at different ways of gathering that information, how people make decisions and how to decide the best people to support them in getting more choice and control. The next step is using person-centred thinking tools to analyse this information further and start developing plans of action.

Working and not working from different perspectives

As soon as there is enough information about someone recorded in a one page profile, we need to use the person-centred thinking tool 'working and not working' to build an action plan to make sure that changes actually happen, rather than there just being a plethora of person-centred information. 'Working and not working serves as a bridge, between what was learned about important to/for and action planning.'[114]

This tool is powerful in three ways:

1. It is a simple way to analyse what is happening in someone's life, whether what is important to him is present in his life, and whether he is being supported in the way that makes sense to him. Problems surface where there are areas of disagreement in people's lives. By looking at what is working and not working from different perspectives, it is clear where there is agreement and where there is difference.

2. It is powerful to look at areas of disagreement in the context of what people see as being the same. It enables people to see things 'all the way round', to stand in different people's shoes and to hear it from their perspective.

3. It prevents us from inadvertently changing aspects of a person's life that are working for them.

'Working and not working' from different perspectives contains two of the core principles of negotiation. When you get each person's perspective on paper, they feel listened to. When you tease situations apart in enough detail, you can find areas of agreement. This enables you to start on 'common ground'.

Dan's story

Dan reviews his progress with his wife using his one page profile and the person-centred thinking tool 'working and not working'. Together they look at each statement on his profile and ask whether it is working (happening in the way described in his profile) or not (not happening, or not in the best way) from each of their perspectives. They use this to think about what actions to take to change what is not working and to make sure what is working keeps happening.

At the beginning of Part II, we introduced Pat who has several long-term conditions. Figure 7.1a shows her one page profile. Pat and her daughter Su used this to think about what was working and not working for Pat (see Figure 7.1b), and then developed actions to address what is not working while keeping what is working (see Figure 7.1c).

One page profile

Me

What people who know Pat say they like and admire about her

Bubbly lady
Confident
Independent
Classy chick and always looks lovely
Never lets her illness get her down
A good friend and listener
Cracking sense of humour
Selfless
Lives life to the full!

What's important to Pat

Speaking and being in the company of her family (daughter Su and granddaughter Jessica) every day and enjoying her `sleep overs' with them.

Seeing friends and neighbours and being involved with her local community.

Being part of other people's lives.

Having a nice home and having the garden looked after by the gardener.

Looking her best in nice clothes and jewellery. Being pampered and having her hair done at the local hairdressers on seniors' day.

To always have enough food in the house!

Getting out and about with her scooter to do some shopping locally.

Going on holiday and sitting on the beach in the sun at least once a year.

Always having some money in her purse.

Having a weekly TV magazine.

Keeping busy and enjoying her many interests such as: good food, gardening, drawing, watching TV (Big Brother and Strictly fan).

Enjoying the odd glass of Liebfraumilch.

Being busy; pottering around can take up a large part of Pat's day.

Making decisions and being organised.

Riding a Harley Davidson for her 70th birthday.

Enjoying life!

How best to support Pat

Share your day with her, she loves being in the company of friends and family.

Don't talk to her about her illness.

Pat will worry if she thinks that Su is having to cope with too much.

Always give Pat plenty of time to get ready in the mornings.

Don't rush her if going out.

Don't fuss over her if she is out of breath.

Be aware that the winter weather does have an effect on her health and she will need more support at this time.

Going with Su to the supermarket once a week and using a scooter trolley to do a `big shop'.

Pat enjoys going out at least once a week to have a break from being in the bungalow.

Make sure events are written down in the diary. Pat likes to plan ahead and be organised; she jots down any questions she needs to remember on her memory board.

Pat is well organised with her medication and medical appointments.

Figure 7.1a Pat's one page profile

What's working?

Living in my bungalow with warden support (who is also a good friend).

Being supported by Su, my neighbours, the district nurse and my private gardener.

Aids and adaptations in the bungalow.

Owning a mobility scooter.

Using the memory board to write.

Pat

What's not working?

Mattress variator controls are out of my reach, which I need to use due to increased immobility during the night in/out of bed.

Unable to reach the curtains/blinds to open/close them.

Mobility scooter being kept at the back of the bungalow.

Accessing the shops to do my weekly 'big shop'.

Not having a break from being in the bungalow. It would sometimes be nice to stay over at Su's and Jessica's.

Worrying about Su taking time off work to accompany me to hospital appointments.

family

Knowing that mum has good support and friends near her.

Aids and adaptations in the bungalow that will help mum stay independent.

Purchasing the mobility scooter and mum gaining confidence in using it.

Knowing that mum feels independent and knowing she doesn't have to rely on other people all the time.

Improved health.

Mobility scooter being kept at the back of the bungalow.

Worrying that the stairs in my house cause difficulties for mum.

Mum not getting out and about.

Figure 7.1b Pat's working and not working

Who?	What?	By when?
Su	Arrange to have a lock fitted on the mobility scooter and buy a storage cover so that it can be kept at the front of the bungalow so that it is accessible for Pat to use to access the local shops, hairdressers and post office etc.	By the end of the week
Pat and Su	Rearrange the bedroom so Pat can move about more easily at night and access the controls for the mattress variator.	By the end of the week
Su	Extend all the pull cords on the curtains and blinds so that Pat can open and close them independently.	By the end of the week
Pat and Su	Su to take Pat once a week to the supermarket, where she can get a scooter trolley and do her own shopping.	Weekly
Pat and Su	To also purchase a freezer which means Pat can stock up on the basics, which would help relieve her worry around not having enough food in the house.	By the end of the week
Pat	Pat said she felt confident enough to attend hospital appointments on her own and actually enjoyed organising her transport to/from the hospital. Pat uses a memory board to write down any questions she would like to ask, and keeps a diary of her appointments and a list of her medication.	Ongoing
Pat	Pat felt that the risk of her managing the stairs at Su's was worth while in order to have the opportunity to have a break from her own home.	Ongoing

Figure 7.1c Pat's actions

4 plus 1 questions

Using the 4 plus 1 questions reinforces a positive habit – that of valuing mindful observation and learning

Michael Smull[115]

This is another tool for reflection and learning about what works and doesn't work. It asks the following questions:

- What have you tried?

- What have you learned?

- What are you pleased about?

- What are you concerned about?

The answers to these questions lead to the 'plus 1' question, which is:

- Based on what we know, what should we do next?

These questions are powerful to use in meetings and reviews, or to reflect on a particular area of someone's life with him when he faces a particular situation or challenge. It can be an easy way to update one page profiles and develop more detailed person-centred descriptions. This is an efficient way to gather collective learning and to make this visible to everyone. One approach is to put up sheets of flipchart paper, each with a different question, and ask people to write on them. This is a way to ensure that everyone's perspective is heard and to make sure that issues are addressed and not overlooked.

The '4 plus 1' questions are a quick way to work out better ways of supporting people, and staff are less likely to continue to do what is on the 'what are we concerned about' list.

In an assessment, treatment and support service, they have changed their reviews to use two person-centred thinking tools: what is working and not working from different perspectives, and using the '4 plus 1' questions. Figure 7.2 is an example of their paperwork.

Helen

Helen is supporting her husband, Arthur, as he is approaching end of life. She was feeling overwhelmed by the strain of this difficult situation as she tried to cope with the huge changes this made to their lives. Helen decided to use the '4 plus 1' questions to clarify her situation and regain some control (see Figure 7.3).

Using these person-centred practice tools decreases the risk that we will 'throw the baby out with the bathwater'. They help us pay attention to maintaining what is working. 'Working and not working' is also the foundation of the person-centred reviews process described in Chapter 10. But before we get there, we need to make sure we capture how people respond when they take action so we can learn more deeply about what is important to and for them in the future.

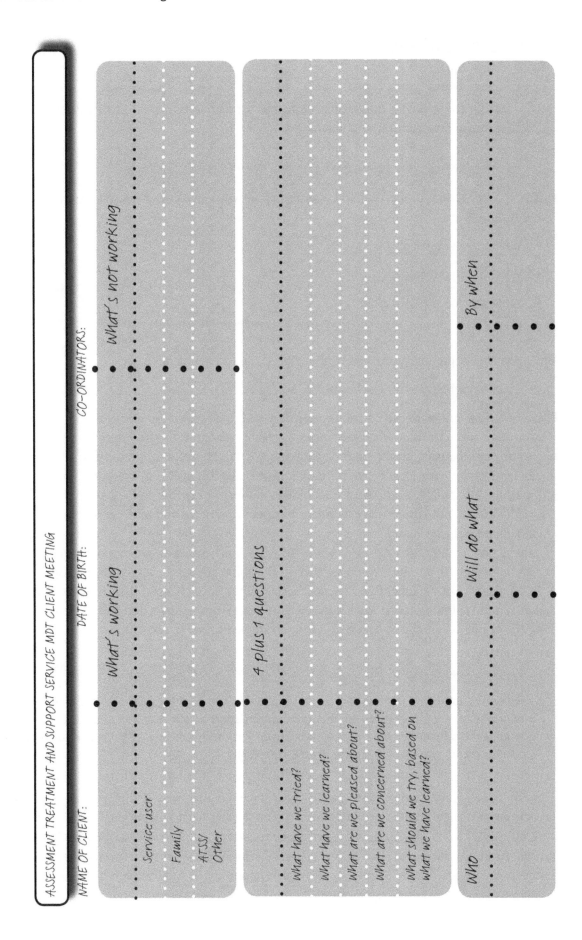

Figure 7.2 Paperwork example

4 plus 1 questions

What have we tried?

- Respite care for Arthur
- Support from family – son, daughters and daughter–in–law
- Domiciliary care service four times a day

What have we learned?

- I take on the burden of Arthur's diagnosis
- I have begun to take on some of the 'male' tasks around the home
- Arthur using respite services may be necessary in the future and that I do not need to visit him as much as I did in the past
- I have worth as an individual and that my self–worth is important to me
- It is important to me to be acknowledged as a person in my own right, separate to me as Arthur's carer

What are we pleased about?

- I am pleased about our personal budget
- I am pleased with the district nurses
- I am pleased about Angela, my volunteer from Hull Churches Home from Hospital
- I am pleased about my social worker who visits every three months

What are we concerned about?

- Arthur can feel abandoned when in respite
- The current situation may continue for a prolonged period and this is not sustainable for me as a carer
- My own health
- What the future holds for me
- Arthur is developing dementia and this will become progressively worse. How will I cope then?

What do we need to do next?

- I will continue to feel empowered
- I will visit the hairdresser once a week
- I cannot let his illness rule me
- I will use respite care
- I will look after my own health and keep well

Figure 7.3 Helen's (carer's) example of end of life

Chapter 8

Person-Centred Thinking Tools for Deeper Learning

> Acting on this kind of learning can have a substantial impact on the quality of life for people with severe disabilities using long-term services. However, it can happen only if the learning is valued, recorded, and acted on.
>
> *Michael Smull*[116]

To make sure that we give people every opportunity to have more choice and control, we should commit to learning continuously in a deeper way about what is important *to* and *for* the person, and the balance between the two. This deeper learning can be focused on particular areas in the person's life – for example, around relationships and community or around work and careers. It involves reflecting and reviewing an individual's progress by asking what else we need to learn and figure out together. It is helpful to know what a person's hopes and dreams are and we should make sure that people involved in this process are the ones who are closest to her.

Learning log

Amy's learning log

Amy hated medical appointments. A nurse who worked with Amy recorded what happened at her medical appointment but not what she did to help Amy cope with waiting around for it. Rather than have Amy wait in the doctor's office, she took her through a drive-through car wash. Amy, who did not communicate with words, was happier and more excited in the car wash than anyone had ever seen before. The creative and skilful way that this nurse supported Amy was not part of her nursing notes until the 'learning log' format was developed.

The 'learning log' is a process to learn about new activities or situations. Staff notes and records confirm what activities have taken place but rarely record what was learned. People who support someone on a day-to-day basis are learning important information about what works for the person. Usually this gets lost as it not expected to be recorded and this knowledge then leaves when the person leaves.

Learning logs are an opportunity for reflection (see Figure 8.1). Recording what works makes it more likely that the activity or event will happen again. They are most useful when people are trying out new things, or being supported by new staff. It is crucial that someone (for example, the team leader) reviews the learning logs with the team regularly, and together people figure out what they are learning about the person and the support they provide. This results in doing things differently. The information from the learning log has to be used in the same way as the 'working and not working' information is used.

Person-Centred Thinking Tools for Deeper Learning

- Those things that are working need to be maintained. These can be added to information on 'how best to support the person'.

- Those things that are not working need acting on to change them.

Table 8.1 illustrates Richard's learning log for managing his pain and trying to sleep. He used this with his partner Deb as a way to evaluate what he was trying around his sleep and what they needed to figure out or change.

Table 8.1 Learning log for managing pain and trying to sleep

Date/time location	What we tried	What worked well?	What didn't work?	Actions or questions
Away from home	Taping arm and shoulder with sports tape. Using cooling spray.	Tape helped support it, less pain and a bit more sleep. Taking most of the tape off when arm first felt itchy. Spray gives brief relief.	Last bit of tape was left on too long, so the skin ripped off – skin on arm now incredibly sore too, so even harder to get comfortable.	Was it that the tape was left on too long? Was it an allergic reaction? Make doctor appointment to go through ultrasound results and arrange allergy test.
Home	Putting burns gel ointment on raw arm. Swapping sides of the bed in the middle of the night so arm could hang out of the bed.	Confident the gel won't cause any reaction. Swapping sides brought a few hours' sleep. Deb happy to be able to do something to help.	The gel doesn't relieve any sting and it's painful to put on. It makes Deb squeamish putting it on.	Ask a chemist for something else.
Away	Sleeping sitting on couch. Icepack. Air conditioner switched on.	Some sleep while on the couch (45 mins out of 3 hrs). Deb didn't wake up. Didn't hurt while sitting up.	Uncomfortable and painful for back. Icepack horribly cold. Air conditioner really noisy so woke up anyway.	Can I get a physio appointment up here to see if they've hypo-allergenic tape and can show us how to tape it properly?

Table 8.1 *Learning log for managing pain and trying to sleep* cont.

Date/time location	What we tried	What worked well?	What didn't work?	Actions or questions
Away	Physio appointment. Using barrier gel under tape. Taping shoulder. Staying up really late. Painkillers before bed instead of when the pain starts.	Taping helped for a while, got a bit more sleep. The skin stayed on! Slept to begin with.	Started to get irritated after 12 hrs rather than 24 as told. Awake most of the night. Pain killers only last about 1.5 hours.	Are stronger painkillers an option? Phone surgeon to be put on a cancellation list. Make massage appointment.
Home	Acupuncture and massage.	Massage helped relieve other sore muscles. Acupuncture relieved a lot of pain initially.	Hate the sensation of the needles.	Ask about other acupressure point techniques that don't involve needles.

The one page profile can then be updated with the new learning and developed into more detailed person-centred descriptions, as well as creating actions for change. Where the same people are doing the same activity in the same circumstances over and over, the learning log will slowly lose its power and purpose. Just automatically replacing progress notes with learning logs, and then not summarising and acting on this learning, will breed what Michael Smull calls 'cynical discontent'.

Pete's learning log

Staff supporting Pete at Beeches – a day service for people with learning disabilities – were struggling to learn about what was important to Pete and what good support looked like from his perspective. They decided to use the learning log to replace their traditional notes (see Figure 8.2). They used this information to begin his one page profile.

Once a month at a team meeting the manager and staff looked at the learning logs to decide what they had learned and where that needed to go on Pete's one page profile. The following information came from this learning log. What does this tell us about what is important to Pete?

- Not to be bored or have to wait around (for example, for taxis)

- Pizza

What does this tell us about how best to support Pete?

- If Pete goes pale it may mean that he is going to have a seizure, so support him to lie down as soon as possible.

- Make sure Pete has an opportunity to look at a menu before he gets to a restaurant, as sometimes menus are difficult to read.

- Ensure that Pete has books, and other activities (for example, his iPod) for car journeys.

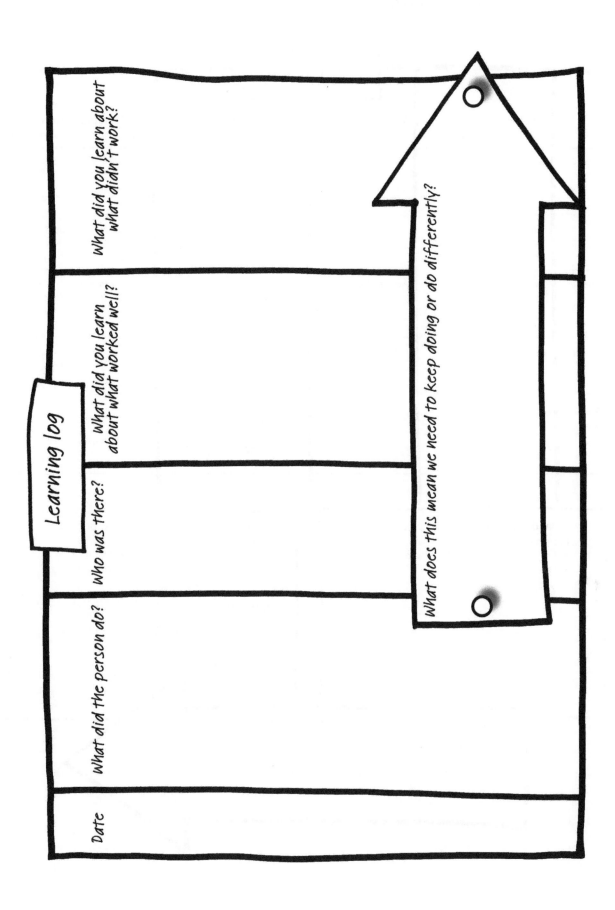

Figure 8.1 Learning log

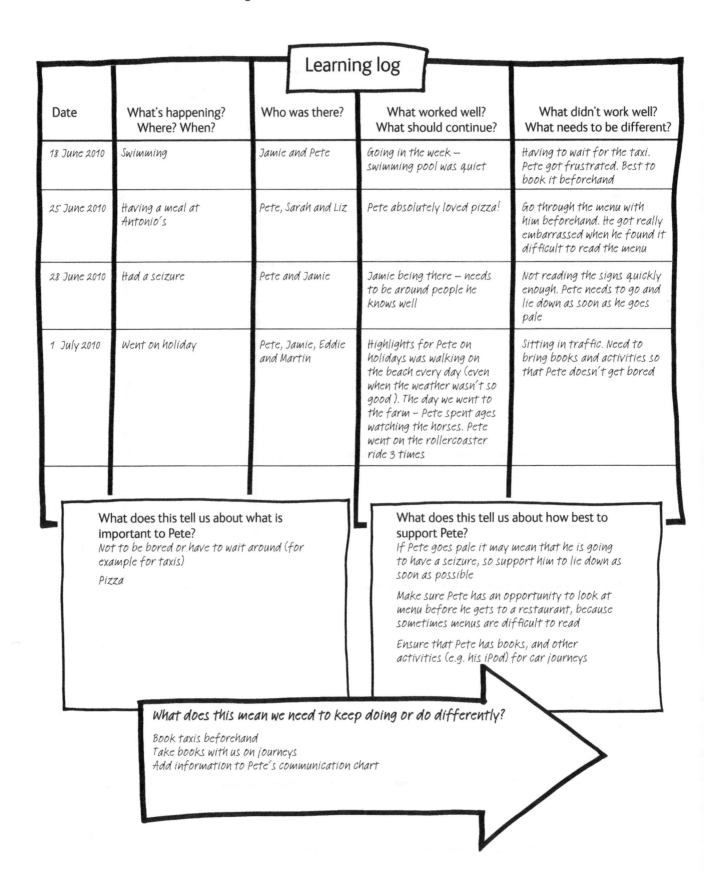

Learning log

Date	What's happening? Where? When?	Who was there?	What worked well? What should continue?	What didn't work well? What needs to be different?
18 June 2010	Swimming	Jamie and Pete	Going in the week – swimming pool was quiet	Having to wait for the taxi. Pete got frustrated. Best to book it beforehand
25 June 2010	Having a meal at Antonio's	Pete, Sarah and Liz	Pete absolutely loved pizza!	Go through the menu with him beforehand. He got really embarrassed when he found it difficult to read the menu
28 June 2010	Had a seizure	Pete and Jamie	Jamie being there – needs to be around people he knows well	Not reading the signs quickly enough. Pete needs to go and lie down as soon as he goes pale
1 July 2010	Went on holiday	Pete, Jamie, Eddie and Martin	Highlights for Pete on holidays was walking on the beach every day (even when the weather wasn't so good). The day we went to the farm – Pete spent ages watching the horses. Pete went on the rollercoaster ride 3 times	Sitting in traffic. Need to bring books and activities so that Pete doesn't get bored

What does this tell us about what is important to Pete?
Not to be bored or have to wait around (for example for taxis)

Pizza

What does this tell us about how best to support Pete?
If Pete goes pale it may mean that he is going to have a seizure, so support him to lie down as soon as possible

Make sure Pete has an opportunity to look at menu before he gets to a restaurant, because sometimes menus are difficult to read

Ensure that Pete has books, and other activities (e.g. his iPod) for car journeys

What does this mean we need to keep doing or do differently?

Book taxis beforehand
Take books with us on journeys
Add information to Pete's communication chart

Figure 8.2 Pete's learning log

Histories: listening to and learning from a person's story

> The excursion through very personal histories is often a way of eliciting the powerful recognition that people are not very significantly shaped by their physical and behavioural impairments nearly so much as they are shaped by their experiences and their lack of experiences.
>
> *Jack Yates[117]*

Understanding someone's history or story with them can reveal insights about what is important to them and suggest future goals or outcomes. People may remember long-lost friends with whom they want to reconnect, experiences they had and want to do again, or times in their lives which they definitely don't want to repeat and what can be done to avoid them. This can also reveal a lot about what the best support looks like for a person, and the characteristics of the best people to offer that support.

There are many ways to approach this through words or pictures. You could ask the person about her past and consider what worked and didn't work well for her. You could draw a timeline with spaces for the person to write or draw significant events (see Figure 8.3). Or you could try a magazine-style quiz:

- What are the top seven significant events that you consider have shaped you and your life?

- Who has been the biggest influence on your life?

- What was your proudest moment?

- Where is your favourite place and why?

- What was your best job?

- What were your favourite passions, interests and hobbies? How have these changed over the years?

- What did you enjoy doing for fun as a young person and adult? What has changed?

As with other person-centred thinking tools, the information gathered through looking at histories can be added to the person-centred description by asking:

'What does this tell us is important to the person?'

'What does it tell us about how to support the person well?'

'What clues does it give us about the person's gifts and contributions?'

Histories could also provide insights into what a person wants for her future. A shared understanding of someone's history can inform how her service could be designed. Herb Lovett describes how he listened to Steven's history to inform service design in his book *Learning to Listen*.[118]

> I spent a day designing a service for Steven, a 16-year-old with autism whose behaviour was considered too difficult to allow him ever to live outside a 'special' institution. The staff on his unit insisted that Steven should not come to this meeting because he would only become upset and disruptive and could not possibly sit through the entire day. They told me Steven had almost no attention span and that he did not speak.

My thought was that no one was going to sit the entire day. Naturally, we would take breaks as a group, and try to make meetings relaxed enough that people who need to stand up and stretch could do so without feeling disruptive. So I persuaded them that Steven should start the day with us, hear the plan for the day and if he needed to leave he could do so at any time without feeling he had somehow failed. And, like anyone else who might take a break, he should feel welcome if and when he decided to rejoin the group.

So when we began, I explained to Steven that we would be going back over his life, that the day would be focused on talking about him, that this might be painful to hear, and that he should, like anyone else, feel free to take a break when he needed to. He gave no indication that I could see that he had heard me.

Just as people had predicted, at the beginning he was restless and noisy, and someone left with him for a while. When he came back, people were talking about his childhood, but I asked them to add an extra piece. When they said that he had been placed in another foster home at age three, I asked everyone present to guess what it would be like to experience that. I asked people to give adult language to a three-year-old's feelings at having lost his birth family and a foster family, and being confronted with a new family yet again. If you were Steven, how would you feel? People came up with some insightful and deeply felt guesses: 'I would feel I was bad. I would wonder why I was being punished. I would think no one loved me.'

As people were talking, their tones changed. Instead of the staccato, just-the-facts way we had been looking at his life, people took longer to speak up. Some people were considering their own experiences as children as they thought about Steven's life. The room got quieter. Steven stopped pacing and sat quietly. By the end of the meeting, when people were talking about how a person this estranged and systematically rejected needed personal experiences of love and acceptance, Steven had curled up with his head in someone's lap, calm and intent.

It seemed to me that Steven had done two things. First, he had demonstrated to people how long he could concentrate on things when things were worth attending to. Second, he had served as a barometer for the group. When we began, people were pessimistic and unfocused. They were sure that 'he couldn't...he will never...' Their predictions were not as specific as they were negative. But as they became more aware of Steven as a person, they looked more at who he was rather than what he was not. By the end of the day, they were clear about what he needed and what they could do to help him get it. Having experienced so much rejection, we wondered if he would want to live with a family. Not every teenager claims to need one, but we thought Steven did. He needed to have his abilities respected so that he could start looking for work. As the group's optimism and sense of purpose increased, Steven steadily became calmer. Just as he had listened to the heart of people's discussion, they were beginning to learn they could listen to the hidden heart of his behaviour.[119]

Hopes and dreams for the future

Our deepest dreams tell us something important about who we are, about our purpose in life, about what we are called to bring to our world, our country, our community, our family and friends. Sometimes we lose touch with our dreams: we can get caught up in things; our wishes to be perfect or rich or famous or to have lots of stuff can hide our dreams from us. In this moment, we can ask ourselves: 'what is my dream? What do I really want for my life?' We wait quietly for whatever answer comes today...and then: 'what does the dream tell me about my gifts?'

John O'Brien, Jack Pearpoint and Lynda Kahn[120]

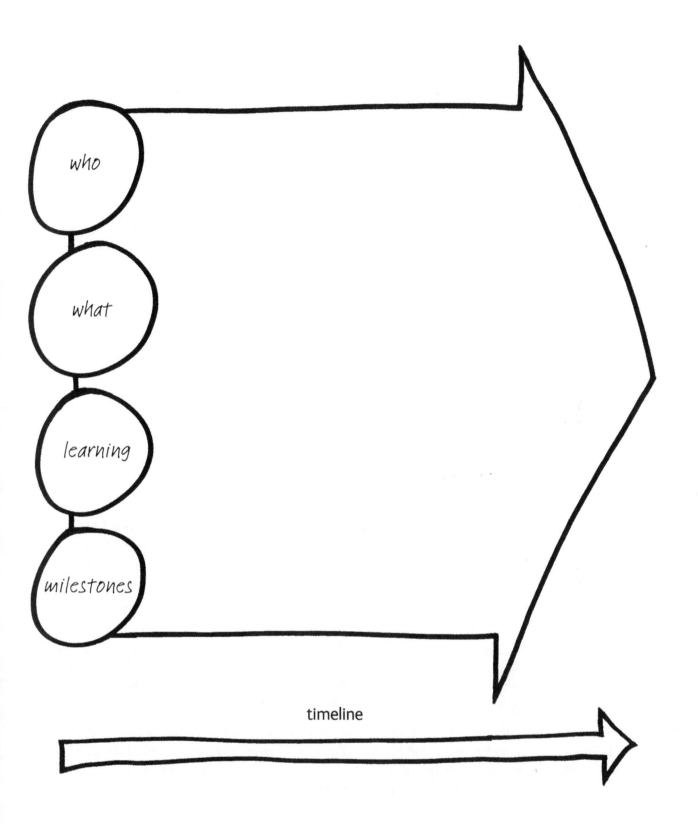

Figure 8.3 Histories

People can approach thinking about the changes that they want to make in their life in different ways. In neuro-linguistic programming, people are described as having a preference to *move away* from something, or *move towards* something. A simple example is that if you wanted to lose weight, which photo on the fridge would you find more motivating? A photo of yourself or someone else who was fatter than you want to be (moving away) or yourself or someone else who was your ideal weight (moving towards)?

For some people, the best way to think about making change is by looking at what is working and not working now. Then ask what it would take to change what is not working, and therefore moving away from it. An alternative approach is to help people think about a positive and possible future – if life was as good as it can be.

Here are some questions that can help a person to think about their dreams and ideal future. Answers could be written on paper, drawn or put together as a collage on a 'vision board'.

If I woke up and my life was exactly how I wanted it to be…

- Where would I live? With whom (if anyone)? What would my home be like?

- Who would be in my life?

- What would I do for fun?

- What would I do for work, volunteering, or making a contribution in another way?

- Where would I go – during the week, on holiday?

- What else would I do – during the day, in the evenings, at the weekends?

- What else would I have in my life (for example, possessions)?

- How would I feel if all this was happening?

Sometimes the phrase 'If I could, I would' resonates better with people. Gill supported Madge to think about this when Madge was approaching the end of her life. This gave Madge an opportunity to think of anything she still wanted to do or achieve, and then to think with Gill about what could be practical and possible for her to do.

One of the things Madge really wanted to do when they explored the 'If I could, I would' question was to have a mini-break in London and see a show in the West End.

> I had a ball. Sally and I went to see *The 39 Steps* at the Criterion Theatre. It was wonderful. Another highlight was a cream tea at Harrods. I had a cup of tea and a mousse. Unusually for me, I really enjoyed sitting down to eat with Sally. I never thought we would make this trip happen but by taking a step back and thinking this through but we did it – fantastic.

Sometimes it is helpful for people to think about their fears alongside their hopes. Gill supported Madge to think about her hopes and her fears. Figure 8.4 shows what Madge talked about. This gave Madge and her family a way to plan for how Madge could realise her hopes and to try avoid her fears. This was a very important conversation for the family to have together.

PATH is the person-centred planning tool that most strongly focuses on the future, and is another way to help people think about their contribution or aspirations and to then develop goals from these. This will be explained more in Chapter 12.

Learning about being part of the community: presence to contribution

Thinking about histories and hopes and dreams can help us learn more about the person, their contributions and how she would like her life to be. We can also learn more deeply about particular areas of the person's life – for example, around health, employment or community connections.

'Presence to contribution' is a person-centred thinking tool that can help with this by asking people to think about the activities or interests they have in their community and how these could be developed further. This helps people work out what it would take to go from simply turning up to an activity and being present, to being fully involved and making a contribution (see Figure 8.5).

Sam and his relationship circle

Sue worked with Sam who lived at a care home in Lancashire. She had started using person-centred thinking tools, and had talked to Sam about what was working and not working in his life. The key thing that wasn't working for Sam was that he lost contact with all his old mates since he spent three months in hospital and then came to live in the home four years earlier. Sam particularly missed his connection with the bowling club he had belonged to for a number of years.

Sam was helped to develop his relationship circle. He was supported to write to some of his old friends, and as they responded, Sam gained the confidence to think about how he could reconnect with the bowling club, which wasn't far away from the home. There was a spring in his step as he anticipated the possibilities!

The challenge now was finding the right staff member to support Sam to go and watch the bowling. They needed a match between his interests and how he wanted to use his hours, with staff characteristics and interests. Sue and Sam's supporters used the matching tool to find the right person. They looked at the one page profiles for staff which included their hobbies and interests and found that Greg, a new member of staff, looked the perfect match for Sam as he, too, was a keen bowler. Sam agreed.

Within a month, they went off to the bowling club together. Sam cannot bowl because of his hip injury, but he enjoyed catching up with his old friends while Greg would play a few games.

After a couple of months, it was as though Sam had never been away. Greg and Sam went once a fortnight and they both enjoyed the company. Sue was now challenged to think about how she could support Sam to have a real sense of purpose, given that he was unable to bowl. Sam said that he would give the dominoes a go and that worked out really well. Sue, Greg and Sam used the 'presence to contribution' tool to think more clearly about Greg's role (supporting Sam to feel part of the bowling community and to make a contribution) and to think together about what the steps to that would be, and how they would know that they had been successful. Sam now writes the monthly newsletter for the bowling club. Prior to retiring, Sam was a keen writer and produced the church newsletter each week, so he feels that he is giving something back.

Hopes

That I will have a long period of remission.

To keep as well as I can for as long as I can.

To keep going to the market each week.

To stay out of hospital.

Spend time with my friends at the luncheon club.

Continue going to the tea dance at the Trafford Centre with Jane and Jim each month.

To go away on holiday by the sea. A little cottage in Wales would be lovely with Ian, Sally and the grandchildren.

That I will die quickly and not put my family through a long drawn out end.

Fears

Being in pain.

Being housebound or even worse bed bound.

Having to be admitted to hospital.

Not seeing Sam again.

That I make my children unhappy.

That I lose the health I have and have a long drawn out death.

That I become incontinent – this terrifies me.

If I looked so gaunt it would pain my family and friends to look at me.

Figure 8.4 Madge's hopes and fears

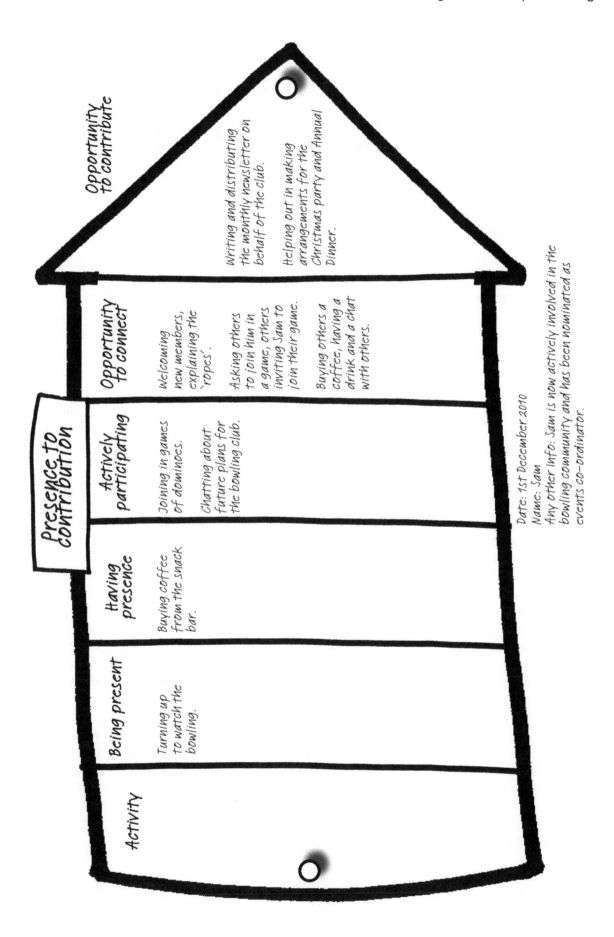

Figure 8.5 Presence to contribution

Chapter 9

Deciding Which Person-Centred Thinking Tool to Use and How to Build a Detailed Person-Centred Description

Staff need to understand person-centred thinking tools and person-centred plans, and coach their colleagues in using them to deliver self-directed support. The tools offer a way of learning and understanding the balance between what is important to and for a person; to enhance voice, choice and control; to clarify roles and responsibilities; and to provide analysis and action.

When you first start working with someone who needs support, how do you determine which person-centred thinking tool to use? We believe the best way to begin is to look at what is working and not working in the person's life and then match the tools to the issues that are raised. We will show you how to do this, and then how to take that information to start building a person-centred description of how a person would like to be supported.

Kenny's story

Kenny, 64, lives in a home which supports people with dementia. Kenny used to love sport and played every sport he could. His mum, Ethel, said 'if sport had been his exams he would have been top of the tree in them all!' He was a professional football player for Blackpool Football Club as a young man, and then went into the textile trade as a salesman until retiring at 54 due to early onset dementia. He loved golfing holidays with his mates and he spent many happy weekends away with his wife Jean in their caravan – his pride and joy. Kenny and Jean didn't have any children, but says Jean, 'we were always content to just have each other and our group of friends'. Kenny was a very confident man who could go and chat with a roomful of strangers easily. He no longer uses any words to speak and is unable to move around unless supported by two staff members or in a wheelchair due to a fall which led to a broken hip a year ago.

Kenny seems bored, restless and unhappy in the home. Kenny's family and staff decided to try and do something about this, and looked at what was working and not working for him. Kenny could not directly tell people what was working and not working for him. Instead, his family and staff made a best guess at what this could be, and decided to use learning logs to test their guesses out. The list of what was working and not working from different perspectives was sobering and grim. Through the conversations of what was working and not working, it became clear that while Kenny was well looked after, what mattered to Kenny was not present in his life, and this felt sobering and grim (see Table 9.1).

Table 9.1 *Kenny's 'working and not working'*

Perspective	What's working	What's not working
Kenny (our best guesses)	Jean and Mum visiting often. Watching DVDs with his wife Jean. Chocolate. Long soaks in the bath.	Having nothing to do. Sitting alone for long periods. Not being able to walk around without help. Not going outdoors. Not being able to watch what is happening in the kitchen.
Family	Kenny always looks very smart and is well cared for. Kenny's physical health is good. His skin is much less irritated than it was. The new cream is working well.	Not everybody understands how Kenny communicates. He is bored and restless a lot of the time, with nothing to do. He only gets old magazines and newspapers to look at, nobody reads the paper to him. Kenny rarely gets outdoors.
Staff team	The care Kenny receives. The diet supplements. Pureed diet. Drink thickener. Pressure relieving mattress.	Kenny's boredom.

Together the team and family thought about opportunities for Kenny to try new things so staff could learn more about what would make life better for him. For example, before Kenny lost his mobility, he was always on the go. He used to stand and watch what was happening in the kitchen. The staff thought about finding out whether this was still something Kenny wanted to do, and how to do this safely. The group also considered what it would take for Kenny to go out and buy some magazines from the local shop each week and have a daily morning newspaper delivered as they knew he would pick up old newspapers and magazines to look through them whenever he could.

They used 'what is not working' to decide what they needed to do and which person-centred thinking tools would help.

This was all put into a detailed action plan stating who was going to do what and when they would have completed it. Pam began Kenny's one page profile using the information that had been gathered from the discussions with the family and what was working and not working. She also worked with staff to use learning logs, and made sure that every two weeks these were reviewed and the information was used to add to the one page profile.

This was the beginning of changes for Kenny. People now know how he communicates, and what matters to him. The staff and family are looking at different activities in which Kenny might be interested, based on his hobbies and interests in the past. He is back being part of what happens in the kitchen, and has a safe place to sit. He has his own paper and is supported to go out of the home to buy his magazines (see Table 9.2).

Table 9.2 Kenny's 'what is not working' and 'person-centred thinking' tools

What is not working for Kenny	What we need to learn or do	Which person-centred thinking tools could help
Not being able to go in the kitchen anymore.	Learn how Kenny could be safely involved in the kitchen, and be part of what is happening.	Learning log. Then use this information to begin a one page profile.
Staff do not know how Kenny communicates.	Learn about how Kenny communicates from people who know him well – his family. Make sure that all staff are communicating consistently with him.	Communication chart. Then look at a decision making agreement to increase the number and range of decisions that Kenny can make.
Not going out.	Support Kenny to buy his own magazines each week and have a daily newspaper delivered.	Review progress on this using 4 plus 1 questions in a month's time. Then develop a history map to discover more about what Kenny liked to do in the past. Then look at developing a community map of other places that Kenny may enjoy going to and being part of (possibly connected to where he used to go in the past).

The person-centred information about Kenny started with a few lines about what was important to him, gleaned from the 'working and not working' tool:

- seeing his wife, Jean, and mum, Ethel, every week
- eating chocolate
- having magazines and newspapers
- long soaks in the bath
- getting out and about
- being part of what was going on; for example, being in the kitchen.

At first, advice on how best to support Kenny had information about how his food needed to be pureed, about his sensitive skin and the care and cream that this required, and about his diet supplements and his pressure-relieving mattress. Since then, his one page profile has expanded to include the communication charts (under 'How best to support Kenny') and more detailed information about the magazines he likes and the support he needs to go to the shop. Next the team is adding a decision making agreement to his support section.

From a one page profile to a person-centred description

A person-centred description usually starts on one page, with a one page profile, as Kenny's did. A person-centred review is another way to have conversations about what is working and not working, and to start a one page profile (see Part III for more information).

To develop a detailed person-centred description requires gathering additional information and learning, synthesising this with what you already know, and organising this information in a powerful and easy-to-follow way. We have shown how person-centred thinking tools are an excellent way to gather more information about what matters to people and how they want to be supported. Kenny's team learned more about him by using learning logs and communication charts, and then looking at decision making agreements, and then a community map. Using each of these person-centred thinking tools directly led to actions, as well as providing information. Pam looked at the information from the person-centred thinking tool and asked:

'What does this tell us is important to Kenny?'

'What does it tell us about how to support Kenny well?'

'What clues does it give us about Kenny's gifts and contributions?'

Over time, this can develop into a detailed person-centred description with information about what is important to the person, how best to support the person (with information about communication, decision making and matching) and to keep listening to what is working and not working for the person and acting on that (see Figure 9.1). This information could form the basis of a support plan, or a job description for support staff, or as a way to continue to review the services that the person is receiving (that is, is what is important to the person happening and is the person being supported in the way they want to be) or to inform a person-centred plan.

Developing a detailed person-centred description

There are some contexts when keeping the information just to one page is important; for example, in Maureen's story in Chapter 4, the fact that the information was on one page made it easier for health staff to use. They may not have had the time to look at a detailed document.

In other situations, it is vital to move beyond one page and develop more detailed information, particularly where people have complex support requirements that people need to follow precisely. Remember that having a detailed person-centred description is not the outcome; it is a vehicle for capturing learning to lead to change.

As you are developing the detailed person-centred description, keep the following things in mind:

- Remember to add detail: the initial information gathered will often be single words to describe what is important to and for the person. We now want to develop this into fuller thoughts, with more detail. For example, if 'chocolate' was written in the 'important to' column, then this could be developed further by saying 'having milk chocolate every day, especially Galaxy'.

- Remember to separate what is important to you from what is important to the person. If it is important to those who support the person that he takes a shower every day, but it is not important to him, then reminding him to take a shower goes under what other people need to know or do, not under what is important to him.

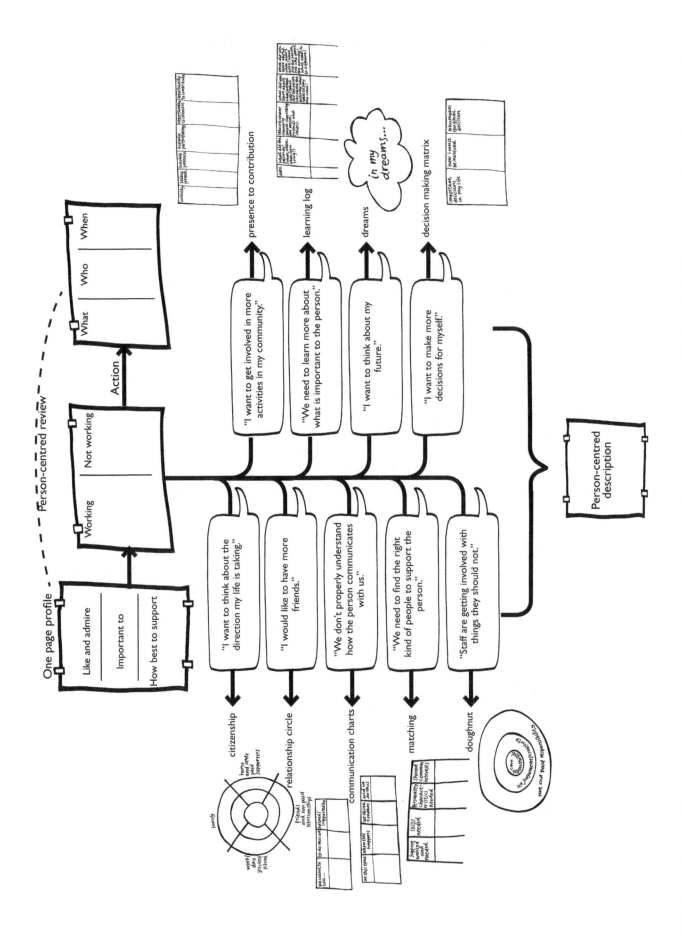

Figure 9.1 From a one page profile to a person-centred plan

- Don't forget to put what needs to be absent from the person's life, what he dislikes as well as putting down what he does like. For example, under what is important to Katherine, it says that she hates to have her teeth brushed. Under what we need to know or do, it says it is important to her parents that her teeth are brushed every day.

- Remember that if someone needs a lot of assistance in getting things done and can't tell people how they like to have it done, you need to write that part of their routine in detail in such a way so that someone who has never met the person could still get it right.

- Remember that if the person-centred description has information that the person does not want everyone to know, you must see if you can develop public and private sections to the plan. The private parts of the plan are only available to those who need to know. Where there are issues of safety, this may not work, but where there are issues of intimate personal care, it almost always works.

The 'bottom line questions' for person-centred descriptions

- From reading it, does it make you feel like you know the person?

- Does it give you enough information that you could support the person well even in a new situation?

- Is there a balance between detail and brevity? Is there enough detail to understand what is meant and who the person is, but not so much detail that the person-centred description will not be read?

- Is it written in everyday language that is easy to read?

Conclusion to Part II

Knowing, understanding and using person-centred thinking tools provide a structured way for staff to personalise the services they offer. This loop of learning, acting and then learning more is supported by undertaking the necessary exercises to understand the balance between what is important to and for the person; enhancing the person's voice, choice and control; clarifying roles and responsibilities of the people supporting them; analysing and acting on information about what works and doesn't work; and then learning more deeply about their dreams and aspirations.

We have shown you the different person-centred thinking tools in action and introduced a process for deciding which ones to use for supporting people. This rich information can be captured in a person-centred description, which can eventually form the basis of a person-centred plan or support plan. Kickstarting the development of these descriptions can be begun in a person-centred review or a person-centred planning meeting, which is the focus of Part III.

Part III

Person-Centred Reviews and Person-Centred Planning

> A well defined understanding of important to and for…and a regular review of 'what's working/not working' that actually guides action is a necessary condition for any form of service provision.
>
> *Department of Health*[121]

A person-centred description is the blueprint of how people want to live and be supported, and therefore constitutes the day-to-day job description for staff – both what needs to happen and how. Change takes place by using person-centred-thinking tools like 'learning logs', and '4 plus 1' questions to reflect and learn, and by continuing to ask what is working and not working from different perspectives. A person-centred review is a meeting that combines two person-centred thinking skills and tools: an understanding of the balance between important to and important for the person, with what is working and not working.

Person-centred reviews can kickstart the development of a person-centred description, or build the depth of this information. The purpose is to create shared actions for change, based on a reflection and analysis of what is working and not working for the person and others. A person-centred review brings together people who are providing support from different roles or places, with family and friends. It places the person who is being supported firmly at the centre.

This part of the book introduces the person-centred review process, including outcome-focused reviews where they are used for people who have personal budgets (Chapter 10). We go on to show how this process relates to the care programme approach (CPA) used in mental health services (Chapter 11) and explore an alternative meeting process to capture person-centred information through various person-centred planning styles (Chapter 12). Person-centred planning starts with a meeting, but fundamentally differs from person-centred reviews in both context and process. Person-centred reviews began with the question: 'How can we make our existing statutory reviews more person-centred?' Person-centred planning starts with the questions: 'Who are you, and who am I in your life?' and 'What can we do together to create a better future?' We also explore the different contributions of person-centred reviews and person-centred planning in relation to service competence and community competence.

In Chapter 13, we show how information gathered in person-centred reviews and person-centred plans can grow into more detailed person-centred descriptions and support plans.

Introduction to person-centred reviews

> I've done thousands of reviews in the traditional sense. These have ranged across two or three people to unwieldy numbers, which, when you are chairing and writing is cumbersome. [They end up] being, isolated and focused on anything but filling in the review document and ensuring it's signed, authorised and feeding the huge computer database – the statutory requirements. Even as an experienced social worker, I still question myself in some reviews. They are long, laborious and boring: everyone doesn't want to be there, many don't turn up, and families often don't feel reassured that this is not another paper exercise... My first time in facilitating a person-centred review was completely different. It felt like my first parachute jump: I was thinking on air, it was happening and I couldn't do a great deal about it except rely on my training, skills, knowledge and values. That's exactly reminding me why I'm here. They were the two most successful reviews I have ever completed, and now, several months later, they still have their effect. Brilliant.
>
> *Paul, social worker*

Reviews are part of the statutory requirements for most services. Many of us have sat in reviews where people have not been listened to, things have not moved forward and there has been little to inspire or motivate real change. Fundamentally, they did not work for people receiving services.

Person-centred reviews are a way to change this: they put the person at the centre of the review of their support, basing actions on what is important to the individual and what is working and not working for them and others. The process of a review can meet all the statutory requirements, but the spirit, the atmosphere and most importantly, the outcomes, are very different to traditional reviews.[122]

> *Service users and carers have reported this to be a more uplifting, empowering, fun and powerful reviewing method in comparison to their experience of a periodic process which was tedious, inconsistent and focused on blue pieces if paper and not 'me'.*
>
> *A care manager*

Disabled people, carers and people from councils describe these key elements of a great review:[123]

- A great review ensures that people are living the life they want to. The review process acknowledges and celebrates what is working well. It encourages people to aspire to improve their life, and identifies what is not working well, and what needs to change.

- A great review maps a journey. The review looks at the steps already taken and what needs to happen to build and sustain this. The review process identifies next steps and sets realistic actions to achieve by the next review.

- A great review is outcomes-focused. The review looks back at the outcomes or changes that the person wanted to achieve in their support plan and checks whether these have been achieved. Decisions are made about how the support plan needs to be updated and whether a more detailed reassessment is needed.

- A great review gathers and shares information. The review is a way to ensure that people have all the information that they need and that the council has the information it needs.

- A great review is person-centred. The review goes at the person's pace and supports people to think about their life – what is working, what could be possible and what needs to change.

WHAT A GREAT REVIEW LOOKS LIKE

In 2003 we worked on the question: 'Can we develop a review process that takes the same amount of time, involves the same people, still meets statutory requirements, but is person-centred in both process and outcome?' The answer was 'yes' and our experience of 'essential lifestyle planning'[124] meetings provided the basis for the approach. The first person-centred reviews took place with four young people in Hull.[125] From these small beginnings, the person-centred review process was adopted by the *Valuing People* support team in their work with young people and adults who have learning disabilities. In the last five years, it has extended to include people who use mental health services, older people, people who have long-term conditions and people at the end of their life. Person-centred reviews have also started to be used in the USA, Canada, Australia and some European countries.[126]

The response from people who use services and families has been extremely positive.[127] A small study evaluated what people using services in the north east of England thought about the person-centred review process and compared these with their experience of traditional reviews. People clearly preferred person-centred reviews.[128]

Why would I ever want a normal review again?

Peter, who uses services in the north east of England

It was informal, really relaxed and all about what Phil wants. A refreshing change.

Derek, a dad

Most professionals are juggling enormous demands on their time and using person-centred reviews is a way of working that does not take more time, but has a very different outcome. For many professionals, this is a more satisfying way of working.

I have watched appreciatively at the emergence in the work place of person-'centredness' and the range of person-centred thinking tools that are out there. It's exciting for me as a speech and language therapist because communication lies at the centre of all of it. I have attended more person-centred planning courses than I care to list and have learnt a great deal; not just stuff to enhance the lives of the people I support but also stuff that has affected me both personally and professionally. My first thought as I turned up for day one of the person-centred reviews training was what could be different or further developed in person-centred reviewing? Quite a lot it turned out! This is exciting stuff. It keeps the person at the heart of it all in a position to communicate who they are and what their experiences are like. It empowers the other participants with opportunities to express themselves... It still meets statutory requirements. Person-centred reviewing is, in my opinion, invaluable.

Esther Gibson, speech and language therapist

Department of Health guidance recommends that person-centred reviews are used in transition and all adult services as a way to get started with person-centred change.[129] Many local authorities have already adapted their review paperwork and IT systems to reflect person-centred reviews.[130]

Leading thinkers and academics are welcoming their introduction as a way of supporting people. Alan Simpson, senior research fellow and lecturer in mental health at City University, London, says that person-centred reviews are about shifting perspective and providing a genuinely more involving approach:

> The Care Programme Approach process was traditionally a medically-driven process; a system-driven process, even a managerial tickbox process, with service user involvement almost an afterthought. Clinicians were making the decisions – sometimes very well-intentioned – but [person-centred reviews] are about shifting that whole perspective.[131]

Peter Beresford, professor of social policy at Brunel University, has gone on record to say that he thinks the roll-out of the 23 mental health personal health budgets pilot schemes will be 'the opportunity for person-centred reviews'.

> I do have a lot of hope…because [with personal health budgets] people with mental health problems could have almost anything they wanted, so assessments really could be person-centred. It could be another brick in the wall in taking us beyond a response to mental health issues that now is so tied to people being placed in a diagnostic category. Person-centred reviews can help us get back to a humanistic understanding so we see the person rather than the diagnosis.[132]

David Coyle, senior lecturer at the Department of Mental Health and Learning Disabilities, University of Chester, says that there should be nothing stopping professionals from using a person-centred approach except their own reluctance to change or recognise its benefits: 'We have got everything we need to do it so anyone who wants to will be pushing at an open door.'[133]

The difference that person-centred reviews make for people is significant. For Dennis, it was as simple as having a warm bath – something many of us take for granted:

Dennis' person-centred review

At Dennis' person-centred review, he talked to Lucy, his care manager, about the support he received. When asked 'what is working', Dennis talked about his friendship with his neighbour and visits from his family. When asked 'what is not working', he said he felt staff talked over his head and that he got cold when he had a wash: 'I feel like a package and not a person'. Dennis was washed in a cold bathroom because his carer got too hot.

Dennis said the things he wanted in the future including taking up his steam train hobby, getting the monthly steam train magazine and visiting his daughter in Weymouth. Lucy and Dennis thought together about what needed to happen to change things and came up with a list of actions including talking to the manager of the service before looking at using his budget to purchase different support. Another action was writing in detail how he wanted to be supported, in a way that all of the staff who supported him could follow.

A few months on, the individual actions agreed at Dennis's review were starting to have an impact. Dennis was warm in the bathroom now and he had enjoyed working with Lucy to put together his one page profile. He could tell that staff had read it and some were using it to think about how they supported him.

A person-centred review for George meant that he could stay living in his own home:

George's person-centred review

George, 69, is fun-loving, sociable and has a great sense of humour. He lives alone in a bungalow and doesn't have contact with his family. He uses a wheelchair and has difficulties maintaining personal care and the hygiene of his home. He wasn't able to sleep in his bed because he couldn't get to it and he didn't have any clothes, meaning he couldn't get dressed. Even though he had a social worker, housing officer, district nurse and carers in his life, they were generally unable to go into his home because of the risk to their own health. His health and home deteriorated, and he was at risk of being evicted.

George's social worker Liz decided a person-centred approach might benefit him as it was clear that he wasn't happy as he was. Together they looked at what was working and not working in George's life and how best to support him.

Now, as well as physical changes being made to his home environment, the support George receives from his carers has changed too – from visits at specific times of the day, to a block of 20 hours which can be used more creatively. George feels less agitated and happier in himself; sleeps much better in his own bed instead of his wheelchair; and his home and hygiene have been transformed. He has also achieved something he has wanted for a long time – he now owns a dog.

Person-centred reviews can also have a huge impact on the, staff, professionals and managers providing the support for people. Take, for example, Sheila and Steve, co-owners of a private residential care home in northern England.

Sheila and Steve using person-centred reviews

When Sheila and Steve took over as the co-owners nine years ago, they were shocked at the institutional way it was run. With backgrounds in learning disability services for the local council, it was completely contrary to their way of working which focused on promoting independence and giving service users choice and control. 'Historically some homes like ours had been run like institutions because it was more convenient to do so,' said Sheila, who is also the home's manager. 'For example, beds were made in the morning and if the residents were unwell or tired they weren't allowed to use their beds during the day because everything had to be kept just so. Staff couldn't see anything wrong with that but we thought it was appalling.'

The home and staff have come a long way since then and they were one of the first residential care homes to start using person-centred reviews with older people 'It was a culture shock for staff at first but they adapted when they realised it was for the benefit of the people living here,' said Sheila. 'The traditional review was just asking a certain number of questions. For me, a person-centred review is the difference between me saying to someone 'You are coming here, this is how we do things, you'll soon get used to our routine' to 'How do you want life to look and how do you want us to support you?'

'Does someone want to get up when they wake up? Do they want to be woken at a certain time? Do they want breakfast in bed or in the dining room? Do they want to be involved in activities? It's looking at an individual and finding out what they want and what's important to them. We might know what's important for someone – nutritional food, enough fluids etc. – but we have to find out what's important to them.

'My role is to make everyone's life as happy as it can be. I don't have a magic wand, but to the best of my ability I give people what they need to be happy. It's about giving people what they want, not what you think they want and using person-centred thinking and person-centred reviews certainly helps us do that.'

Chapter 10

The Person-Centred Review Process

A person-centred review uses person-centred thinking tools to explore what is important to a person, what support she needs, what is working and not working from her perspective and other people's perspectives and agrees actions for change. The process involves the person herself, key people who have to be there to meet statutory requirements and, what is very important, anyone else that the individual wants to invite. They last up to 1.5 hours – no longer than a traditional review should take (although some people try to do traditional reviews in much less time).

Preparation is vital.

A facilitator will support the person whose review it is to consider how she wants to be at the centre of her meeting, and what it would take for her to feel as comfortable as possible to contribute her information, views and be as in control as she wants to be. This also involves thinking about who she would like to *invite* to the review (for example, friends and family) and the people *required* to be there.

Elizabeth, a team leader

When Elizabeth (a team leader) began to introduce person-centred reviews with people using the mental health services, she warned them to 'expect it to be slightly different', while explaining to them how they would take part. For people with who use mental health services, preparing for a review depends on how well they are and whether they feel that they are in a place to cope with a process that is more open and more focused on them. Elizabeth said that she knew their view and opinion was much more in the forefront and 'that can be scary when you are used to having things done to you'.

Mark and Thomas preparing a person-centred review

Mark helped Thomas and his family prepare for his annual person-centred review by inviting the people who knew him best, including family and friends. Using poster-sized paper and recording what was said in simple language and pictures, they helped Thomas map out what people like and admire about him – his positive characteristics, what is important to him, what he is good at and enjoys and some ideas for the future based on his qualities, skills and interests. This was then reduced to A4 size using the computer and presented at the person-centred review.

Families also need an opportunity to prepare, especially those who have had typically negative or passive experiences in the past. They need to know what will happen at the meeting and what contribution they can make. One father prepared for his daughter's review by drawing pictures that symbolised what he liked and admired about her. At the review meeting, he copied the pictures onto the paper as part of his contribution.

For social workers and other professionals who may be used to attending reviews and just reading reports, this means knowing the process and the kinds of headings that will be used to obtain information about what is working and not working for the individual. This is an opportunity for them to contribute their knowledge to create a shared understanding together, rather than a way of writing more reports under new headings. It is vital that staff and professionals are there and contribute to the whole of the meeting, not just come to share some information and then leave the review.

The person-centred review process naturally begins with introductions, and then people are invited to share positive information about the characteristics or contribution of the focus person. This reflects that underpinning value of focusing on capacities in person-centred practice. The facilitator works to 'pitch this' so that it feels empowering, not patronising. More than anything, this begins a meeting with a clear sense of it being different to traditional ones. This feels very different for an individual who is more used to attending meetings which focus on what is wrong in her life. This helps to remind those at the meeting to think about the person beyond her diagnosis and to see her as an individual with capacities, gifts and contributions.

At this stage, the typical reviews would involve social workers and professionals reading their reports. However, in a person-centred review, the person shares her own perspective, and then everyone adds their information (including family and friends). So, rather than sitting formally around a table, information is shared and built together. Sometimes flipchart paper is pinned on the walls in the room and everyone is given a pen so that they can write their thoughts on each in a more relaxed way. Another way to do this is around a table, with A4 sheets of blank paper with a question written on the top of each sheet. These are circulated around the table for people to add their information. The way that information is shared is decided with the person, taking into account the number of people coming to the review and where it will be held. The aim is to create a comfortable atmosphere which gives everyone an equal opportunity to have their say, and for this information to be recorded.

Information is recorded around the following types of questions:

- What is important to (the person) now?

- What is important to (the person) for the future?

- What does (the person) need to stay healthy and safe and well supported?

- What questions do we need to answer?

- What is working and not working from different perspectives?

The 'what questions do we need to answer' sheet is where people ensure statutory requirements are addressed. It is also a place to record any questions or issues that the person or her supporters want to work on or work out.

Once the information has been recorded and shared, the next stage is to use it to explore any differences in opinion and generate actions based on what is working and not working for people and moving towards their desired future. In this way, the person-centred review makes it more likely that the person will have what is important to her in her life and move towards the future she wants. Actions are agreed that keep what is working happening for the person and changes what is not working for her. It also uses this person-centred information to build a detailed person-centred description, as described in Chapter 9.

The questions that the facilitator may ask in this part of the review are:

- What needs to happen to make sure that what is working in your life keeps happening?

- What needs to happen to change what is not working for you?

- How can we address each of the 'questions to answer'? What else do we need to learn?

- What can we do together to enable you to more towards what is important in the future?

The next part of the process is to think about solutions and develop actions. With what is working for the person (and others), we simply ensure that this continues. You may be able to address what is not working for people within the current service and resources. We may need to use person-centred thinking skills to find out what we need to do differently, as Pam did with Kenny, in Chapter 9 (see Table 9.2, p.100).

This process is also used with 'what else we need to learn', by looking at the 'questions to answer' and then thinking about any person-centred thinking tools that could help address the questions.

Where there are areas of the person's life that are not working and not within the sphere of influence of the people in the room, then other people need to be involved to figure it out. For example, this could include working with people from the housing department if the person wants to move, or finding a supported employment service if the person wants to change or find a job. All of this should lead to detailed actions that change what is not working for the person, add to our learning and keep improving how we are delivering personalised services that truly offer choice and control.

One action from a person-centred review is likely to be for someone to take the information and learning and either work with the person to create a one page profile or add it to her existing profile to create a more detailed person-centred description. The record and information from the person-centred review is written up or photographed and produced in whatever way is required.

The first part of the review either records for the first time, or builds on what we understand about what is important to the person and how she wants to be supported. We then compare this to how the person is living now by asking what is working and not working from her perspective and others, and think about what else we need to figure out or learn. We look at what the person wants in the future, and what we can do to move towards that. The actions agreed should change what is not working, add to our learning about the person and move closer to the life the person wants in the future.

Mark's story

Mark is a social worker and he and his colleagues decided to make person-centred reviews the mainstay of what they do.

'When I was first a social worker, we tried to roll out person-centred plans and do assessments in a person-centred way but didn't have corporate sign-up at the time. Then *Valuing People* came along and there was more of a general move to that way of working, but it didn't come into the care management process. Now, with the push for personalisation, our team has had the opportunity to be trained in person-centred thinking and reviews. This is the best chance we've had in a long time to cement it, really make it part of the care management process and take it past critical mass.'

Mark said that all the social workers and community care officers at his base are now using person-centred reviews. 'We've had really positive feedback from the people we're doing the reviews with and also from their families, supporters and providers. It's gone down really well. We did our best to try and engage with people from the ground up, including community managers, social workers and co-facilitators. It's about getting people together to do the hard work and get things written down.'

Caroline was the first person with whom Mark undertook a person-centred review back in November 2008. The people who attended were members of Caroline's support network including her support worker and friend. As a first step, they took a picture of Caroline and wrote a list about all the good things they liked and admired about her. This included comments like 'willingness to try new things', 'caring of others', 'good cook', 'good advocate for others', 'good friend' and 'works hard'.

Person–centred review process

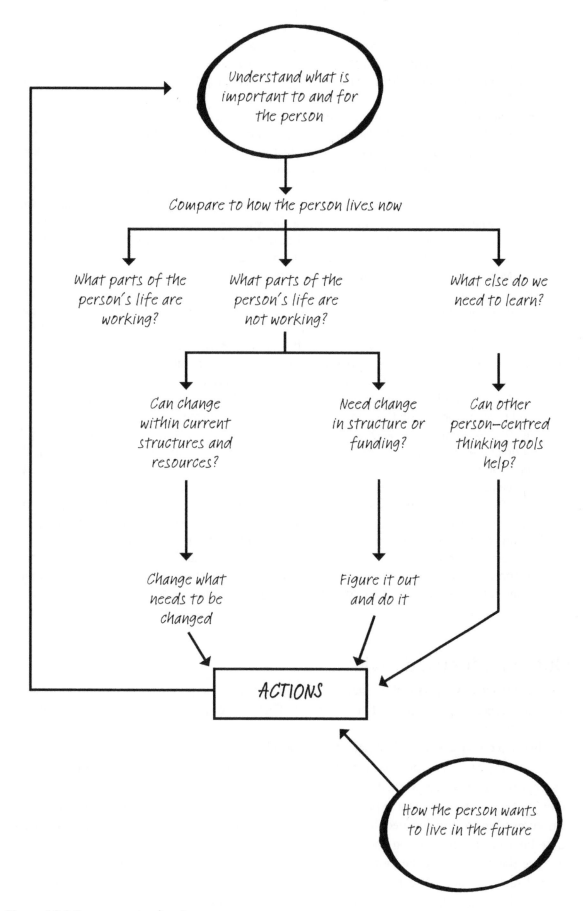

Figure 10.1 Person-centred review process

Mark said asking people what they like and admire about someone is a great part of the person-centred review process: 'Picture it: you've got everyone sat around the room and you're asking them to write down the thoughts about the individual they're reviewing... people are a bit like rabbits in the headlights at first. What is lovely is seeing people move from that fear to engagement. By the end, people really enjoyed it and got into it.'

Once that was done, the team and Caroline also talked about what was important to her now and in the future. This included things like 'keeping in touch with friends', 'volunteer work' and 'having answers to questions that bother me'; and 'having a correct placement so not having to move backwards', 'work' and 'who I live with'.

For Caroline, things like 'volunteer work, staff friends and college' were all considered working, while 'job, seeing ahead and contact with relatives' were considered not working.

Towards the end of the review, the team created a list of actions which meant lots of things to do for Caroline and her supporters in the year ahead. They broke the actions up into what they were, who would do it and when. Some examples included Caroline writing a letter to get a new job coach by the end of the week; writing a letter to her mum by the end of the following week; looking at a new house to share with staff support by the following month; and looking at ideas for a holiday by next summer.

Mark said it was important to make sure someone had responsibility for taking things forward. 'We review these actions once a year, but if we get to a year later, and the actions haven't been done, then what's the point? Get them done, and in time: that's so important.'

Facilitators were also really important to the process: 'It's a little scary to move to this format for reviews, especially for new staff, students or community care officers. We found it works if you team up and do it together and give that person time to build up confidence, so that eventually he or she will be able to take that lead role in facilitation.

'We've found this approach is working really well for with people with learning disabilities, and people who are on the autistic spectrum. The old formalised reviews can be a difficult process for people to engage in. But doing it in a person-centred way is richly engaging for people: they are staying all the way through and getting really involved. The end result is that we have many more person-centred goals and the potential for positive outcomes for the individual.

'The main thing we've found – and we've learnt a lot – is that the review process is evolving all the time. The person-centred tools – like the 'working and not working' tool – run really well. They're simple to use and people like them. The person-centred review captures all the key performance indicators we need as a local authority. We get a really good action plan, with the appropriate checks and measures that deliver the outcomes people want. It's getting us to go back to actually changing people's lives.'

Outcome-focused reviews

When someone has a personal budget, there is an additional requirement of reviewing how the personal budget is spent against their outcomes. This type of person-centred review is called an outcome-focused review.

This outcome-focused review process was developed in early 2009 by a group of disabled people, family carers and people from eight councils who knew that the best way of developing a successful process that worked for people and councils was to work together as a group of individuals each with relevant experience. They saw it as essential to ensure that the end product was acceptable to disabled people and families, who sometimes find assessments and reviews to be bureaucratic, patronising and stressful experiences. Having disabled people and carers co-produce the process was the best way to ensure this happened. They started with the person-centred review process and adapted it, so that it reflected a review of the outcomes from the support plan, and included a review of how the personal budget had been spent.

Outcomes are a 'golden thread' which runs through the self-directed support process. It is what people say they want in their lives, or would like to achieve. Outcomes are identified during the assessment and support planning process, and are the basis of the review. The person-centred review process looks again at the outcomes, asking what is working and not working for people around each outcome, and looks at how their personal budgets have been used. The reviews' purpose is to:

1. Review progress in using a personal budget to achieve the outcomes set out in a person's support plan.

2. Share learning about what has been tried and worked or didn't work.

3. Identify next steps to achieve a person's goals.

4. Update the support plan.

5. Make clear if the person's support needs have changed.

6. Help the council to check if the person is still eligible for social care.

In the introduction to this chapter, we introduced what disabled people considered to be a great review generally. The following two points are particular to outcome-focused reviews:

- A great review looks at money. The review is an opportunity to check that the person is getting all the money needed, and that the amount of the personal budget is right.

- A great review gathers necessary data (see Table 10.1). The review is a way for councils to ensure that they have the data they need so that records can be updated as necessary.

Table 10.1 *Outcome-focused review process*

Element	Purpose	Resulting action
Recording the most important outcomes from the support plan.	To make clear the goals that the person wants to achieve.	Agree the support plan
Organise the outcomes into categories using outcome domains.	To show how outcomes are linked to policy aims and objective outcomes.	Provide data for council performance management systems Provide information to inform commissioning decisions.
Review what is working and not working for each of the personal outcomes that the person chose when developing their support plan.	To review each outcome and reflect on what has worked well and what needs to change. To acknowledge and celebrate success. To think about what may be needed to maintain what is working. To identify what is not working to begin to think about what needs to change.	Identify any safeguarding concerns that need investigation.

Table 10.1 Outcome-focused review process cont.

Element	Purpose	Resulting action
Ask how people are spending their budget.	To review how the money is being spent. This is not a detailed audit of receipts. It is a light-touch review of the ways that people said that they would spend their money in their support plan. It is designed to show whether more detailed financial checks are needed.	Decide whether more detailed financial checks are needed. Identify any financial concerns that need investigation. Provide information to inform commissioning decisions.

Sandrine mentoring personal budgets

Sandrine is personal budget mentor in adult services in the south west of England and helped many people aged 65 or over with outcome-focused reviews of their budgets. Each person's review came six to eight weeks after the initial assessment.

'It gives people who are being supported time to think about what they want to keep or change in their lives,' she said. 'In a way, everyone with regular support has been through a personal budget review which should put the emphasis on support planning options rather than eligibility criteria.

'A big difference from the person's point of view is the review should address their needs and wants – what is important to them – to provide more flexible and less prescriptive support.

'Now it's a more holistic approach and people have more choice and control. By reviewing the plan, we are reviewing the outcomes of what we are trying to achieve, compared to "what did we get?" It's the next step to making someone happier, rather than "what do you need?" In the past, the review was more of an administrative exercise, ticking the boxes, looking at whether the person was still eligible. Now it starts with a conversation with the person about what's important to her and for her so that she feels listened to.

'It can be just something small like the care worker making sure the older person's cat is in for the night because she will worry if it's not in and then not sleep well. It's about how well-being has an impact on the person's quality of life and these little details are important to that.'

After any person-centred review, there will be more information and learning about the person, what is important to and for her and what she wants in the future – this builds in to a person-centred description, but in outcome-focused reviews, this information can be added to the support plan.

We have shown that person-centred reviews are a very different way to have a meeting. A person-centred plan may begin with a meeting, but the context and process is very different, as we explain in Chapter 12. But before then, we want to show how person-centred reviews can be used in mental health services, which is the focus of Chapter 11.

Chapter 11

Person-Centred Reviews and the Care Programme Approach

> This is not a learning disability process or tool, it's a way of thinking, working and supporting someone. What the professional says is or isn't working may not be what the individual thinks, and this gives them the chance to say so.
>
> *Elizabeth, children and adolescent mental health outreach team leader*

Person-centred reviews can – and should – be used with everyone using services.[134] In the context of mental health services, it can change a typical care programme approach (CPA) review for the better. CPA reviews were always intended to be person-centred, but this is often not the experience of the people who need support.

In a traditional CPA review,[135] professionals meet with the person and possibly family members. Everyone present can take turns to speak and professionals may refer to or read out reports they have compiled, but many people have reported that they felt intimidated by the process, and so might not express how they are really feeling. The whole process is very much from the point of view of the consultant, mental health nurse or social worker. Although the person is present in the room, the whole process is much more about meeting the objectives of the consultant rather than providing a service that makes sense to the individual.

Marianne Selby-Boothroyd talked with people who use mental health support, to find out what their experiences were of reviews, in a variety of settings including CPA meetings, key worker meetings, recovery star meetings and review meetings while in hospital.

> The group talked about how reviews can still cause a great deal of stress, anxiety and resentment. This was felt most strongly about CPA meetings where examples were given of having to wait to be invited in to your own meeting, not being allowed to bring your advocate or friend into your meeting and professionals coming in and out of the meeting, staying only for the bits that concern them. One person described the shock they felt when they were once offered a cup of tea at their CPA meeting. It would appear that refreshments and putting people at their ease are not the norm!
>
> Reviews take place in a variety of ways – from informal 'key worker' meetings which take place on a monthly basis to the formal 6 monthly or annual CPA meetings. What was common however was the lack of control felt by the individual over both the structure of the meeting and to varying degrees of the decisions made within it.
>
> > 'If I suggested my CPA was held in a café instead of at the hospital, they would think I was really mad and probably section me.'
>
> The quote above was made by someone in relation to trying to take some control over their CPA meeting. Whilst it was said as a joke, it reflects the feelings of many that their

mental health can be used by professionals as reasons to not work in partnership with the individual, further exacerbating the lack of control felt.

However, even the more informal meetings between the person and their key worker can still feel like control is held by the staff member, 'it depends on who the key worker is and how they do it'. The use of the Recovery Star to review and plan with people was seen both positively and negatively. When used well, it was seen as great in identifying and celebrating people's achievements. However, it was also described as a tool which can be used simply as a checklist, preventing wider discussion of how the person actually feels, particularly when things aren't working so well.

A key issue which was raised repeatedly by various people, was the belief that 'knowledge is power' and that very often it is the individual who feels the least knowledgeable and out of their depth. This obviously completely contrasts with the fact that it is actually the individual who is the expert on their own life and mental health. Examples were given including not understanding the terminology used by medical professionals and the use of long sentences which are confusing. People described not wanting to ask too many questions in case they were seen a being awkward or difficult. One person said that being offered a course in his mental health condition when diagnosed would have helped him understand better what was happening and professional's roles in supporting him. Another person talked of the benefits of developing a psychiatrist's communication chart!

Shared language was seen as really important – the same words can mean different things to different people. By not checking out what each person's understanding of the issue is and most importantly their understanding of what action has been agreed, tension and the label of 'non-compliance' easily surfaces. Someone gave a really good example: 'Rob's CPN had been focused for some time on ensuring Rob ate healthily. Through Rob's CPA meeting, it had been identified that Rob should learn to cook healthy, nutritious food. Rob, however, did not want to learn to cook and resented that this action had been decided within his review meeting without his agreement. The staff supporting Rob felt resentful that they were seen as failing in encouraging Rob to learn to cook instead of getting the takeaways he really loved.

When Rob and his support staff sat down one day and asked the CPN why they were so focused on Rob's eating habits, it transpired that actually, the CPN was not overly bothered about what Rob ate as long as he ate regularly enough not to suffer any side effects from his medication. Once everyone was clear on what each other's understanding about the issue was they were able to agree a way forward which meant that the CPN, the support staff and, most importantly, Rob, were happy.

At a person-centred review, every question is aimed at the individual and at looking at things from his perspective. David Coyle, a senior lecturer at the Department of Mental Health and Learning Disabilities, University of Chester, says that when he and his colleagues have undertaken person-centred training and developmental work in mental health, some professionals felt that they were already doing it, 'bandying the term person-centred about without really knowing what it is.' He says that a proper person-centred review lives with the person so that their support is reflective and has synergy with their day-to-day needs. It's not 'we will have a look at this in six months' time and see where we are' as if by magic something will have changed.[136] Social workers and professionals must be trained in person-centred approaches in order to understand the difference between the two. Otherwise they think that they are doing a CPA review aimed around the person, but it's still aimed around the service.

Elizabeth and Henry

Elizabeth is a team leader for a Child and Adolescent Mental Health Service intensive outreach team. She has been working with Henry, an 'in-patient', for quite some time. She felt that his views weren't being heard. She was asked by his CPA coordinator to facilitate his CPA review, and Elizabeth set about doing this in a person-centred way.

Henry had a person-centred description which set out what was important to him, what helped keep him safe and well, and how those things can be achieved with the support of his family, friends, carers and supporters. When preparing for his review meeting, Henry and Elizabeth talked about how he might share this with the other professionals around the table. Henry liked this idea, but didn't want to do the talking because he finds speaking in front of others difficult – he is self-conscious about not always being understood. He and Elizabeth came up with the idea of using a red hand that he could hold up if he found things difficult to deal with at the review meeting.

The CPA was held in the 'traditional' way with everyone talking around a table. Elizabeth supported Henry to be more involved and to take the focus away from a service-led review. Afterwards, Elizabeth and Henry discussed how it had gone and what could be different. He thought using the red hand was good, as was being able to tell others what he wanted by using his person-centred description. But what wasn't so good was that professionals arrived late and left early, the room layout didn't work for Henry and the review meeting notes were taken by someone in a way that no one else could see them.

Henry and Elizabeth talked about how his next CPA could be different and Elizabeth discussed ways of doing this with his CPA coordinator by using a person-centred review process.

Elizabeth realised that most of the people she supports – including those with mental health problems and challenging behaviour – found CPA meetings stressful, so she decided to train in person-centred reviews, believing that this would work better for all concerned. She looked at the statutory requirements of a CPA review and its various headings – finance, housing, mental and physical health, activities and family/social/community support – and realised that they could comfortably fit with the headings used in the person-centred review process.

Elizabeth prepared Henry for his next CPA review by going over what they would use and how they would be doing things. They also talked about how he wanted to be involved. She put the previous CPA action plan on to flipchart paper and added columns for a tick or a cross. Henry filled this in as they went through the plan, ticking something if it had been achieved and putting a cross if not. They had sheets for people to sign in, to say what they liked and admired about Henry, and for questions to ask and issues to raise. They set the chairs in a semi-circle facing the action plan with Henry and Elizabeth sitting together to one side at the front.

When everyone had arrived and signed in, Elizabeth pointed everybody out so that Henry could say if he knew them and, if he didn't he felt able to ask them to introduce themselves. Elizabeth said that to watch Henry do this was a lovely moment because he already had taken some control and looked more confident.

Between them, they went through the CPA action plan, and what was working or not working. Elizabeth read out the action points, Henry put a tick or a cross and if necessary the point was discussed. Anything that needed to be carried over or required further discussion was added to the 'questions to ask' sheet. They formulated the new action plan using the headings from the previous CPA plan and the issues raised. Again the headings were taken from the traditional CPA formulation.

At the end, Elizabeth handed out feedback forms to help her continue to develop this process.

'This meeting had a very different feel about it from the first. All the professionals and others involved directed their comments and conversation to Henry so that it was far more open and genuine. From my perspective it very much took the emphasis away from the services leading the meeting and it empowered Henry.

'Henry enjoyed being more in control, but was not sure how he would feel about taking further control next time. It was good that he felt he could challenge or question others and had the confidence to do so. Once again he was disappointed that professionals were late and left early. He would rather they hadn't come at all.

'The feedback from Henry's parents and the professionals was very positive and the psychologist presumed that all CPAs were done this way. The site lead was so enthused by the process that she has told others which has led to me being asked to do a presentation to the CPA development group.'

The group of people, staff and managers, that Marianne Selby-Boothroyd brought together to think about reviews, also described their positive experience of more person-centred reviews.[137]

'We were treated like royalty… I felt like a brand new woman.'

Good support and good reviews are happening and where they are – there are most definitely common themes. The ability to just listen cannot be underestimated. Too often, the value of people's lives feels measured by the number of tick-boxes completed. Meetings and reviews which feel like conversations and are marked by a lack of paper were seen as a good thing. People talked about the importance of being supported by people who have true empathy and are genuine. Being able to choose who supports you is key and is not yet happening routinely. Being supported by people who have similar interests or who understand cultural/faith issues; being supported by people over time and not having key workers changed because they are getting too close were both seen as really important.

Great reviews affirm people's strengths and skills. People talked about it being important that staff were good at recognising people's skills and sharing these. One person said that it was really important to her to acknowledge her achievements in her reviews and to see her progress.

The group developed some statements about how to make sure reviews are as person-centred as they can be (The best reviews…) and what needs to be considered before, during and after reviews, and what good support looks like in reviews, and generally.

The best reviews…

- happen on a day and time which suit me

- give me the time and space to talk

- happen in a place where I feel comfortable

- celebrate my achievements

- are when I feel listened to – I don't feel like it is just a tick-box process

- happen when everybody uses the same language; we understand each other and have a shared purpose – me!

- do not include people who are invited without me knowing or agreeing

- acknowledge that the people supporting me need to know me; talking to a stranger isn't helpful

- focus on the here and now as well as the future; they don't keep bringing up the past.

Before the review...

- Enough notice should be given to everyone attending. The choice of date, time and venue should be led from the individual.

- Remind the person of the review, leading up to it, to help him think about and plan what he wants to talk about.

- Encourage the person to invite whom they want – especially family and friends. Talk with him about the things he is happy to talk about with family and friends and the things which he would rather not discuss.

- Make sure that the person knows everyone who is attending.

During the review...

- Set up the room so that it is comfortable and inviting.

- Think about who is doing all the talking – if it's you, be prepared to stop!

- Decide who is chairing the meeting.

- Spend time talking about the social stuff as well as the serious stuff.

- Ensure that there are enough breaks so that people can stop to smoke or get a drink.

- Ensure that enough time has been given to enable people to clarify/check anything?

- Have actions been clarified and checked?

After the review...

- Is there clear information on what happens next?

- Are there clear, accurate notes of the meeting? Have these been produced in a timely manner? Have people had a chance to comment on the accuracy before the next meeting?

- Are minutes amended if people don't agree with what is in them?

- Where support plans are written, are they in the first or third person? Which is more meaningful to the individual?

Good support is...

- keeping your word – if you say you will do something, do it

- respecting each other, seeing each other as adults and as equals

- recognising that it may be your job, but it's my life so it needs to work for me

- understanding that having experience and genuine understanding really can make a positive difference

- making sure it is easy for me to say when things aren't working and, if I need to, to complain (not just told to put it in writing)

- being flexible, genuine, honest and realistic

- better when both people have shared information about themselves, that it is not just a one-way process

- comes from someone who knows me

- acknowledging me – even when you are busy doing something else

- remembering 'who this is for'

- knowing that listening and talking is what's important – ticking boxes isn't

- having a shared purpose and language – checking out that we understand each other is really important

- ensuring that the choice over who supports me is mine

- acknowledging that shared interests and experiences are important and do matter.

Certitude, a London provider of social care support for people who have learning disabilities and people with mental health needs, have developed a new approach to CPAs which reflects these statements and the person-centred reviews process, placing control and decision making back with the individual. Staff are trained on how to support people to identify what is working and not working in someone's life – from different perspectives where appropriate, as well as what is important to them for the future. They run training and coaching sessions for people in 'managing their CPAs', focusing on supporting people to move from passive recipient to active participant.

This kind of shift in power relationships may be uncomfortable for some. Some critics of person-centred practice are concerned that it focuses too greatly on the individual's choice over the social worker's, potentially neglecting the safety and well-being of a person or those around them.

However, this is a misunderstanding of person-centred thinking, which seeks to find a balance of what matters to the person and the support required to stay healthy and safe. Social workers or professionals may have a well-placed concern for the needs of the individual based on their previous experience of the person, and worry that if they don't do something, the individual's needs won't be met, but investment in the person-centred review process means finding that the balance can become clearer and easier.

Current mental health policy *No Health without Mental Health*[138] and *Refocusing the Care Programme Approach*[139] means that there is the requirement for an organisational and system transformation to deliver person-centred support so that service users move from being viewed as the objects of care to contributing citizens. The time for person-centred practice to be taken fully on board in mental health has come.

Chapter 12

Person-Centred Planning

> Person-centred planning is a way of organising around one person to define and create a better future... Typically in person-centred planning, the person involved invites people who know and like them to come to a meeting. One or two facilitators guide and record the discussions and decisions. After the meeting, people do what's been agreed. This hardly sounds revolutionary. But the frame which is put around the meeting, the questions the meeting asks and the way the meeting is organised often mean that new possibilities emerge, new understandings develop, new alliances are formed and people's lives take a definite turn for the better.
>
> *Pete Ritchie[140]*

Person-centred thinking tools, descriptions and reviews are becoming the expected practice in personalised services.[141] As we have shown in Part I, these processes emerged from person-centred planning and sit alongside the other styles of PATH, MAPs and 'personal futures planning'.

Since person-centred planning first appeared in government policy in 2001,[142] a perennial question has been 'which style of person-centred planning should I use?' The ideas of 'service competence' and 'community competence' are a way to think about the different contributions made by the approaches to person-centred thinking and planning. Service competence means ensuring that services are able to deliver personalised support which reflects what matters to people and how they want to be supported. Community competence means creating communities where everyone belongs and contributes.

We need to achieve both for two reasons. The first is to ensure that we achieve new levels of performance within services, so that they consistently and efficiently deliver what people want them to. Second, it is so that we can passionately explore what is possible within communities.

Service competence

> We want everyone, regardless of the presence of disability, to live in their own communities. But we want more than presence; we want community life where each person's contribution is welcomed and appreciated and where each person is supported in a web of relationships. To achieve this for everyone, we need both service competency and community competency. Most people with significant disabilities will need (and most will want) paid support. That support must be provided in a respectful way that also helps make and sustain community connections (service competence). To establish and maintain the committed relationships that are at the heart of community life we will need structured, intentional efforts that organise, mobilise, and maintain them (community competence).
>
> *Michael Smull[143]*

'Essential lifestyle planning' has now been deconstructed into a series of person-centred tools, which, along with person-centred reviews, are a way to mainstream person-centred practice and achieve service competence. As we have seen in Part II, to deliver personalised services requires that each staff member understands and acts on what is important to the individual, how the person makes decisions and what good support looks like from her perspective. Person-centred thinking tools and reviews can help us learn and deliver this.

Person-centred thinking tools and reviews can help people get 'a good service life', where people have choice and control on a day-to-day basis. Where people have sought to make their existing paperwork 'more person-centred', and where staff need a written record of how to support an individual, these approaches have offered a way to achieve this. Therefore person-centred thinking is a crucial place to start in implementing personalisation, but it must not be the end. People should have much more choice and control over their service and day-to-day life using person-centred descriptions and reviews; however, the boundaries between the person and their roles and place in the community are unlikely to significantly change.

Other approaches to person-centred planning and thinking will be needed to enable people to think about their contributions to community and to take up valued social roles. These are community connecting tools[144] and the person-centred planning styles of PATH, MAPs and personal futures planning, which we define later in the chapter.

Community competence

The current Coalition government wants to build a 'Big Society'. PATH, MAPs and personal futures planning are ways to contribute to creating a big, inclusive society starting at an individual level for marginalised people. The title of the most recent book on PATH and MAPs suggests that these styles are person-centred ways to build community.[145] These styles of person-centred planning work most powerfully in the hands of people and families who bring their networks together to create change, and require skilled, independent facilitation. PATH and MAPs are group processes and sometimes these groups or networks are called *circles of support*.

> Evidence shows that when people feel they have control over what happens to them and can take action on their own behalf, their physical and mental well-being improves. When individuals and groups get together in their neighbourhoods, get to know each other, work together and help each other, there are usually lasting benefits for everyone involved. Networks and groups grow stronger so that people who belong to them tend to feel less isolated, more secure, more powerful and happier.[146]

A 'circle of support' brings together an individual who wants change in her life with her family, friends and neighbours, to think about how they can use their connections and resources to create change together. Although initially focused around an individual, a circle that uses PATH, MAPs or futures planning is likely to benefit everyone who participates, in the way described in the quote above. People from services can be part of circles of support, but do so in their own time. Bringing people together significantly increases the chance of positive change.

> A plan done alone can make a difference, as can a plan made within a family circle or within the boundaries of a single organisation. But a planning group that includes people with a variety of connections and interests has more knowledge and information to draw on and more immediate possibilities for action.[147]

John O'Brien, Jack Pearpoint and Linda Kahn illustrate this with a diagram (see Figure 12.1).

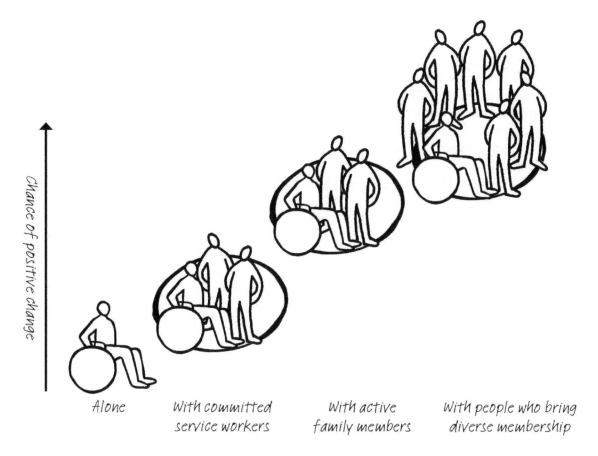

Figure 12.1 Chance of positive change (O'Brien, Pearpoint and Kahn 2010)

As well as a circle of committed people who meet regularly, independent facilitation is crucial to person-centred planning. 'Some people might imagine that if someone facilitates their own plan she has more choice, control and status, but the reverse is true. Having a facilitator to help you plan is like having someone cut your hair – they can see all the way round.'[148]

Facilitators are expected not just to learn their craft well, but to demonstrate the practice and values in how they live their own lives, as John O'Brien says:

> Practitioners need to feel the effects of these processes in their own lives, by making plans for themselves with their own circles of support, however those circles may be shaped. Practitioners owe it to the people they serve to personally exemplify courage in defining their own dreams and recruiting others' support to pursue them. They also accept responsibility for making a continuing investment in improving their own understanding, knowledge, and abilities as listeners, as facilitators, as organisers, and as learners through reflection-in-action.[149]

PATH, MAPs and personal futures planning have a strong future focus and were originally designed for use – outside of, or at the edges of – services, one person at a time, using a graphic meeting format. John O'Brien, one of the co-developers of PATH, MAPs and personal futures planning, describes these styles as an art or craft and talks of the dangers of seeking to assimilate these styles of person-centred planning into the service system, stressing instead that they be kept marginal to the system.[150]

The accountability in person-centred planning is always to the person, not the service, as Pete Ritchie describes: 'Person-centred planning is an event in the person's life, not a procedure of the service system. As much as possible it takes place in the person's world, with the service system seen as part of the environment... The facilitator is accountable to the person who is the focus of the plan.'[151]

Pete describes John's experience of person-centred planning:[152]

John's story

John is a man in his 40s who lives on his own with support from a housing association. His parents live a few miles away and they have just gone on holiday together to Cyprus. John is a part-time college student and is learning to use computers. Most evenings he visits a couple of close friends who live locally and they often play pool. John is currently looking for work either as a cook or a gardener.

For many years John lived in a privately managed small hostel for people with mental health problems. He had to fit in with the other six people. Bed was at 9.30 p.m. and lights out at 10.00 p.m. He went to a mental health day centre during the week. At the weekend he only got out for half an hour. The social worker used to come to see him and ask how he was getting on. John would say 'I'm not coping' and she would say 'you'll just have to grin and bear it'.

John was referred to Connect Housing when the manager of the private hostel retired. He moved into a shared house managed by the housing association and around the same time he got a new social worker. John was invited to use person-centred planning to think about his future and how he wanted to lead his life.

John invited various people to come to the first meeting – his parents, his social worker, someone from the day centre, someone from the housing association and a couple of friends. They used a large sheet of 'wallpaper' to record the discussion and the decisions. As John says: 'It was a bit strange. People were saying good things about me. I managed to get through it all. Dad came out with a lot of good things. It was a blank sheet before we put pen and paper to it. What came out if it? A lot! My past is my past – let's look forward. My future holds a lot this year.'

Since then, John has moved to his own house; stopped going to the day centre; taken a college course; established some close friendships with people living locally; taught a friend to play pool (he's too good now, he always wins); learned to manage everyday tasks like cooking stir-fries and doing the ironing; and worked out some coping strategies for the ups and downs ('I've been going in even if I feel miserable – I never skip art.').

The group has kept meeting every few months to help John take stock and plan ahead: 'I look forward to these meetings...when they're finished I'm glad to get home. We've had about four meetings, everything's come out positive. Every time it came round I got more confidence about dealing with the bad things.'

John's story illustrates some of what is different about person-centred planning:

- Different people come – John's friends and family are equal contributors in the meetings, alongside professionals. As John says: 'This was the first time that they've felt involved. Before then it was just decisions made.'

- People come by invitation – it's up to John to say who he wants at the meeting, nobody has an automatic right to be there. John in turn has been invited to help a friend of his to plan.

- There's a different style – the two facilitators keep the meeting focused on helping John work out what he wants to do and how he wants to go about it. The meetings are positive and lively and the graphic recording helps to track and summarise the discussion.

- Everyone is involved in follow-up work after the meeting – John's task last time was to sort out getting a computer and setting it up.

- The meeting asks different questions. John's negative reputation preceded him to the housing association. It would have been easy to focus on John's problems and on how to 'fix' John or where to 'place' him. Person-centred planning focused instead on John's gifts and capabilities and on where he wanted to go with his life.

- There is a very practical respect for John's preferences. John said he wanted to live on his own. 'My parents weren't quite sure. Now my Dad comes on a Sunday, helps with the grass cutting. He's taught me to play golf.'

- John said he wanted his own garden, and this is now an important part of John's life.

Person-centred planning is not about doing things to John or for John – but nor is it about saying 'here you go, John, you're on your own now, you can do everything yourself.' It's about people who know and like John, doing things with John and recognising that John – like all of us – needs other people's support to be his own person. 'Living on my own is perfect. I can do what I want, come home when I feel like it…it's my weekend.'

PATH, MAPs and personal futures planning

As you can see from John's story, the focus was on discovering and creating a future where John was part of his community, living his life, his way. This focus on positive and possible futures and community contributions is common to PATH, MAPs and personal futures planning, yet each has a different emphasis and process.

Here are their defining features.[153]

PATH

A group process for discovering a way to move toward a positive and possible goal, which is rooted in life purpose, by enrolling others, finding strength and finding a workable strategy. Both PATH and MAPs can be applied to individuals, families, groups and organisations. Neither are specific to disability though both are widely used by people with disabilities, their families and human service organisations.

MAPS

A group process for clarifying gifts, identifying meaningful contributions, specifying the necessary conditions for contribution and making agreements that will develop opportunities for contribution.

PERSONAL FUTURES PLANNING

Aims to generate powerful images of a rich life in community that will guide a search for opportunities for the person to take up valued social roles and develop service arrangements to support the person in those roles. It collects and organises information by looking through a set of windows for change that describe, for example, the person's relationships, important places, things that energise the person, the person's gifts and capacities and ideas and dreams of a desirable future.

So far in Part III we have introduced person-centred reviews and how they relate to CPAs and to personal budgets (outcome-focused reviews). Person-centred thinking, planning and reviews all share and reflect in their practice the values described in Part I. Person-centred thinking and reviews can enable services to achieve personalised services where people have choice and control. In this chapter we describe this as 'service competence'. Creating inclusive and competent communities will require more than service competence. It will require focused effort on community connecting, circles of support and person-centred planning.

In Table 12.1 we clarify and summarise the difference between two meetings – a person-centred review and a person-centred planning meeting – before going on to explain how person-centred thinking, reviews and planning contribute to support planning.

Table 12.1 *The difference between a person-centred review and person-centred planning*

	Person-centred review	Person-centred planning (PATH or MAP)
Why – the purpose of the meeting	To ensure that services deliver personalised services, based on what is important to the person and how she wants to be supported. To review what is working and not working for the person and others, and to agree actions that build on what is working and change what is not working. Person-centred reviews also kickstart or build the depth of information in a person-centred description.	To achieve a significant change in moving towards a desired future and community membership. Person-centred plans can also set the direction and provide information for a support plan (as part of a personal budget) or personalised care plan.
Who attends	Professionals and staff who provide a service to the person are required to attend. The individual, supported by the facilitator, will also invite other people – for example, family and friends.	The person, supported by the facilitator, invites who she wants to come. People make a voluntary commitment to come, in their own time, based on their personal relationship and commitment to the person. Service staff are often invited by the person, and usually attend in their own time.
How often do meetings take place	As prescribed by the service – this could be a six-week review after a new service has started, or an annual review.	As often as required to achieve the purpose, and to check on actions from the plan. This could be monthly.
How long do the meetings take?	Between an hour-and-a-quarter and an hour-and-a-half.	The initial PATH or MAPs process could be two to three hours, and follow-up meetings could be shorter.
When and where the meeting takes place	Usually at a service venue. The facilitator will ensure that this is as comfortable and welcoming as possible. The time would usually be during the working hours of the service.	At a place and time that works best for the person – their home, or a community venue. Very rarely at a service location, often in the evening or weekend so that everyone can attend.

	Person-centred review	Person-centred planning (PATH or MAP)
Who facilitates the meeting?	A trained facilitator, who usually has reviews as part of their existing role – for example, reviewing officers, social workers, health professionals. Where providers are leading on person-centred reviews, people try to achieve a degree of independence, for example, first line managers doing reviews for people in other parts of the service (that they do not directly manage themselves). Some services are 'outsourcing' this role to independent people or groups – for example, peer supporters, family members, person-centred planning coordinators or people in advocacy organisations.	A trained, independent facilitator. Not connected to any services that the person receives.
What happens during the meeting	Sharing or expanding information about what is important to the person and what good support looks like. Then analysing what is working and not working from the person's (and others') perspectives. The meeting ends with actions to change what is not working and deepen learning.	The first meeting will usually be a PATH, MAP or personal futures plan. Follow-up meetings will review progress and keep focus on the vision and actions. All meetings end with actions to move towards the desirable future.
How is the information recorded?	On flipcharts or paper, depending on what works best for the person. This information then adds to or develops a detailed person-centred description, and also informs the required information or data collection from reviews.	A graphic record is created.
How are actions followed up?	People will be identified to work on the actions with the individual. There is usually a process or person for following up on actions in between person-centred review meetings. Service managers will be expected to ensure that staff complete actions.	By the facilitator and the person in between meetings as required; however, people share learning and information about actions at each meeting.

Chapter 13

Person-Centred Thinking, Planning and Support Planning

Person-centred thinking and planning are fundamental to great support planning. Within the context of personalisation, a support plan (or in health, a personalised health plan) describes on what the person is going to spend their personal budget and how this will achieve his goals or outcomes. Good support planning is crucial to the success of personal budgets. 'Implementing individual budgets require(s) major shifts in staff and organisational culture, roles and responsibilities. Intensive support and extensive training will be needed, particularly in developing specialist support planning and brokerage skills.'[154]

Listed below are some of the stages of the self-directed support process, showing how outcomes are developed, agreed and reviewed in adult social care and the importance of support planning and outcome-focused reviews.[155]

A) Assessment

The initial assessment will identify areas where a person has an eligible need for social care. This covers questions like: with which areas of your life do you need assistance that are eligible for social care money?

B) Support planning

For each of the needs identified in the assessment, the person then decides how he wants this to be addressed in his support plan, and the outcomes he wants to achieve. To develop a support plan, the person will need to discuss questions such as:

- Within these areas of your life, what is important to you?

- What is working and not working for you at the moment?

- What do you want to change?

- What are the most important goals that you want to achieve?

C) Agreeing the support plan

To complete a support plan, the person needs to record the outcomes highlighted in the support planning process. The support plan shows for each goal how the support arrangements will enable these changes to happen. The council, or health professional, and the person agree the plan to confirm that the money can be used in this way.

D) Review

The person-centred review process looks again at the outcomes (called an outcome-focused review, described in Chapter 10). It asks what is working and not working for the person and checks how much progress has been made towards the goals.

Table 13.1 provides some of the information required for great support planning and how person-centred thinking tools can help to provide this.

Table 13.1 Support planning and person-centred thinking tools

Areas of information in a support plan	The person-centred thinking tools that can help provide this information
1. What is important to you/the person being supported? Great support plans give a good sense of the real person – their personality, interests and hopes for the future.	A person-centred description provides this information.
2. What do you/the person want to change? Support plans say what the person wants to change about his life. This may include changing where he lives, changing how he is supported, or changing how he spends his time.	'Working and not working' from different perspectives.
3. How will you/the person be supported? Support plans say what kind of support he is going to use to make the changes that he wants to make. It should say how the person will make sure that he stays safe and well.	A person-centred description provides this information.
4. How will you/the person spend the personal budget? The plan must set out how the person is going to spend his budget to meet his outcomes.	
5. How will the support be managed? The plan must explain how any support the person pays for is going to be organised. This means saying who is going to manage it and how the person will sort out the payment of salaries or other necessary practical arrangements.	
6. How will you/the person stay in control of life? Great support plans clearly say how the person will stay in control of his own life. This means looking at what decisions he will make, and where other people make decisions for him, how they make sure that he is involved and has agreed to them.	Communication charts Decision making agreements
7. What are you/the person going to do to make this plan happen (action plan)? The plan should set out real and measurable things that will have happened in the future so that it is possible to see whether the plan is working or not.	

In this story, Nan was assisted to use person-centred thinking tools as part of developing her support plan.

Nan's story

Nan, 94, has always been very active. When she lost three of her own children, she opened her home up to other kids who didn't have parents. These days, she is living with her daughter, Anita, as she is deaf, registered blind and can no longer use her legs the way she used to. It's meant that there have been times in her life when she was sitting around all day feeling frightened, lonely and fed up... She had to call on Anita to do a lot of things for her that she felt she could have been doing for herself: 'I was just sat there, doing nothing...I wanted to do things and felt I could because up here (in my head) and down here (in my body) don't grow old together... I wasn't ready by a long way to have "had it"... I couldn't see what Anita was doing in the kitchen, and I thought to myself, "Gee, I'd love to be out in that kitchen, too, but instead, here I am on this settee." That's just not me.'

Her daughter Anita could see her mum was miserable, but was finding the situation really hard. She couldn't leave Nan, but still had to look after other members of her family. Everyone was always calling on Anita to help. They only had three hours of help from an agency per week, and that was barely enough time for Anita to get down to the supermarket.

A social worker talked to Nan and Anita about personal budgets and the different ways that they could develop a support plan. Nan and Anita thought together about:

- what was important to Nan

- what qualities, talents and connections Nan had

- how best to support her

- what she wanted for the future

- what was working and not working from Nan's perspective and Anita's perspective.

Since receiving her personal budget and going through the support planning process, Nan now has a personal assistant – Rachel – to support her every day. Anita showed Rachel everything about Nan, including how to give her medication. With Rachel's help, Nan can wash the pots and do her gardening and she's also planning a holiday. It means that Nan can accompany Anita and her husband to the seaside, but can do her own thing and just meet up at meal times. 'Rachel is like a sister. That sets Anita free and that's how I want it. I feel like I'm 49 again.'

Nan says she is a lot happier now and Anita thinks that her mum has a new lease of life. 'Rachael has not just set Nan free from her old age, but has also helped me have more of a life too. Before, I'd have to wait for Tony to come home and sit with Nan before I could go anywhere. Now with Rachel, I can just go and do it. We are very, very happy.'

Nan said she doesn't ever want to go into a nursing home. She wants to stay in her own home where she knows where things are and she can see her family. 'Everyone has to get old, but some can get there better than others. Why be miserable?'

Person-centred plans are also an ideal opportunity to use person-centred planning. Here the plan is solely to enable the person to create a vision of his future and how his budget can help achieve this, working together with family and friends. Here, Charlotte describes how her son Ben used his PATH and worked with his circle of support to create his support plan.

Ben's story (as told by his mum, Charlotte)

Ben did his support plan with a small group of people whom he wanted to help him. He had already done a PATH with his family and friends so took this with him and proudly pinned it to the wall. With great pride he explained to our circle all that he intended for his future, the basics of which was to have a life just like anyone else.

The importance given to Ben and to what *he* wanted in life during the development of his support plan meant that he took an interest from the start and, although he didn't fully understand the procedure, he totally understood the implications and the possible outcomes: that he was being given the opportunity to be in control of what he wanted to do with his life and to be given the choice of how he would do it through the support of a personal assistant.

Already his self-confidence was beginning to grow. Ben explained what was and wasn't working in his life, what he would like to change as he was supported in deciding how we could change those things. He described the sort of person he wanted as his PA, right down to tattoos and muscles (he wanted to feel safe to leave the house without being victimised by bullies). The PA definitely had to be 'a dude'! He also talked about the courses he would be interested in attending and the type of social activities he would like to do. His long-term aim is to live independently and so we included how he would learn all the necessary skills to make that possible.

Once the support plan was finished, it was sent up to the council to be agreed; I was hoping to get it all through before Ben started college in the September – unfortunately the 'powers that be' weren't accustomed to this type of support plan and we had a further month's delay while they received training! But it sailed through! Nothing was contested and Ben's indicative budget was agreed – we were on our way!

We had decided that three different PAs would not only give him choice and diversity but would also be a good contingency plan for sick leave and holidays. We also put adverts up in the Rugby Club, the Leisure Centre and other places with potential for finding tattooed and muscled dudes. We ended up with many applications to wade through. We started the interview process and, although we both had our designated questions to ask, the main criteria was how Ben related to each person. If he liked them, he was particularly noisy, exuberant and tended to jump all over them. If they couldn't deal with being leapt all over they weren't put on the short list!

Ben didn't like some of the interviewees on first sight and after only a couple of minutes into the meeting, he would just say 'I'm off to play Xbox Mum!' leaving me to go through the formalities, knowing that the person wasn't going to get the job! He has an uncanny perceptiveness of people – those he didn't like I didn't either!!

After many such interviews Ben chose the three he liked best – they were all dudes, one was even a weight lifter, though none of them had tattoos!

With his circle of support, we organised to hold quarterly meetings to follow his progress and achievements and to ensure that he kept to his plan. At present he is surpassing all expectations and his dreams for the future are arriving quicker than anticipated. Many unthought-of opportunities have arisen and been taken which have only enriched his life, including driving lessons, taking part in a television advert, a role as an extra in an *EastEnders* episode and 16 hours a week paid work at McDonald's.

If the person already has a person-centred plan, then it is a head start in creating a support plan with them. For example, this is how a PATH can contribute information to a support plan.

PATH

Information you will have:

- what the person wants to change and move towards (positive and possible, north star)
- who the key people are in the person's life (enrol).

Information you need to develop:

- what is important to the person
- how he needs to be supported

- how he will spend his individual budget and manage his support

  - how he will stay in control of his life

  - action plan.

In Part II we introduced person-centred thinking tools and how they can build into a detailed person-centred description. In the last two chapters we have introduced person-centred planning and support planning. They are all person-centred practice and therefore share the values described in Part I. We clarify some of the differences between them in Table 13.2.

Table 13.2 Differences between person-centred description, support plan and person-centred plan

	Person-centred description	Support plan	Person-centred plan (PATH or MAP)
Purpose	To share how the person wants to live – what is important to the person and how he wants to be supported. It forms the basis of action planning (using the 'working and not working' person-centred thinking tool or in a person-centred review).	To record the decisions about how the person wants to spend his personal budget to achieve his outcomes.	To describe a desirable future as part of the community, and the actions that people are undertaking to achieve this.
Who has/could have one	A person-centred description is important for everyone who receives health or social care. It could be part of a personalised care plan or support information.	Everyone who has a personal budget.	Anyone who wants one.
Who uses it	People who support the person to ensure that they are delivering to him a personalised service.	The person and people who support him.	The person, his circle (friends and family) and anyone with whom the person wants to share it (for example, staff).
How it is developed	Through using person-centred thinking tools and 'growing' this information from a one page profile. Person-centred descriptions can be started through a person-centred review.	Through using person-centred thinking tools or a person-centred plan.	Through a person-centred planning meeting (for example, a PATH or MAP).

	Person-centred description	Support plan	Person-centred plan (PATH or MAP)
Who is involved	The person, staff and information is sought from family.	The person could develop the support plan himself, or involve family or friends, or get support (for example, peer supporter).	The meeting has an independent facilitator. The person chooses whom to invite.
What the structure or format is	The headings are *Like and admire* (or a variant of this) *What is important to* the person *How best to support* the person (this usually includes subheadings – for example, *Communication* and *Decision making*).	People can use whatever headings they want, but their plan must meet specified criteria. The support plan will always state what the person's outcomes are, and how he will use his personal budget to achieve them.	A graphic record, using the headings from PATH, MAPS or personal futures planning.

Conclusion to Part III

Person-centred reviews are a highly effective way of helping people to listen, learn and engage with each other. The success of the meeting relies on everyone's preparation, participation and the skills of the facilitator. It is crucial that facilitators receive appropriate training and support. However, it is also vital to remember that however successful and person-centred the meeting is, if every effort is not made to complete the actions, then it is an unacceptable breach of trust. Neither a good meeting nor a plan is the outcome we are seeking – it is positive change for the person.

An exciting consequence of using person-centred reviews is that people are asking for positive and flexible outcomes which challenge current patterns of provision. It is important that this is shared with the people who can act on this, through implementation groups, or senior managers, and that facilitators also provide information about direct payments and individualised funding. Simply changing the way we do reviews could lead to change at many levels. Person-centred planning starts with a very different kind of meeting, and commitment, as John O'Brien says:

> At it's core, it [person-centred planning] is a vehicle for people to make worthwhile, and sometimes life changing, promises to one another.[156]… The promise of person-centred planning, is a way to expand the power that people have, to move towards their desirable future, and to be contributing members of their communities. The change comes about through the work of a circle of support (planning circle).
>
> Planning alone does not change people's lives. Person-centred planning offers people who want to make a change a forum for discovering shared images of a desirable future, negotiating conflicts, doing creative problem solving, making and checking agreements on action, refining direction while adapting action to changing situations, and offering one another mutual support. But without people working together in a sustained and careful way in the world outside the planning circle, change can not happen.[157]

Both person-centred thinking and person-centred plans can form the foundation of great support plans. When someone has a personal budget, he develops his support plan to record his decisions about his future, and how he wants to use his budget to achieve his outcomes.

Jennie's story, as told by her mum Suzie, shows how person-centred reviews, person-centred thinking, person-centred planning and support planning can be used together to create significant, and lasting change.

Jennie's story

Jennie is 20 and, has a warm personality; she is fun with a cheeky sense of humour, a real zest for life and is great company.

Even though it is sometimes hard for Jennie to articulate her thoughts and feelings, I admire her determination to communicate with us about whether she likes an activity, place or a person.

After Jennie was diagnosed with autism we received four nights of overnight respite care a month, and that began our journey with services.

In 2004 I learned about the world of person-centred thinking and planning. I was a bit cynical about the idea of person-centred planning at first and felt it was just another fad to come over from America and I was concerned that local authorities and provider organisations would not 'get on board' with the concept. But as soon as I realised its potential I jumped into it one hundred per cent. I went on a course for families, and developed a person-centred description of what is important to Jennie and how best to support her, with the help of everybody in her life who knew her best. Everyone involved in Jennie's life has a copy of her person-centred description. When she was at school a mastercopy stayed in Jennie's home/school communication book in her school bag so that comments and suggestions could be added by anyone at any time who knew Jennie really well. I didn't want it to be this pristine plan that was stuck in a drawer and as everyone got into the habit of using it, it became a 'living' document about Jennie with scribbles and crossings out – 'Jennie doesn't do this anymore she prefers this' – so we were constantly learning and everyone was using it and keeping it up to date.

I started worrying about Jennie's future and the transitions she would go through from finishing school, post-16 education and leaving children's services and moving into adult life. We were one of the first families to be offered a person-centred review (Year 9 review). There are a few important things I remember that came out of it. In particular it was the start of us looking at planning for Jennie's future. When we were developing her person-centred description I realised that I was making all the decisions for Jennie and that the emphasis needed to shift to Jennie being involved in making some of those decisions herself, whether I liked them or not!

We had also drawn a relationship circle for Jennie and it hit me that Jennie's circle included family but no friends. Although friendships had not been that important to her, I thought we had a responsibility to look at this. So I raised this as an issue at the Year 9 review and asked everyone whether there were any relationships that Jennie seemed to be enjoying, and this began work with Jennie to develop friendships. Her friendship with Rowenna came from the work that we did at this point. They are still friends today.

A year later Jennie had her Year 10 review. Both reviews made a huge difference to the way Jennie was included and talked about in a positive way. One of the main things to come out of the Year 10 review was the idea to set up a circle of support to help us achieve the future we wanted for Jennie and this has been pivotal. One of the long-term issues for me is that I'm not always going to be here to support Jennie. I wanted to make sure that there were enough people in her life with the same interests and concerns for her future as me, and who knew her well enough, who could make the right choices about what she wants when she is older. This was the reason behind setting up the circle of support.

Being a member of someone's circle of support is a voluntary role, so we asked everyone at Jennie's review whether they would like to participate. Jennie's step-dad Dave, brother Matt and I joined the circle, as did our friend Julie and colleague Helen. Debbie, a friend and colleague, also volunteered. She is a close and valued friend and has two sons with autism so brought a different perspective, as a friend looking out for me, and a professional perspective too. Another friend, Carol, who used to be one of Jennie's support workers, also volunteered and attends meetings when she can. Jennie's dad, Derek, joined the circle at a later stage. It is a brilliant combination of family and friends who know Jennie well and have her best interests at heart. But also the circle has a good personal and professional quality, particularly with Helen and Julie having person-centred and service backgrounds. Once the circle of support was established it started to take that weight off my shoulders.

In the first six months of the circle, Helen suggested we do a PATH for Jennie and we used this to start looking at Jennie's future. It was a very visual process, with two facilitators, who drew up a huge poster showing a PATH and all the things Jennie would need to journey along it. We started off by looking at our hopes and dreams, then what was positive and possible, and then looked at the steps we would need to take in two years, one year, and six months, to reach that point. So, in effect, you start off by looking into the future and then work backwards to set the goals and deadlines to achieve that future and this is all written up on the PATH. Using the PATH taught me that it is important to think really creatively because it encourages you to aim higher.

The PATH was really useful because it kept us focused on what was important to Jennie and the possibilities that were out there. But I personally found the PATH quite a challenging person-centred planning process to use because I had to change my attitude from thinking 'this is ridiculous, it's never going to happen' to 'if you don't strive for the ultimate then you are never going to take little steps to reach your hopes and dreams'. This is when we started to think about personal budgets. To cut a long story short we got a resource allocation for Jennie, and used information from her person-centred description and PATH to put together a support plan. Everything we had learned about Jennie, from person-centred thinking and planning, pointed to the fact that it was crucially important for Jennie to live on her own supported by people who understand her. We based our decisions on our collective understanding of Jennie.

We also did a community map and the circle members were tasked with looking at local activities, groups or places that Jennie could visit or be part of that were linked to things that we knew from her person-centred description and her PATH were important to her; for example, could she visit an art gallery or take art classes, were there any groups where she could develop friendships? It was about making sure that she had a full, rich, active life and was spending time with people who were important to her; the sorts of things that we would all strive to have in our lives.

This was all recorded in her support plan. As well as recording what is important to Jennie, the support plan outlines how her personal budget will be used; sets out her 'perfect week'; and includes a communication chart and decision making profile. The support plan is a really important document because everything we wanted for Jennie in the plan was costed, so it had to be signed off by us and the local authority.

Life for Jennie, who is now living in her own flat, is fantastic. In fact, I would say that Jennie is really happy most of the time and it is a delight and a relief for me to see that. Jennie had a few difficult months settling in and so did I in letting go. She has a really happy, active life and is supported by great people. She is enjoying the independence away from us. If you had said to me 10 years ago that this would have happened I would never have believed it. I was worried that by then she might be in an institutional setting or in supported living with people she didn't like or, worse still, didn't choose to live with, but now all the worry has gone which has been amazing for me.

Part IV

Person-Centred Thinking from Prevention to End of Life

This part focuses on how person-centred practice can be used in people's journey of support through adulthood – from prevention (Chapter 14) or the management of long-term health conditions (Chapter 15) to reablement (Chapter 16), recovery (Chapter 17), support at home and in residential care (Chapter 18) and at the end of life (Chapter 19). The common thread that runs right the way through all of this support is managing risk in a way that still means people achieve their desired outcomes. This is the focus of the final chapter (Chapter 20).

Chapter 14

Prevention and Well-Being

> Our vision for prevention: Empowered people and strong communities will work together to maintain independence...those actively involved in care are the best people to decide how these services should change... Happier, more socially connected individuals have more pride in their neighbourhoods, which can enhance quality of life, health and well-being.
>
> *Department of Health[158]*

The government's vision for adult social care says its ambition is to foster conditions in which communities and others can develop a diverse range of preventative support that reduces isolation and improves health and well-being.[159] This will build community capacity, promote active citizenship and help better manage demand for formal health and care.

One way to deliver this vision is to improve an individual's connection with the community around them by developing their social relationships – this is a key component of improving well-being.[160] Therefore, if you think of prevention in terms of taking care of a person's well-being, you can help develop personalised and person-centred support by considering what makes her feel good and function well.[161] Person-centred thinking tools like 'Presence to contribution' (Chapter 8) have a role to play here.

In the last few years, there has been a shift in focus in psychology from illness to well-being. The 2008 Mental Capital and Wellbeing Project, as part of the UK government's Foresight programme, commissioned research[162] to develop a set of evidence-based actions to improve personal well-being. The research reviewed the emerging literature in positive psychology and drew from the government's Foresight Challenge Reports, produced by academic experts, on learning through life, mental health, well-being and work, learning difficulties, and mental capital through life. The actions identified were social relationships, physical activity, and awareness, learning and giving.

Connect...

Make connections with the people around you, with family, friends, colleagues and neighbours: at home, work, school or in your local community. Think of these as the cornerstones of your life and invest time in developing them. Building these connections will support and enrich you every day.

Be active...

Go for a walk or run. Step outside. Cycle. Play a game. Garden. Dance. Exercising makes you feel good. Most important, discover a physical activity which you enjoy, one which suits your level of mobility and fitness.

Take notice...

Be curious. Catch sight of the beautiful. Remark on the unusual. Notice the changing seasons. Savour the moment, whether you are on a train, eating lunch or talking to friends. Be aware of the world around you and what you are feeling. Reflecting on your experiences will help you appreciate what matters to you.

Keep learning...

Try something new. Rediscover an old interest. Sign up for that course. Take on a different responsibility at work. Fix a bike. Learn to play an instrument or how to cook your favourite food. Set a challenge you will enjoy achieving. Learning new things will make you more confident, as well as being fun to do.

Give...

Do something nice for a friend, or a stranger. Thank someone. Smile. Volunteer your time. Join a community group. Look out, as well as in. Seeing yourself and your happiness linked to the wider community can be incredibly rewarding and will create connections with the people around you.

Person-centred thinking tools can help people think more about how they are doing in each of these well-being areas, and what they could build on or improve in (see Figure 14.1).

Even if people's lives are relatively in control and are 'OK', there is always something that can be done to reflect on and improve well-being, as Jaimee shows in Table 14.1.

Table 14.1 *Improving well-being*

What am I doing already? What is going well?	Way to well-being	What could I do to increase or improve my well-being?
Attending book club with colleagues every six weeks. Speaking with family in Australia via telephone and the internet once a week.	Connect.	Set up fortnightly catch-ups with my non-work friends. Save up to fly home once a year to re-connect with family and friends in person.
Going to the gym twice a week.	Be active.	Go for a jog during the lighter evenings after work. Get off a tube stop early and walk.
Keeping a diary.	Take notice.	Take my lunch breaks away from my desk to enjoy the seasons. Switch off my phone when catching up with friends and when having meals with my husband.
Visit a gallery or museum once a month.	Keep learning.	Enrol in an evening class to learn a new skill like cooking.
Unofficial social coordinator at work.	Give.	Remember to send celebration cards (birthdays, new babies, anniversaries) to family and friends on time. Make more time to chat with our neighbours.

Figure 14.1 Well-being chart

This approach can also be used by teams to improve both individual well-being and create a 'healthier workplace'. The team in the following example rated themselves in each of the five areas on a scale of 1 to 5, with 1 meaning no activity and 5 doing as much as possible. They looked at where they scored 1 or 2 and prioritised these for actions. As a result of this:

- Sanjay decided to pay more attention to how he could have a healthier lunch and make sure he walked for 20 minutes in his lunch hour.

- June decided to set up a book club with three other friends.

- Helen decided to read a book about mindfulness and see if she could do 10 minutes of yoga most days.

- Andy decided to de-clutter his apartment and give what he did not want away on 'Freecycle'.

- As a team they decided to support each other to take at least 30 minutes for lunch in the kitchen area rather than eating at their desks. They also agreed to review how they were doing individually and as a team at their monthly team meetings.

Other person-centred thinking tools can help 'drill down' into particular areas. For example, if you're helping someone to improve their well-being by connecting with people, you could use a 'relationship circle' to look at who is in their life at the moment, and what they could do to develop the relationships they already have. The 'community mapping' tool shows where a person spends time already, where they are connected, and the other places where they might want to be in their community. The 'presence to contribution' tool plans steps to help people be and feel part of their community. The 'working and not working' and '4 plus 1' tools can help reflect on what you have been trying in order to be more connected.

> Having strong social relationships, being physically active and being involved in learning are all important influencers of both well-being and ill-being. By contrast, the processes of giving and becoming more aware have been shown to specifically influence well-being in a positive way. A combination of all of these behaviours will help to enhance individual well-being and may have the potential to reduce the total number of people who develop mental health disorders in the longer term.[163]

The actions people take to enhance their well-being – for example, by staying fit or maintaining social and psychological needs – are important for staying healthy. They are also integral components for effectively managing long-term health conditions, which we explore in the next chapter.

Chapter 15

Long-Term Conditions

> Personalised care planning is about addressing an individual's full range of needs, taking into account their health, personal, social, economic, educational, mental health, ethnic and cultural background and circumstances. It recognises that there are other issues in addition to medical needs that can impact on a person's total health and well-being.
>
> *Department of Health*[164]

The five ways to well-being explored in the previous chapter could help prevent some health and mental health problems. When people do have long-term health conditions, then the emphasis is on helping them to be informed about and manage their condition as much as possible, and to maximise control over their care choices. 'Individuals with long-term conditions have no choice but to live with their condition as best they can. They need to learn to self care as well as manage their condition on a daily basis.'[165]

Jane uses person-centred thinking to feel more in control of her life and to manage her long-term health condition, ulcerative colitis.

As I started to use person-centred thinking, I realised there were so many things I found upsetting about how people treat me and my condition, and the presumptions that people make (on my behalf). But I would never say anything and then usually ended up feeling frustrated with myself.

It was such a good feeling (and emotional at times) documenting how I'd like to be supported and what didn't work for me. The hardest tool to work on was hopes and fears because it took some time and effort in being honest with myself. I had to take a really good look at my life and work out what has happened and what I want for my future.

I went through an amicable divorce and the realisation that my ex-husband wasn't going to be there as a support around my colitis scared the life out of me. After our split, I had been in remission so I'd not given this aspect of my life a second thought until it flared up again.

I shared how I was using person-centred thinking tools with a friend, Julie, who helped me to think about my actions. Using the tools and talking to Julie made it feel simple and clear... just simple strategies like if I'm going out for dinner with someone new, just explain that I'm a vegetarian, which is so much easier than saying I can't eat meat because my bowel can't cope with it...and how to communicate to my colleagues when I'm feeling very unwell and need to head home to bed!

We put this together into a 'one page health profile' (well, it was one-and-a-half pages to be exact). I was really proud of it and felt oddly emotional over a couple of A4 sheets of paper. But here was the information I wish I'd been able to pull together when I was first diagnosed so that everyone knew where they stood and how I wanted to cope and manage my colitis.

Jane's profile

Me

My health history

My ulcerative colitis was diagnosed 8 years ago as right-sided distal colitis (on the right side of the 1st section of my bowel) but in summer of '09 colitis spread to my entire colon.

What's important to me...

- Being with honest, supportive and trustworthy people who can make me smile even when I don't feel like I can.

- Spending time with my family and friends. Spending good quality girly time with Shell, Claire and...my sister-in-law Jo.

- I like to try and see my family once a week.

- Being an ex-chef I'm passionate about food, so I love to eat out as often as I can. I like to eat in Town Bar once a week, and treat myself to eating out in a nice restaurant in Manchester once a month (but always like to try somewhere new).

- Cups of tea throughout the day – builders' brew strength with milk.

- I'm a huge Manchester City supporter (watch matches on TV, see live matches when I can afford it).

- Wearing Converse (I would live in a pair of Converse every day of my life if I could; there actually is a pair for every occasion).

- Running 3 times a week, especially listening to the Arctic Monkeys on my iPod.

- Travelling – seeing new places and experiencing new cultures is uplifting.

- Listening to music – I love music (especially Manchester music) going to gigs/concerts.

How best to support me...

- **About food** I am the expert about me, my colitis and my diet, so please don't try and advise me on what I should or shouldn't be eating. I know what my system can/cannot cope with each day, it's not me being fussy or watching my weight. Please trust my own judgement on this subject and know that I'm doing what is best for me on that day for my body, and ideally avoid taking Tramadol which you all know I hate.

- **Talking about ulcerative colitis** Don't confuse IBS with ulcerative colitis – I find it frustrating when people tell me they have IBS from time to time, they are NOT the same condition.

- **About stress and tiredness** I refuse to 'opt' out of life as a whole so don't tell me that I should avoid certain emotional stresses. I am working on finding ways of coping with it not avoiding it.

  Don't worry if I lie in bed all day watching movies and sleeping, it's me recognising I've done too much and could really do with the RandR. When my body gets run down that's when a flare-up can take over.

- **About cups of tea** At home and at work, the answer to 'Would you like a brew Jane?' is always yes! If I say 'I think it's a peppermint tea day today' (no milk and leave the bag in the cup please) it means that I am having a bad day, and that is the easiest way of me letting you know.

- **When I am ill or in hospital** Don't feel you always have to visit me at home when I'm poorly, a text with a kiss on it will always put a smile on my face and just to know you're thinking of me is enough. If I get admitted into hospital, please take time to visit (even if it's for a few minutes). I hate being in hospital and feel very alone and isolated, so knowing I will get visitors means the world to me, but don't bring me anything...it's thoughtful but not necessary.

  At hospital I really hate using enemas. They don't always help and usually aggravate an already sensitive area, so if there is an alternative please offer it.

  Always cc me into consultant appointment review letters, treatment letters and hospital admission letters. When you are in the situation it's very easy to forget some of the information that's being discussed about you.

  Always trust me when I know my body needs i.v. of steroids, when a flare-up gets to 'that stage' when only i.v. steroids will do. My GP is understanding of this, and it would be really helpful during a severe flare-up if crucial days are not wasted trying to decide if I need a bed, when I should just be brought in and put straight on a steroid i.v. to reduce my suffering and pain.

Figure 15.1a Jane's one page profile

What's working?

Having a direct line to my consultant's office, so it saves time when I need help. At the moment Infliximab is working (fingers crossed).

Being able to sit with Rachel (colitis specialist nurse) whilst having i.v. meds and being able to chat about anything that's worrying me.

What's not working?

Having to re-learn what my food intolerances are.

Getting tired easily and learning when to 'give in' and rest.

Having to explain to everyone when I'm having a bad day. It happens so often I feel like people lose interest when I mention it.

The effect that emotional stress has on my gut and bowel...makes me very unwell and then it's hard to get the colitis under control again.

Next steps?

Explore how I can prevent and manage emotional stress – and still have a life!

Try books and internet sites first.

Keep a food diary to notice my intolerences.

Figure 15.1b Jane's working and not working

Several initiatives have or are exploring use of person-centred approaches in health practice:

- The Diabetes Year of Care[166] (a partnership between the Department of Health, Diabetes UK, The Health Foundation and NHS Diabetes) put people with long-term conditions in the driving seat of their care and supported them to self-manage. This was achieved through having true collaboration in the care planning process and making sure people had all the information they needed – for example, knowing the results of tests before consultations.

- The Co-Creating Health[167] initiative provided self-management support for people with long-term conditions and embedded personal care planning into primary and secondary care.

- The Expert Patients Programme[168] supports people to increase their confidence, improve the quality of their life and better manage their long-term condition through a peer-led self management programme.

- Information Prescriptions help maintain independence by guiding people to relevant and reliable sources of information about their long-term condition in consultation with a health or social care practitioner.

- The government's Personal Health Budget pilot, which runs until 2012, extends this through offering people a personal health budget as a means to give them more choice and control over the healthcare they receive.

Person-centred thinking and personalised care plans

Some of these initiatives involve personalised care plans, which are based on a conversation between the person and their healthcare practitioner about the impact that their condition has on their life, and how they can be supported to meet their health and well-being needs in a 'whole life' way.

The key elements of good personalised care planning are:

- having a clear purpose

- timely and relevant information beforehand

- clear goals and outcomes

- detail about how the person will meet their outcomes

- contingency planning and risk management

- how and when the plan will be reviewed.

When someone has a personal health budget, the personalised care plan should also include how the budget is going to be spent and managed. Early work on personalised care planning and personal health budgets stressed that planning conversations need to address what is important *to* and *for* people; what is working and not working; and what they hope to achieve. There was also recognition that there has to be a huge cultural shift and change in thinking about power within the workforce to support people to really be in control of their health.[169]

Person-centred thinking tools help conversations between the person and the health practitioner, and are a way to record their decisions and outcomes.

In Chapter 5, we met James and saw his decision making profile. Here is some information from his personalised care plan to show how person-centred thinking helped him decide what is important *to* and *for* him, what is working and not working, and his decisions and actions from this.

HOW MY CONDITION AFFECTS ME

- I have a lot of pain in my hands, which can affect the amount of exercise or the things I can do.

- Transferring to a bed or sofa is difficult and I need support with this.

- I can have episodes of Autonomic Dysreflexia though this has decreased in frequency since having a live-in personal assistant.

- Sometimes my pain medication can make me feel tired and drowsy, limiting time with family or friends. This time can also be affected by accessibility issues.

WHAT ARE MY WISHES AND PREFERENCES FOR MY TREATMENT AND SUPPORT?

- Having a consistent live-in personal assistant who knows my routines, equipment and me! They must be a high quality carer with specialist knowledge.

- Having a specialist physiotherapist.

WHAT IS IMPORTANT TO ME?

About life

- My computers. I have three laptops, two computers and a server. I use them for web development, gaming, programming, using the net and watching TV. I have voice recognition on one of my PCs and on one laptop.

- Seeing my mum once a week. She comes to see me as her house isn't very accessible. Seeing my friends Al, Paul, Simon and Gav at least two or three times a week. I enjoy going to the pub, cinema or comedy nights.

- Seeing my London-based twin brother Tom, middle brother Rob and step-sister Gemma twice a month. I would like to be able to go and visit them.

- Seeing my dad twice a month. He usually comes to me but I have been to his house a couple of times. I have also been to his local pub, which is very accessible. Having a lightweight manual wheelchair to enable me to get around myself. There is a big difference in how people react to you in a manual wheelchair compared to an electric one.

- Playing sports. I love to play wheelchair rugby once a week and play in tournaments.

- Being able to travel and stay in hotels. Having a mobile hoist and an adapted car has enabled me to do this in the past few months.

- Having a live-in PA. This provides me with flexibility, consistency and allows me to travel. Active Assistance, a specialist agency who provides live-in carers for people with spinal cord injuries, provides my current PA, Carla.

About my health

- *Improving my stamina and fitness so that I am able to do more things during the day without getting too tired.*
- *Avoiding being admitted to hospital and losing time to being unwell. This means eating well, avoiding urinary tract infections, chest infections and deep vein thrombosis.*

WHAT IS WORKING AND WHAT IS NOT WORKING

Table 15.1 shows what is working and not working in James' life.

Table 15.1 *Working and not working*

What is working	What is not working
My general care and support.	Not seeing enough of my family and friends.
My personal care, transferring etc.	My stamina not being what I want it to be
My physiotherapy and exercise that	and not being able to cope with long days.
helps me with my stamina.	Living in a big, shared environment,
My social life has improved,	having a lack of privacy and not being
particularly where I live.	able to redecorate to my taste.
Playing wheelchair rugby.	Not being able to control my bed
	with environmental controls and
	having to ask for help with this.
	The pain in my hands.

WHAT DO I WANT TO CHANGE? WHAT ARE MY PERSONAL OUTCOMES?

Table 15.2 shows what James wants to change and achieve, and how he plans to do this.

Table 15.2 *What I want to change and achieve*

What I want to change, my priority issues	The outcomes I want to achieve	My ideas for achieving these outcomes
Improving my fitness and stamina levels	Tolerating 12–14 hours in my wheelchair without getting too tired so that I can do more than one thing per day. Being able to push myself to Morrisons, which is about 500m away but does involve kerbs, roads and a hill. Standing in my standing frame for one hour twice a week to improve my general health, particularly digestion etc. It would also reduce the pain in my neck and the risk of osteoporosis.	Working with my physio to ensure my posture is correct in my new wheelchair and it is set up correctly for me. Improving my sleep pattern by doing more during the day, avoiding afternoon naps and listening to music to help me get to sleep. Taking up swimming – maybe going every one to two weeks. I have the equipment but need an extra two hours/week of support from a person additional to my PA. Either seek additional funding for two hours per week agency support or ask Mum if she can help.
Changing where I live	Find my own fully adapted or adaptable bungalow to live in with a live-in carer by autumn 2010. It must be in the area I want and have at least two bedrooms, garden and local amenities like a pub, shops and a takeaway.	Explore both renting and buying a property. Check my local Homeseeker application is active and speak to My Safe Home about an income support mortgage.
Managing the pain in my hands	To be pain-free in my hands so that I can push my manual chair further and improve my stamina and fitness.	Referral to a specialist pain clinic in London. Have a hand massage once a week at physio. Explore whether my PA can train to do this at home.
Staying out of hospital	Improve my general health and avoid being hospitalised or having ambulance call-outs for urinary tract infections or episodes of Autonomic Dysreflexia.	Having my own live-in PA has already reduced my hospital stays and emergency admissions. This has to be maintained. Making sure I take my medication at the same time each day. Eating and drinking well.
Maintaining and developing my independence	Feel confident in using a Flip Flow valve on my catheter and potentially changing my own catheter. This may reduce nursing team support.	Speaking to my consultant at my next appointment about a Flip Flow valve.
To get back to driving	Pass my disabled driver's test within 12 months.	Investigate the nearest specialist driver centres and the process of applying.
Seeing more of my family and friends	See my friends twice a week at the pub or cinema. Visit London every 3–4 weeks to see my family who live there.	Arranging things in advance.

HOW TO SUPPORT ME TO LIVE MY LIFE AND MANAGE MY HEALTH CONDITION

I need support with the following day-to-day things. This support is mainly provided by my live-in personal assistant.

Maintaining a safe environment – I need some assistance to stay safe in my living environment. I live in level-access accommodation with a separate furnished room for my PA. I have the following equipment to support me and my PA with this:

Electric wheelchair

Manual wheelchair

Lightweight manual wheelchair

Standing frame

Rowing machine and electric leg bike

Track hoist

Mobile hoist

Adapted van – Fiat Doblo

Shower chair

Neuro 4 electrical stimulator

Mattress and adjustable bed

Slide sheets

Hand strap for eating

Rugby chair – sit in sling

There are risk assessments in place to ensure both my PA and myself are safe. Please see additional Safer People Handling Risk Assessment and General Risk Assessment.

I need support with personal care including showering, shaving and some assistance to dress myself. My PA supports with this.

I need support with mobility and using associated equipment.

My PA prepares and cooks my food. I am able to eat and drink most things myself using my specialist equipment. I like to do my food shopping with my PA.

I have a reduced lung capacity so I need to do daily lung exercises. I sometimes need assistance to cough. My PA assists with this.

I generally do not need any help at night, unless I am unwell and on bed rest. I then need to be supported to turn.

My PA supports me with any of the things I do for leisure, supporting me to get there and while there.

My PA also supports me with my medication. My medication is not delivered so they collect it from my local pharmacy and assist me to take it.

MY ACTION PLAN

Table 15.3 shows James' action plan.

Table 15.3 *My action plan*

Outcome	Who	What	By when
Tolerating 12–14 hours in my wheelchair without being too tired and having to go to bed.	James and physio James and PA	Set up posture correctly in new manual wheelchair. Look into local accessible swimming pools	Feb 2010 22 January 2010
Standing in my standing frame at least twice a week for at least an hour each time.	James	Speak to my mum about being the second pair of hands while I am using the standing frame.	20 January 2010
Find a place to live by autumn 2010.	James	Check that my Homeseeker application is active and speak to My Safe Home about an income support mortgage.	Feb 2010
Be pain-free in my hands.	James and physio James and consultant	Have a hand massage once a week at physio. Explore the possibility of my PA being trained to do this at home. Referral to a specialist pain clinic in London.	Ongoing March 2010
Improve my general health and avoid being hospitalised or having ambulance call-outs for urinary tract infections or episodes of Autonomic Dysreflexia.	James and PA	To continue with maintenance of bowel and bladder routines with a consistent approach. To take medication at the same time each day.	Ongoing
Feel confident to use a Flip Flow valve on my catheter and potentially changing my own catheter.	James and consultant	To discuss the use of Flip Flow valve at next appointment.	March 2010
Pass my disabled driver's test within the next 12 months.	James	Investigate the nearest specialist driver centres and the process of applying.	April 2010

Other person-centred thinking tools that can help people think about and manage their health condition

MY HEALTH: WHAT HELPS AND HINDERS?

Figure 15.2 is a simple table for people to think about their current treatments and lifestyle by considering what helps and what hinders.

GOOD DAYS AND BAD DAYS WITH MY HEALTH

Thinking about good days and bad days around health can help people to identify what helps in having more good days and fewer bad days and what they can do to about this (see more about this tool in Chapter 4).

My health: what helps and what hinders

What helps me be as healthy as possible?	What hinders (makes my health worse) or stops me from being as healthy as I can?

Figure 15.2 My health: what helps and what hinders?

✓

Thinking about my history

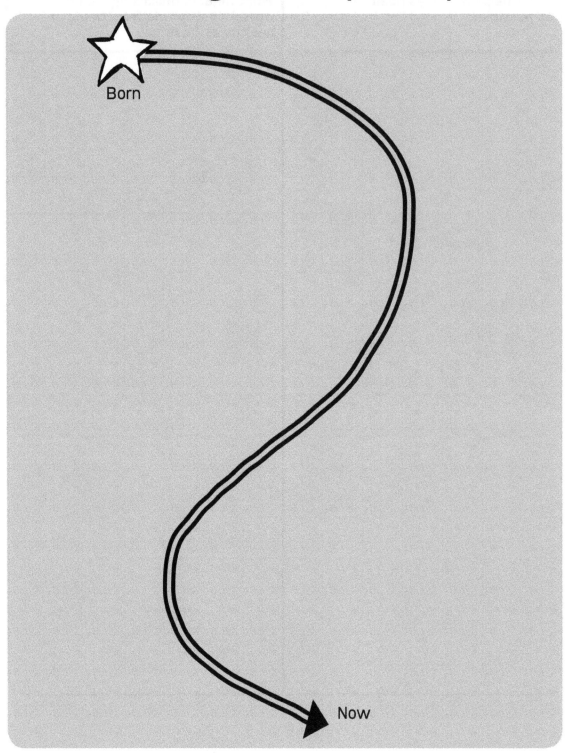

Figure 15.3 My health history

People can record their health history to reflect what has worked and not worked around their health in the past, and whether there are lessons and ideas that could help now (Figure 15.3).

HOPES AND FEARS

This helps people talk about their hopes and fears for the future around their health condition and what this could mean to their lives overall (Figure 15.4).

Person-centred thinking and dementia care mapping

Jane used person-centred thinking tools to help manage her long-term condition with help from a friend while James' support came from a health professional, who integrated person-centred thinking tools within his personalised care plan. However, there are many people with long-term conditions who are supported in residential care.

The following story about Jenny shows how person-centred thinking was integrated with dementia care mapping.[170] Dementia care mapping (DCM[171]) is a process which helps a professional observe life through the eyes of a person with dementia. It involves watching someone unobtrusively over an extended period of time to see how they respond positively and negatively to events that happen to, and around, them. The results of DCM can change the way the person with dementia experiences care and support, while also assessing the staff who deliver that care and identifying staff training needs.

During a DCM evaluation, a 'mapper' will sit with a group of people in the communal areas of a care home. They will observe up to five people with dementia, continuously over six or seven hours. After each five-minute period, the mappers will note the behaviour, mood and engagement of the person or people they are observing.

Figure 15.4 Hopes and fears

Jenny's story

Jenny has lived in a residential home for the past six years. She has dementia and staff members were finding it difficult to cope with her behaviours. She wandered around the home day and night punching staff members, other people living in the home and the walls. Three staff members were required to support Jenny when she needed assistance with personal care but she would constantly hit out at them. When Jenny was not walking about the home, she would remain in her bed all day and refuse her medication. Jenny would not let staff near her and refused all physical contact. During this time, she never communicated verbally. The situation saddened the staff and they felt that they were letting Jenny down. They were barely meeting her basic human needs and she had no quality of life.

The manager asked Hull's two dementia care mappers to spend time with Jenny so that they could find ways to understand her. The mappers spent two days observing Jenny as she walked around the home. The results were shared with the care staff of the home. They found that there was very little interaction with her. But when care staff did speak to Jenny, her mood rose and she would smile. She also appeared to enjoy rubbing the wallpaper and her clothing, which were textured. It was noticed that Jenny interacted with music that was playing by clapping and singing along to it. The mappers also observed that Jenny picked up a bundle of towels and carried these around with her.

Discussion took place with the staff to explore how Jenny's quality of life could be enhanced. The mappers described how use of their person-centred thinking tools could support the staff to use the learning from the map to make a real difference to Jenny's life. Staff explained that because of the home's routines, they had not noticed what Jenny was actually doing other than walking around. They were constantly asking her to sit down to keep her safe. Once staff members were able to understand Jenny's behaviour, they were able to suggest potential activities around the home that Jenny may like to do. Staff members' ideas included a tactile/rummage box – to meet Jenny's sensory needs – and to find out what type of music Jenny enjoyed.

Staff members asked to explore Jenny's life history, as this could explain some of her behaviours and would also to find out what her interests and hobbies were. They found out that she loves Mars bars and when she lived in her own home she would buy them in bulk.

Learning what was important to Jenny and what great support would look like for her would ensure that she had a better quality of life. A one page profile was developed with Jenny, her staff and her family and the learning from the map was included on this. They found that touching and feeling things was really important to Jenny. She holds a piece of ribbon and will run it through her fingers when staff members are assisting her in the mornings.

Over the past year, staff members have become more aware of how Jenny is getting those little things that are important to her. There has been a real change in Jenny's behaviour and both her family and other agencies involved with Jenny have commented that she is a new woman. Jenny appears content and is involved in meaningful activities around the home such as folding the laundry. The manager explained that when the initial map took place, Jenny would not even go outside but now she loves to walk around the garden with staff.

Jenny's one page profile explains that when Jenny tells you she hates you, it is because she is frightened. This sometimes happens when she hears loud noises. Reassure her and stroke her arms. Jenny also has a communication chart which is crucial as Jenny uses only a few words.

What is important to Jenny

Jenny loves all types of music, she will sing, dance, clap her hands and tap her feet to the music.

To talk about her son-in-law Martin and be listened to well – sit with her.

Touching and feeling things really matters to Jenny; she has her own basket with different fabrics in.

Jenny enjoys tea and coffee in a mug; milk with one sugar.

To eat her meals in the lounge; the dining room doesn't work for her.

She has a great appetite and loves anything sweet – especially puddings and Mars bars.

Jenny enjoys a bubble bath; she doesn't mind which product as long as there are bubbles.

Jenny must have a walk around the garden each day.

To sit by the window.

To get up between 9.00 a.m. and 9.30 a.m. – no earlier.

To be called Jenny, not Jen or pet names. This would irritate her.

To hold her piece of ribbon when getting ready each morning.

Jenny

What those who know Jenny say they like and admire about her

Thoughtful

Caring

A real character

Affectionate

Loving

How best to support Jenny

Know that Jenny will not respond to you if you do not include 'Jenny' in the sentence when speaking to her.

When Jenny tells you that she 'hates you', it is because she is frightened. This sometimes happens when she hears loud noises. Reassure her and stroke her arm.

When Jenny has her medication, stay with her as she chews her tablet. She needs encouragement to drink plenty of fluid with them – orange juice is her favourite.

Jenny's drinks must be served in a mug.

Know that Jenny holds a piece of ribbon when getting ready each morning and will run this through her fingers while staff assist her to get ready.

When walking to the toilet with Jenny she sometimes backs away from the toilet door; she must never be forced. Leave it and go back later.

Jenny's bubble bath and toiletries are in her bedroom. These should be kept on the top of the wardrobe. Jenny has eaten and drunk these products and this causes her to have an allergic reaction.

Figure 15.5 Jenny's one page profile

When this is happening	When Jenny does this	What am I communicating to you?	
		We think it means	We need to do this
Anytime	Puts her clothing into her mouth	She is thirsty	Offer her a drink – tea or coffee with a drop of milk; one sugar is favourite – must be in a mug
Meal times	Doesn't lift her knife and fork, looks at her plate	She needs help cutting some of her food	Jenny is embarrassed that her fingers are bent with arthritis. Sensitively offer to cut her food – quietly
Going to the bathroom	Backs away from the bathroom door	Jenny is anxious	Leave it and go back later
When using the lift	Begins to shout	The gap between the floor and the entrance to the lift makes her anxious	Reassure her and link her as you get into the lift

Figure 15.6 Jenny's communication chart

The mappers returned to map Jenny again a year later. The results of the map showed a real improvement not only in the home environment, but also in Jenny's well-being and happiness.

Each time the mappers returned back to Jenny's care home, they observed that real changes started to happen within the home, both in the environment and the staff culture. Staff members appeared more motivated and interested in the people they supported.

'We've learned more about the person. You think you knew the person before but you didn't really.'

Support worker

'"The mappers" suggestions and pointers using the person-centred tools support the map to move forward. We didn't know what to do with it before.'

Shift leader

'We thought we were doing the best we could until we found out what was important to the person.'

Support worker

'The dementia care map on its own was brilliant. It helped us to think about activities for the people living here, but now, it has now made such a difference to find out what is important to individual people.'

Registered manager

'The format we have now has surpassed our expectations by providing us with a more simplistic and easy to understand approach. The person-centred thinking tools give clear and concise information that is easy to read. This approach is now the way forward in our delivery of a far better service that combines person-centred thinking fully.'

Registered manager

The mappers observed a change in the way staff and the people they support interact with each other. This gives a measurable increase in enhancing people's care and support experiences, making a significant difference to the lives of the people living in the care home.

In this chapter we have shown that when people have long term-conditions, person-centred thinking tools can help people develop personalised care plans – in partnership with healthcare practitioners – that meet their support needs in a way that suits their 'whole life'. This extends to dementia where care mapping in residential homes can help people have a better quality of life. In the next chapter, we look at how person-centred practice can provide a different approach to recovery.

Chapter 16

Person-Centred Thinking in Recovery

> Recovery and being person-centred: one is an aspiration for a journey, and the other is the tool for getting there.
>
> *David Coyle*[172]

Recovery and person-centred approaches share the same values, with the same underlying positive set of assumptions about people and their capacity to lead their own lives, to change and grow. Many professionals have argued for a long time that mental health services have tried to 'contain' mental illness by focusing too much on doing things *to* patients, or *for* them, to reduce disturbance, rather than working *with* people, to develop more personally meaningful ways of living.[173]

By the end of the twentieth century, the assumption that professionals could 'fix' mental illness was waning and increasingly was overtaken by the view that people should participate in, if not actually lead, their own 'recovery'.[174]

The *recovery model* is rooted in the idea that people with mental health issues can live rich, fulfilling lives and that this is not necessarily reliant upon the elimination of the illness, but its effective management. With government policy firmly set on personalising care and providing the structures for people who need care and support to exercise choice and control – as well as an increasing acceptance that health improvement outcomes are as important as the processes leading to improvements – the time has come for person-centred approaches to be adopted as an important way to achieve recovery. 'In a high-quality service, the principles of recovery and the concepts of hope, self determination and opportunity that come under its umbrella underpin the practice of all those offering care and treatment.'[175]

Fiona has bi-polar disorder and started to use person-centred thinking tools to think about her situation and what she and others could do to help her stay well. This included a one page profile which provides specific detailed information about how to support a person – on her terms. For some people it can also be developed to inform future support – for example, for people whose support needs will vary at different times. This can simply be described as 'What to do when I become unwell'. Fiona found it useful to have a written description of how people would know when she started to become unwell and what they needed to do about it.

Fiona and her partner, Alex, also spent some time thinking about and recording what they had learned about keeping well and preventing relapses. Table 16.1 is her 'Stay well plan' and it asks 'What helps me stay well?' and 'What contributes to me becoming unwell?' and then provides space to create an action plan.

Fiona's story

Table 16.1 *Fiona's 'Stay well plan'*

What helps me stay well?	
Time with Alex	I have been particularly well since Alex and I have been together. We make sure that we create space and time to just 'be' with each other – either in the house or going out for a walk every day, out for a meal or to the cinema at least once a week.
Time with friends	Friends are really important to me. Our friends are spread around the country so we have to be really proactive about seeing them. We try to make sure that we have people come to stay, or plan visits or days out at least once a month. The friends that we see every month are: Lucy and Tim Sue and Simon Malcolm.
Work	Work is a really important part of my life – it is not just a job but part of who I am. I work long hours but the work I do is an important focus for me.
Exercise	I love going to the gym and try to plan this into my week (1 hour at Jim's Gym each week). Exercise definitely keeps me positive and feeling good about myself and that helps me stay well.
Sleep	I need to make sure that I get 6–7 hours a night or at least one sleep-in at the weekend!
Acupuncture	This is great for my general well-being, as well as a key treatment if I do get ill. I see my therapist, Mr Joseph, every month.
Spotting warning signs and taking action	I do get warning signs that I am getting ill: • not sleeping • overworking • avoiding being with friends or going out • controlling food • over-exercising. Alex and my friends and key work colleagues have an agreement that they will tell me straight if they think that any of these things are becoming a problem. See my communication chart for details.

What contributes to me becoming unwell?	
Lack of light	I am most likely to get depressed in the autumn and winter.
Over work	I can get into a downward spiral of overwork (working 45 hours a week, and staying away from home more than once a week).
Lack of exercise	Not getting enough exercise affects my mood any my self-esteem.

Not getting enough sleep	Too little sleep (less than 7 hours) over a prolonged period (more than 2 weeks) can start a downward spiral and lead to depression.
Ignoring warning signs and taking action	The most important contributing factor to my becoming unwell is that I ignore the warning signs and keep going as though nothing is wrong.

OUR ACTION PLAN TO HELP ME STAY WELL

The key to my staying well is that Alex, my friends, family and work colleagues are honest and open about how they perceive my mood. We figured this out several years ago and everyone who is close to me is comfortable doing this.

There are some specific actions we will take:

- *I will continue to have regular acupuncture. This helps my general well-being and will enable early symptoms to be picked up by the doctor.*

- *Alex and I will keep in close contact with Social Services and be clear if we need additional support.*

- *Alex and I will work together to make sure that I am able to go to the gym. We share child care responsibilities at the weekend and make sure that we each have the chance to sleep in on one of the two weekend days.*

- *We will make sure that we continue to plan time with friends and family on at least a monthly basis, both having people to stay and visiting friends around the country.*

- *We will monitor my mood closely in the autumn and winter and plan a week's holiday in the sun if necessary (or it feels like a good idea!)*

Finally, we have agreed that in the unlikely event that Alex is worried about my mental health and we cannot agree that I need support or agree a way forward between us, that he will:

- *contact Social Services*

- *contact Barney and Terry who will support me to get the support I need*

- *contact Morris who will help sort out work issues.*

A person-centred approach to records

These changes for professionals and people will be reflected in what is written about people and how their 'story' is recorded. For example, psychiatry has traditionally devalued the person's voice by promoting diagnostic jargon. Given the power imbalance between professionals and their 'patients', many people ended up describing their own experience in the technical language of psychiatry and psychology, as if their own story was inadequate.[176] 'Arguably, the emergence of the user voice is one of the most powerful developments in mental health, worldwide, in the past 30 years. Such groups are reclaiming their story and personhood through the act of "speaking up" or "speaking out".'[177]

A truly empowering and person-centred approach[178] would be that all assessments and records of care are written in the person's own voice. If the person is unable or unwilling, then the practitioner records what has been agreed, but still in the person's voice, much in the way that a secretary would in taking minutes at a meeting.[179] The supported self-assessment process in personal budgets aims to be an example of this approach, where people are seen as the experts in their own lives, and therefore the best people to assess what they can and cannot do, with whatever support people need to do this. 'Traditionally, the person's story is "translated" into a third person, professional account, by different health or social care practitioners. This becomes not so much the person's story (my story) but the professional team's view of that story (history).'[180]

In listening to the person's story, professionals are often only interested in their own line of enquiry, through their lens and understanding of 'the problem' and therefore listening for 'signs and symptoms'. The person is the expert on her own life, and history, and the way that this is shared and represented is uniquely hers. 'How can you know more about a person after seeing him for a few hours, a few days or even a few months, than he knows about himself? He has known about himself for a lot longer!'[181]

> Good social work is done with people and not for them. That requires mutual respect and trust; keeping the person at the centre of the work; enabling them to define desired outcomes; and supporting them to develop their own solutions.
>
> *Charles Leadbeater[182]*

Using person-centred thinking in existing recovery-based approaches

Person-centred thinking tools can be useful for both people using mental health services and professionals using recovery-based approaches, like Wellness Recovery Action Plan (WRAP)[183] and the Recovery Star[184] where the ethos and values underpinning them are the same.

WELLNESS RECOVERY ACTION PLANNING (WRAP)

WRAP is effective for promoting and supporting individual recovery.[185] There are five areas that combine to create a strengths assessment and a resource to support recovery. These include:

- *wellness toolbox* for identifying strengths, supports and resources

- *maintenance plan* for looking at the routines and activities that help the person stay well

- *early warning and identification of triggers*

- *crisis planning* to set out what the person would like to happen if they become unwell

- *post-crisis planning* to help the person recover after being unwell.

Tony's WRAP plan

Tony came out of hospital with his WRAP plan in a folder. For the three weeks that he was an inpatient, an occupational therapist worked with him to look at the questions in the 'wellness tool box'. This gave some good, basic information for Tony's one page profile. This profile was a summary of the key information in the WRAP plan, and Tony shared this with his family to help them understand what they could do so support him.

His main support was his wife, Marie, and son, David. They decided to look at the information in the WRAP plan and think about what was working and not working now, both from Tony's perspective and Marie's perspective. This revealed that Tony needed a balance of activity and rest during his week, so together they created a weekly timetable. This also meant that Marie could book in regular time to see her friends, which was important to her. They decided to review it every month, when David came over to dinner. The family also used the 'early warning information' and the crises planning information from the WRAP plan to create a 'stay well' plan. This clearly described what was likely to happen if Tony was becoming unwell, and what the family needed to do to respond to this.[186]

One of the things that Tony found difficult was making decisions about spending money. His wife was anxious that when he became unwell, he would spend and spend, which resulted in huge credit card bills. They were still paying off the last credit card bill from before Tony went into hospital. David, Tony and Marie talked about their decision making about money, and recorded this using the headings of a decision making agreement.

That was all a year ago and Tony has been unwell once since then, but says that his structured week has really helped. Marie feels more confident in supporting Tony, now that they have an agreement about decisions and money, and the stay well plan means that they can act quickly if things change.

THE RECOVERY STAR

Clear outcomes are emphasised in the mental health strategy *No Health without Mental Health*[187] and are required in support planning for the plan to be agreed. One approach is the Recovery Star[188] which is a tool for the assessment of needs and outcomes for adults of a working age.

People rate themselves in ten areas of their lives on a 'ladder' from 1 to 10 (1 being a serious problem and 10 indicating self-reliance). The ratings provide a way to measure progress and help to set outcomes.

The domains are:

- Managing mental health

- Living skills

- Work

- Addictive behaviour

- Identity and self-esteem

- Self-care

- Social networks

- Relationships

- Responsibilities

- Trust and hope

Here are some ways that person-centred thinking tools can be used with the Recovery Star.

LEARNING MORE ABOUT WHERE THE PERSON IS ON THE LADDER

For example, if someone thinks that she is at the 'Believing/Stage 6' level in 'self-care', then she wants to take responsibility for looking after herself well. You could use the 'working and not working' tool to think together about what she is doing around her self-care that is working for her at the moment, and what are the areas that are not working that she wants to change. You could also look at the level and ask what 'positive and possible' change would look like for her?

PATH is the person-centred planning tool that most strongly focuses on the future, and is another way to help people think about their aspirations, and to then develop outcomes from these.

If someone is on the 'Learning' step on the ladder, then the person-centred thinking tool '4 plus 1' questions could be useful. This will help you to think together about what the person has tried and learned, and what she is pleased and concerned about, to inform setting the next actions.

Here are other person-centred thinking tools that we refer to in Part II that can be useful when looking at the other domains.

Thinking about the social networks domain

- Community map

- Inclusion web: another very useful person-centred approach, developed within the mental health field, is called the 'inclusion web'. This looks at both relationships and how the person uses her community.[189]

Thinking about the relationships domain

- Communication chart

- Decision making agreement

- Relationship map

Thinking about the identity and self-esteem domain

- 'Appreciations' and one page profile or person-centred description

DEVELOPING A ONE PAGE PROFILE OR PERSON-CENTRED DESCRIPTION WITH THE LEARNING FROM USING THE RECOVERY STAR

Whatever stage of the ladder the person is at, clearly describing how best to support her is important. If the person is at the 'accepting help' stage, then it is very important to be able to say what this help needs to look like for the person.

The shift to a recovery approach from a more medically or system-focused approach means that rather than having the aims of the organisation or the clinicians as paramount, it's the aims and hopes of the person who needs care and support that are central. Recovery comes from the service user movement where many said that when they came into contact with psychiatric services it felt like a life sentence – they were told 'you are going to have this and be on medication for the rest of your life, you can forget about work or education'. But working in this way means that we are approaching recovery differently, by asking people what they would like to achieve and then helping them do that. Ultimately, the recovery approach is about working in partnership, and using person-centred approaches helps us to do things with people rather than to them. Once they are ready, people can regain skills to be independent through reablement, and the next chapter looks at how person-centred practice can help people be involved in all discussion and decisions about their support, and strengthens natural support networks and community involvement.

Chapter 17

Person-Centred Thinking and Reablement

Reablement services offer considerable benefits for people who are regaining skills rather than being 'cared for' in a traditional sense. An intensive period of coordinated 'enabling' support focusing on outcomes and drawing on the expertise of a number of professionals can achieve positive results, both to the person and to organisations.

Despite a strong focus by government, there are still some systemic, structural and cultural factors that mean that we are not getting the most out of the current investment in reablement.

Nellie's story

Nellie is 86 years old, and, until a recent fall, was an active, lively and fiercely independent person with a good network of support. Since her fall, Nellie lost some of her confidence and strength. She had a stay in hospital and was assessed by the hospital social worker who organised the Council's reablement team to get in touch... She had another assessment and was told that she would have two visits a day when she would be helped to get up in the morning, prepare a meal and get ready for bed.

On the second day at home, she had a visit from a new social worker who did another quite lengthy assessment. Nellie liked the carers, but she met many new people and they weren't able to get to know her given they could only spend a very short time with her to do the essential things. Nobody was able to find out who Nellie was, what made her tick, what friends and support she had around her, or what was important to her.

After five weeks, Nellie's ability to do more for herself had increased, but she was still going to need some support. The social worker visited again and asked more questions similar to the first visit. Nellie was told about personal budgets and asked to fill in a self-assessment questionnaire. She was also told that the current carers could only be with her for six weeks and that she would now be supported by a new care service. She was also told that she would now need to pay something towards this service and that a Fairer Contribution assessor would visit her soon to work out how much. The social worker told her that she would be informed of the amount of her Personal Budget and that they could plan how she used it, but in the meantime he would organise for the new care agency to visit her.

After three weeks, Nellie had still not heard back from the social worker. The new carers were visiting, but they had been told what she needed so they just came and did the tasks. They were nice, but didn't have a real understanding of who she was and what was important to her.

For Nellie, and many other people, there are some difficulties with the way reablement services operate. These factors are best illustrated from the perspective of the person:[190]

- There are too many assessments and these are not coordinated. People are asked the same questions many times and have to meet a lot of professionals at a time when they are most vulnerable.

- People are not actively involved in their reablement plans and have poor information – it remains a service that is largely 'done to' the person.

- Some of the forms people are asked to complete appear to be suiting the needs of the system not the person (for example, some people have to fill in a self-assessment questionnaire twice for no benefit to them).

- People feel like they are on a conveyor belt and that their 'needs' are of interest but not who they are as a person, often because carers are on a tight timescale to complete tasks in the allotted times.

- Reablement services tend to adopt a 'one size fits all' approach with little, if any, choice over who provides the support.

- People who still require some support after a period of reablement are often not told enough about self-directed support and personal budgets. Many people using reablement services are elderly and, while there are many exceptions of enlightened professionals, there is a pervading view that they will not want, nor be able, to exercise choice and control over any ongoing support.

- Reablement services are usually under pressure to meet goals within a set timescale (often six to eight weeks) and need to 'move people on' after that time. But for those who need support beyond that time, there is inadequate preparation for the person to be very involved or to enable that move to be a smooth transition.

- Not knowing until the end of their reablement how much, if any, personal budget they might have, means that there is little time to plan in a meaningful way before an alternative service is needed.

- Many people are still regaining independence gradually and may need longer than the allotted time to achieve goals in certain areas, but often this 'reabling' support doesn't continue, meaning that the chance for greater independence in that area can be lost.

- Skills that the person is learning are often not embedded in the context of his day-to-day life and are often focused on personal care tasks, whereas for many, getting out and about, shopping and having social contact are just as important to their independence and well-being.

- There is little consideration of the value of friends and support networks in maintaining the person's well-being, or activities and opportunities in the community from which he could benefit.

The reablement journey: what could it look like?

If we regard reablement as a concept rather than a service, it is hard to argue that more people should not be able to benefit from a short-term intensive period of support to promote their independence and well-being, thus reducing or removing the need for continued support. We need to think about reablement as something that everybody should have the opportunity to benefit from, but which can exist alongside other support if necessary. Reablement *services* then become one way by which people could achieve certain short-term outcomes, but they are not the only way. In addition, people should not delay planning to meet longer-term needs which are evident, simply because they are increasing independence in other areas through a period of reablement.

The experience of offering personal budgets has shown that people themselves and their families know best what will work for them and can work within a known budget to achieve agreed outcomes. The transparency, flexibility and choice that are available for people with a personal budget now need to permeate into the world of reablement. If our aim is to support more people to need no ongoing support, then for many it will be a short experience, but will be no less valuable for that.

Much of the bumpy ride from reablement to self-directed support is a result of trying to bolt together an existing reablement process with a new self-directed support process. This has worked to varying degrees but there is now a new way of thinking about the person's journey and it is based on the following principles:[191]

- Reablement is not a particular service, but is a journey that everyone should be supported through.

- Reablement can therefore be appropriate for anyone, not just older people who require assistance with personal care tasks, but are just as relevant for a younger person with a physical or learning disability, or people with mental health issues. The way people maximise their independence will be unique to them and may include such things as support to find employment, housing or to use public transport independently, etc.

- People should be able to self-direct the support available to them to achieve the outcome of maximised independence.

- Plans to achieve those outcomes should be owned by the person and they have information about the resources available to them and support to exercise choice and control.

- People should be able to exercise choice in how they are supported to achieve agreed short-term and longer-term outcomes.

- Different teams, services or experts may need to be involved, but people have a seamless experience. There should be minimal hand-overs between professionals or services for a person whether or not they have ongoing support needs.

- Achieving outcomes that maximise independence and strengthen natural support networks and community involvement should be embedded in all support planning and reviews and not just confined to the first few weeks of the person's journey.

- There is one person-centred 'harvesting' of relevant information about the person with their full involvement and consent that can then be drawn upon for a range of organisational purposes.

- People will be involved in all discussions and decisions about their care and support and will own the planning process (see Figure 17.1).

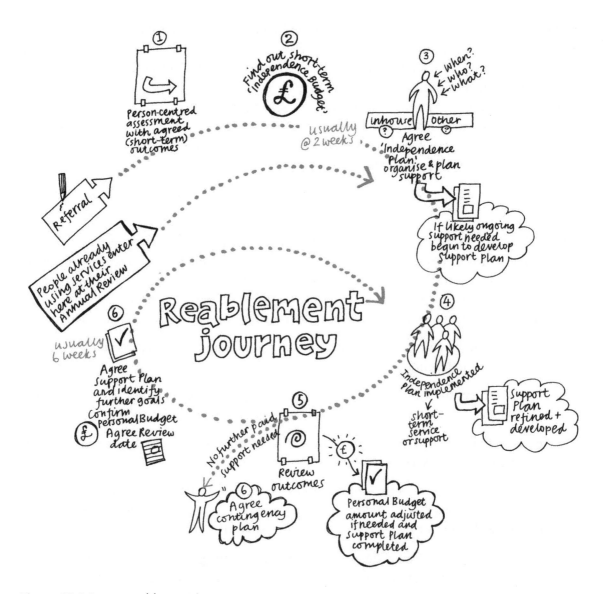

Figure 17.1 A new reablement journey

HOW THIS COULD WORK FOR PEOPLE

In the new model, Nellie's journey would have been very different:

Nellie's reablement journey

Prior to her return home, Nellie would have had a suitably skilled lead worker who asked her all the relevant questions and basic information and was then able to identify and arrange for her to have a fall alarm. This lead worker would stay in that role throughout her journey. She would have been told very early on the amount of money that was available to meet her short-term needs and what this was currently spent on. This person could have helped her understand what that meant and how it could be used, or they could have introduced her to a person from a local voluntary organisation that could have helped her. She could have chosen to reduce one visit from her carers and pay her daughter's train fare so that she could visit and help her get to bed one night. She could have been put in touch with local volunteers who could have helped her with her shopping and helped her prepare simple meals again; this 'befriending' would have put her in touch with new people in her community whom she would get to know. They could have helped her organise a lift to her local church group where she would have met many old friends and had other offers of support.

She would have known that she could start thinking about how she would want to be supported after the reablement carers had left as she was finding out what was important to her, such as having only a small number of different carers and maintaining the contact with her daughter. She might not know exactly how much money she would have available, but she could have started to plan – finding out which were the good care agencies, thinking about buying a microwave or looking into having lunch in the local pub and organising a lift. All these things she could have planned for, all the while gaining as much independence back so that she could do things for herself.

Her reablement journey would not stop after six weeks, but she would continue to work to small goals where she felt she could learn to do things again and this would be agreed with the new carers at the outset. Some tasks she would have learned to do again with the help of some new gadgets, such as preparing food and getting dressed, but in other areas she knew that she just wanted to be treated with respect and have as much dignity as possible. This, she would be able to make clear in her Support Plan which she would have helped to write up.

Table 17.1 *Using person-centred thinking to deliver the common core principles to support self-care*

Common core principle to deliver self-care (Skills for Care)	How person-centred thinking tools can help
Communicate effectively to enable individuals to assess their needs and develop and gain confidence to self-care.	Develop one page profiles while people are in hospital as a way to record and communicate what is important to the person and the best ways to support him. This shows the individual's and staff members' reflections on his needs and what support the individual requires to develop the confidence to self-care.
Ensure individuals are able to make informed choices to manage their self-care needs.	The decision making profile is a way to record important decisions in the person's life and how he can make informed choices about his self-care needs.
Advise individuals how to access support networks and participate in the planning, development and evaluation of services.	Using a relationship circle is a way to describe the networks and people in an individual's life who may be able to offer support. A learning log is a simple way for everyone to record and evaluate progress.
Support and enable risk management and risk-taking to maximise independence and choice.	The person-centred risk tool is a way to enable individuals to think about enabling risk in the context of what is important to the person and how he can be as independent as possible and have choice and control.

Person-centred thinking tools to help the reablement journey

There are a range of person-centred thinking tools that practitioners can use to deliver a more person-centred reablement service.

There is some early pioneering work using person-centred thinking and planning in prevention and delivering reablement services in Lincolnshire. Staff members are exploring using person-centred thinking to deliver the Skills for Care[192] 'common core principles to support self-care' (see Table 17.1).

This is what it could look like for Nellie, if the worker supporting her was able to use person-centred thinking tools:

Supporting Nellie

Jane was assigned to support Nellie on her reablement journey, and before she met Nellie, she was told how much money was available to meet her short-term reablement needs. They met for the first time prior to Nellie's return home. When they met, they talked about Nellie's health and also about what mattered to her as a person, and how she wanted to be supported.

They talked about the money that was available for Nellie's support and thought about the different ways that Nellie could get the support she wanted. They used a 'relationship map' to think about the people in Nellie's life who could help out, and mapped the places that she went to locally through a 'community map'.

This work showed several possibilities. On Nellie's relationship map was her daughter, and they did not get to see each other as much as they would like. One option was to use some of the money to pay her daughter's train fare so that she could visit Nellie once a week and help her get to bed that night. On Nellie's community map was her local church, that she used to attend each week, but had not been to now for over a year. Madge, her neighbour, was on Nellie's relationship map, and Madge was a member of the same church. Through using the relationship map and community map, Nellie and Jane decided get in contact with Madge to see if they could organise a regular lift to church on Sundays and for the Wednesday social afternoon.

They contacted someone from the local voluntary organisation to look at whether volunteers could help with Nellie's shopping and assist her to prepare simple meals again. Jane also mentioned that there was a local 'Timebank' where people traded hours of their time to help each other. Nellie used to be a teacher, and could offer to listen to children reading, in return for help with shopping.

The immediate actions were to talk to her daughter about visiting once a week, put in a fall alarm, talk to Madge and the volunteers organiser, find out more about the Timebank and finally to find a carer to support Nellie at other times. Jane has captured the information about who Nellie is, what matters to her and how to support her onto a one page profile. Nellie and Jane decided together who should have this information. They decided to use this as almost a job description for the carer. The one page profile specified exactly how Nellie wanted to be supported. Jane arranged to use this with the carers' organisation.

Three weeks later, Jane and Nellie looked at what was working and not working about the arrangements that they had put in place. Nellie was most excited about being back in contact with people in the church and she had also joined a group exploring family histories. Nellie had learned to do some tasks again with the help of some new gadgets, such as preparing food and getting dressed, but in other areas she knew that she just wanted to be treated with respect and have as much dignity as possible.

Nellie decided that she would like a microwave or was looking into having lunch in the local pub and organising a lift. Jane and Nellie developed her one page profile into a more detailed support plan with how much money she would use from her allocation to buy these. She planned for all these things while gaining as much independence back so that she could do things for herself.

To make it clear what decisions Nellie made herself and what decisions she wanted to have support in, Jane and Nellie put together a decision making agreement. This, and her one page profile, were used by any carer who supported her so they could learn about and respect what mattered to Nellie, how she made decisions, and how best to support her.

Her reablement journey did not stop after six weeks, and she continued to work to small goals where she felt she could learn to do things again. This would be agreed with the new carers at the outset, and this was part of Nellie's contract with them.

OTHER PERSON-CENTRED THINKING TOOLS THAT COULD BE USEFUL IN REABLEMENT

Person-centred thinking can help the reablement journey as the way people maximise their independence will be unique to them (see Figure 17.2). It allows for people to be involved in all discussion and decisions about their support and strengthens natural support networks and community involvement. In the next chapter, we go on to show how person-centred practice is used for when people do need ongoing and continued support, either at home or in residential care.

Tool	What it does	How this tool helps in reablement
Sorting important to/ for 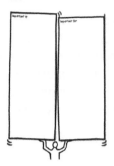	Sorts what's important *to* (what makes us happy, content, fulfilled) from what's important *for* (health and safety, being valued) while working towards a good balance.	Helps us to stay focused on what matters to the person in the context of medical issues and interventions. Keeps the focus on who the person is, not just on the rehabilitation support that he needs. This helps us to see the person beyond the patient and to jointly set goals that take account of what is important to the person and what style of support works best for him. This information can then be used to develop a one page profile and forms the beginning of a support plan and/or a personal care plan if this is needed. A personal care plan looks at the whole of someone's life to ensure that the focus is not just on medical needs but that health and well-being are seen as a whole.
The doughnut sort 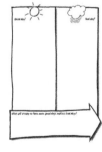	Identifies specific responsibilities: Core responsibilities. Using judgement and creativity. Not a paid responsibility.	Helps supporters and families to know where they can be creative with ideas without fear that they are doing something that would not work for the person they love or are supporting during reablement. Clarifies the roles of the different professionals and agencies supporting people and families through reablement. It helps supporters, not only to see what they must do (core responsibilities), but where they can try things (judgement and creativity) and what is not their responsibility. Helps a person and his family to ensure that they are clear about their role and specific contribution to the reablement process. It is an approach that supports achieving outcomes. Creating clarity around the roles and responsibilities of those who provide support ensures that the right things have priority for attention and move to action.
Appreciation tool	Identifies what we like about people and how to use this information so the person can contribute to his reablement.	What we like and admire about somebody can be a starting point for relatives, staff and allies to see who that person is and appreciate his qualities and strengths. This helps to counter our tendency to focus on how much support the person needs to what he can contribute and make the most of, as he moves on with his life.
Good days, bad days	Helps people reflect on what makes a good day and bad day and informs action planning and goal setting based on what is important to the person and how he wants to be supported.	Identifies the elements that make a day good or bad, to enable the person and his supporters to work out what they can do together to ensure that the person has fewer bad days and more good days. It can be used to help build up a picture of life before the person started on his reablement, how life has changed and what makes sense now in terms of what is important to the person and the support that he needs.

Figure 17.2 Tools to help in reablement

Tool	What it does	How this tool helps in reablement
Matching staff 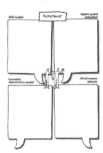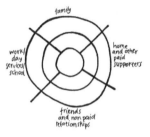	Gives a structure for looking at the skills and characteristics that will make for a good match for a person who is receiving support.	Helps people think about what kind of paid and non-paid support they want and need during reablement and after. This helps to get the match of the style, approach and skills of the reablement worker, as close as possible to the requirements of the person they are supporting and his family. A good match is central to the happiness and motivation of the person requiring support. Helps people to think about the networks and people in their life who may be able to offer ideas, knowledge, resources and support as part of their reablement.
Relationship circle 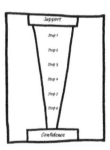	Identifies who is important to the person.	Helps people to think about the networks and people in their life who may be able to offer ideas, knowledge, resources and support as part of their reablement. Helps a person to think about his life before reablement and who was important to him and how he wishes these important relationships to be respected and supported now. A person may also start to think about those people he might have lost contact with and would like to contact again. Helps a person to be clear about what role the people identified in his circle could have in supporting him and what support he may need in order to do this. It helps to demonstrate to other professionals – for example, occupational therapists and GPs – the significance that these people and networks have in the person's life and how he needs to be supported and respected.
Support to confidence 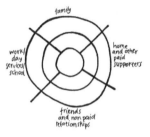	Helps a person and his supporters, in a task-orientated way, to plan the specific steps that matter for the person in building his confidence. Also supports the person being fully involved in saying what he wants to achieve and the best way to use support to achieve it.	Step 1: What you want to achieve and why it is important. Step 2: Where are you now? Where do you want to be? This is a continuum from 1 (being not confident) to 10 (being very confident). It helps clarify the starting point and where a person is aiming to be in the six weeks. Step 3: How can we help you in achieving this? Step 4: Who else could we include? This could be family, friends, health professionals, assistive technology and people in the local community. Step 5: How can we do this together? This is a plan of what we will do; e.g. if the person wants to start back at a local tea dance, what support can we give; what support can we get from others? Step 6: Are you feeling confident to do this without paid support? What conditions need to be in place for you to feel confident?

Figure 17.2 Tools to help in reablement cont.

Tool	What it does	How this tool helps in reablement
Communication charts 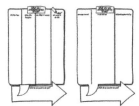	A quick snapshot of how someone communicates. A way of recording detailed information for people who use words to speak and particularly for people who don't.	Helps us to focus on how a person communicates and what we think different things mean and how we should respond. It is vital in helping the person to direct his reablement and for supporters to find ways to keep him central to the process. Respectfully recording and acting on what we know about the way a person communicates should start from admission to hospital and be added to as the person, his family and supporters learn together throughout the six-week reablement process.
Learning log	Directs people to look for ongoing learning. A structure that captures details of learning with specific activities and experiences. Provides a way of recording information which focuses on what needs to stay the same and what needs to be different in how we support people.	Provides a way for people to record ongoing learning (focused on what worked well, what didn't work well) for any event or activity. A simple way to record and evaluate progress. It is often used to replace traditional notes or to help people think about what they want to enhance or change. It provides a way for supporters or those receiving support to evaluate how things are going around specific situations – focusing on what worked and what didn't. Can be used to focus on someone's whole life or specific areas of their life, e.g. someone's health and progress on specific rehabilitation goals or how he likes to spend his time. This is a way of recording that demonstrates real progress or where there are difficulties. Helps to stop the doing 'for' rather than 'with' approach by focusing attention on recording what we are learning about a person as he moves through the reablement process.
Sorting what's working and what's not working now and in the future and family perspectives	Analyses an issue or situation across different perspectives. Provides a picture of how things are right now and for planning for the future. Forms the basis for goal setting and action planning. Acts as a powerful reviewing tool.	Helps people to clarify what they want and what they don't want now and can help people to look to the future in terms of what would work or not work for them. To see what is happening currently from the perspective of the family and professional involved. By focusing on what is working, it helps people to think about the skills and self-care tasks that they can maintain, and the things that are not working can be prioritised in terms of actions. It helps people to think about skills that they could regain during the reablement process and how they can be best supported to do this. Can be used at any time during the reablement process to review progress from different perspectives; the person, the family, the professionals and others. It can also be used as part of a person-centred review.

Figure 17.2 Tools to help in reablement cont.

Tool	What it does	How this tool helps in reablement
4 plus 1 questions	Helps people focus on what they are learning from their efforts.	A set of questions that are used when meeting together, in order to gather collective learning. The questions explore what is being tried and learned with the person, his family and professionals. It focuses on what we are pleased about in terms of progress and the concerns that people have and concludes by asking 'Given what we know now, what are we going to do next?' This is a powerful tool that can be used at any point to review progress and is used by managers to help reablement workers reflect on their practice. It is also an approach that can be used within a person's home to shape information that is being recorded and shared as part of a team approach to supporting him. This provides wider viewpoints of a particular situation leading to tailor-made actions.
Histories	Helps people reflect on the past and how this information can help to shape what they do next.	Helps people who are supporting the person to remember the achievements to be celebrated and acknowledged in a person's life. Informs supporters about factors and expectations that will affect the person who is regaining his life through the reablement process.
Decision making agreement	Helps us to think about decision making and increasing the number and significance of decisions people make.	Enables people to be in control and make decisions about the way they wish to live their life and how they can make informed decisions about their own reablement process. Can inform best interest decision making and advanced decision making.
Circle of influence	Helps the person to identify areas of concern and/or anxiety and what he can do to address them.	Can be used when a person is feeling overwhelmed or powerless. It helps the person to focus his time and energy on the things he can control and helps others to see how they can support in a way that leaves the person with control and decision making that makes sense to him. Can be used early on in the reablement process to shape goals and to ensure that the person is really being listened to at a time when he may be dealing with major life changes. Can be used separately or compositely for the individual and his family to address separate and shared anxieties and concerns; then using this information to form the basis of goal setting and action.

Figure 17.2 Tools to help in reablement cont.

Tool	What it does	How this tool helps in reablement
The person-centred risk tool 	Looks at risk through a framework of focusing on purpose, people, process and progress to ensure that they can achieve what they want, while keeping a balance on being healthy and safe and keeping risk in perspective.	Helps us to enable individuals to think about risk in the context of what is important to the person and how he can be as independent as possible and have choice and control.
One page profiles with action 	A one page profile is a way to set out information about what people appreciate in an individual, what is important to them and how they want to be supported. It leads to looking at what is working and not working for the person and what needs to happen to change what is not working.	Helps us to record and communicate information that we are learning about, and with, the person when he is in hospital. This information can be added to and acted on as the person progresses through the reablement process. An effective way to start to gather information that makes sense to the person at the point of referral from hospital. A good way to share information with each other, especially in reablement, if staff do not see each other when supporting people. Can act as a set of instructions for staff and supporters, about the person's needs and what support makes sense to him to develop his confidence, move towards greater independence, or to direct tailor-made ongoing support. It is at the heart of a Support Plan and can be expanded on should a person need to use a Personal Budget to meet his personal outcomes. Can be used to develop a Personal Care Plan that looks at the whole of someone's life to ensure that health and well-being are seen as a whole.

Figure 17.2 Tools to help in reablement cont.

Chapter 18

Support at Home and in Residential Care

It would be great if we could use some of the fee we pay for our own leisure, maybe have someone for two hours each week to do what we want with us – take me out on the bus, sort out my wardrobe.

I wish I had the same person so I could get them into my routine...you end up having to fit in their routines. I pay a lot of money here...I think it should be my routine that's found out and stuck to.

Helen Bowes et al.[193]

The chapters in this part so far have looked at how person-centred thinking can be helpful for people who are managing a long-term health condition or recovery. We have shown how person-centred thinking can be useful in self-care, like Jane; or as part of support from professionals and personal assistants, like James; or in managing recovery with support from family, friends and professionals, like Fiona; or gaining confidence and independence back through reablement, as in the story about Nellie.

However, when people need ongoing support, person-centred practice can still contribute. For many people, this is provided at home by family carers. There are around six million carers and unpaid carers provide more care and support than the NHS.[194]

Support at home can also be provided by domiciliary care, where staff come into someone's house for short visits to provide specific support. Finally, there is residential care, when people are no longer able to be supported at home.

This chapter looks at how person-centred thinking is being used to support people at home – by carers and domiciliary care and then in residential care.

Support at home: by carers

I am making my first steps giving support to people that I care deeply about. I see the personalisation of services as a fantastic opportunity. My hope is that this approach will enable me to show my love for my family members in this very practical way for as long as it is needed.

A family carer[195]

> To recognise carers as expert care partners is to value both their role in providing support and the wider knowledge and skills they possess as individuals. Doing so greatly increases the likelihood of more personalised, responsive and high-quality outcomes for those being supported; and makes carers' valuable and informed contribution available to other carers, service providers and commissioners. To maximise the benefits of these partnerships, training and development opportunities are as important for carers as they are for those employed in the health and social care workforce.
>
> *Department of Health*[196]

Carers may find person-centred thinking tools helpful in their role supporting loved ones. Alison describes how person-centred thinking tools helped her – specifically those tools which focus on hopes and fears for the future – as she prepared to become her mum's full-time carer.

I was delighted to meet the very competent and smiley [support worker] Jennifer along our very long journey in becoming a carer. Initially, I did fear that the task she set for me and my mum was unachievable and only now that it's over can I admit that I was considering faking the process.

Jennifer asked if I would take time with my mum to talk about her fears, goals, dreams and wishes. My mum is very 'old school'; she believes to talk about one's self is indulgent and unnecessary. Mum feels much the same about wasting the GP's time; she would have a leg hanging off before I could persuade her to bother the doctor. I'm sure you know the type of person I refer to. I only tell you this to paint a picture of the kind of woman we are dealing with: introverted, unconfident (due to the dementia) and generous beyond belief.

Knowing all of this, I dutifully left Jennifer's office ready for rejection. What I found, however, was a part of my mum that I had not discovered yet. The dementia seems to unveil itself weekly in different forms for us, but I didn't predict a turn for the better. Not only did Mum respond well to the idea of spilling her innermost dreams and wishes to me, but she would mockingly scold me for not writing quickly enough as the emotions and memories flooded from this wonderful woman. We were half-way through when my uncle came to the house. I knew for sure that Mum wouldn't want to let him into this private world so I suggested that we pack it away and start again later when we were alone again. With a cheeky smile on her face, my mum leant across and whispered in my ear 'let's sneak upstairs and find a quiet room to finish it now'.

It was an absolute revelation to me. First, it taught me not to presume anything about who she is or how she perceives things. I may have to care for her in ways that I'd never of thought of – wash her hair, remind her to eat and drink – but she is still her own woman. Mum has plenty of wishes and dreams and this task has made me realise that so much more is not only possible, but essential. As a carer, you can get bogged down in the practical day-to-day chores. It's easy to forget why you are there in the first place: to make this person happy.

I have learned so much from completing this task: my siblings and I will try it again in six months to see if our mum's dreams and wishes have changed. One of the most important aspects of this was finding out those desires that I had no knowledge of: the cooking classes and such. It also made me realise how important certain aspects of Mum's life are. Perhaps those things that aren't so high on my agenda so therefore aren't obvious: the importance of having the church in her life and why and how that all came about; and hearing the stories of her childhood that shaped those events and made her the way she is today.

We started this process for me to be Mum's carer a year ago. During that time, we have filled out many forms that made Mum close up, recoil into herself and feel inadequate because of the way they were structured and formulated. Some were trying to extract the same information needed for the Support Plan, but it was only when we used person-centred thinking did we see some results. Only then did Mum truly relax and enjoy the experience: up until that point it was a chore and we both really struggled with it.

I am really grateful to Jennifer for showing me this way of working and for the amount we as a family have gained from it. I would urge anyone doubtful of the benefits to please give it a chance, you never know, you must just be as happily surprised as we were.

Alison was preparing for her mum to come and live with her. Carers also support their family members who are living in their own homes. In Leonora's situation, she is supported at home by her daughters, Carmen and Theresa, who live between 40 minutes and an hour's drive away. Leonora has a third daughter, Elena, who lives in Spain. Carmen and Theresa found person-centred thinking tools helpful to describe exactly how Leonora wants to be supported and to review how this is going both from Leonora's perspective, and from her daughters' perspectives. As Leonora starts to need extra help, they are employing a cleaner, and in the future are thinking about a PA, to supplement the support that their family can provide to enable her to stay at home. Leonora is a 'self-funder' and will pay for this support herself.

Leonora's story

Leonora is an inspirational 90-year-old woman who lives in her own home in the north west of England. You would only need to spend a short time with her to feel the joy for life she exudes.

A fantastic film buff, her knowledge of the movies right back to the 1930s is incredible. Leonora has a vast collection of movies and 'chick flicks', as she calls them, which she loves to watch over and over again. She buys a new DVD from the market every week when she goes for a shop and lunch with her daughter Carmen.

Leonora has travelled the world visiting her other daughter Elena and her family, as their work has meant that they have lived in many different countries. They are presently living in Spain. Leonora has been over to stay a number of times, though she has become increasingly anxious over the last 18 months about making the journey alone.

Leonora's other daughters, Carmen and Theresa, each take turns staying with her so she is rarely on her own for more than a night or two. She has great neighbours, Jean and Brian, who run her errands if she doesn't manage to get out. They are also really good at taking her in their car for hospital appointments.

Tom, Mu and Ian are also good friends who live locally. Leonora loves going out for lunch with them each week. Ian drives and Leonora, Tom and Mu pay for his meal by way of thanks – they go to all sorts of different restaurants. Leonora has a beautiful garden: she spends hours pottering in it. Ian calls once a month to help her keep on top of it. Leonora is renowned for her baking and cooking – her chocolate cake is second to none!

In the last year or two, Leonora's sight has deteriorated and she is registered blind, although she still has some tunnel vision. She has also been diagnosed with diabetes.

She still manages to read the *Sun* newspaper each morning with her coffee and toast. She has a special lamp and magnifier which enable her to read it. Leonora sits in her armchair very close to her large TV so that she can see it. Soaps are her favourite – she must never miss *Coronation Street* or *Emmerdale*. She also loves *Strictly Come Dancing* and *Eggheads*.

Leonora is aware that she needs a little more support these days. She has agreed for her family to look at a cleaning service to help with the household chores and someone to accompany her to go out shopping in the village, paying her paper money and all those little things which matter so much to her. She is very clear about the sort of people she wants to help her and Carmen has conversations with Leonora based on the person-centred thinking tool 'matching'.

Carmen and Theresa developed a one page profile with Leonora, both to make sure all three of them had a shared understanding of what good support meant to Leonora, and to provide information for other people (for example, a cleaner and maybe a PA in the near future) who may provide support (see Figure 18.1).

They also had conversations with Leonora about her hopes for the future. This is what Leonora said:

- to live as long as I can and have good health

- to go to Spain and see my family there

- to have the best DVD collection ever and have them all numbered and written in my DVD Book

- to get my money's-worth out of my newly-laid paving around the house and enjoy it for a long time

- to go to Hollywood and to watch *The Lion King* on Broadway in New York City.

Every six months, the family does an informal person-centred review and looks at what is working and not working from each of their perspectives, including their sister who lives in Spain.

Leonora's family knows that they will need to supplement the support that they are able to provide. They want to plan for and make decisions to buy support or services for Leonora in an incremental manner, with Leonora very much in control, and the family continuing in their caring role.

It is easy for carers not to have their own support needs acknowledged: 'Carers have always wanted better outcomes for the people they care for. However, with many carers suffering poverty, ill health and isolation due to unsustainably heavy caring roles, they also want and deserve better outcomes for themselves.'[197]

Person-centred thinking tools, like 'working and not working', and using them to inform different perspectives, mean carers can ensure that the impact on their own lives that being a carer entails is considered.

One page profile

What people appreciate about Leonora

Great sense of humour.

Very inspirational.

Always upbeat and happy.

Great fun to be around.

Incredibly organised.

Full of joy.   Her straight talking.

What's important to Leonora

- Seeing Ian, Tom and Mu every Wednesday for lunch.
- Chats with Jean and Brian, her neighbours, every day.
- Travelling to Spain to see her daughter Elena, Graham, Kate, Aly and Matt every year.
- Watching old films, she will tell you lots about the actors/actresses: William Holden, John Wayne and Audrey Hepburn are favourites!
- Baking and making soup and cakes.
- Living in her own house.
- To go to church and enjoy the company there (St James) every week with Jean and Brian (next-door neighbours).

- Having a coffee in the café at Sainsbury's after shopping with Carmen.
- Sunday afternoon in Clevelys with Theresa – lunch in the cafe and buying a new DVD are a must!
- Watching soaps – `Emmerdale is the best'. Strictly Come Dancing is another favourite show.
- Going to the hairdresser every week to have her hair set.
- Pottering in her garden and making her hanging baskets each spring.
- Speaking to Elena on a Sunday and Tuesday at 5.00 p.m. each week.

How best to support Leonora

- If you are visiting Leonora at home give more than 1 week's notice. She likes to prepare.
- Leonora uses her magnifier and reader lamp when reading. Always leave her magnifier on the coffee table by her chair.
- Know that Leonora's eyesight is poor. She gets around the house fine but you need to pay attention when outdoors, especially crossing roads or if the ground is uneven because she will trip up easily.
- Remind her to use her white stick when crossing roads.
- Leonora can become disorientated when outdoors and when out shopping; always stay close by her.
- Leonora manages the stairs well at home and will be irritated if you keep asking if she is OK.

- Fill Leonora's dosette box with her medication each Sunday morning and she will take it each day without being reminded.
- Order Leonora's repeat prescriptions on the 20th of each month.
- Leonora only has the central heating on 7.00–11.00 a.m. on the timer. She will not have it on any other time even on bitterly cold evenings. She will be vexed if you try to persuade her to put it on and tell you the gas fire is fine.
- Never move furniture around – she will trip over it. Never move her talking clocks – there is one by her bed and one on the table by her chair.
- Remind her to take her bottle of water up to bed each night.
- NEVER ask to borrow her DVDs or videos.

Figure 18.1 Leonora's one page profile

What's working?   What's not working?

Leonora

What's working?	What's not working?
Living in my house Theresa and Carmen staying over every week. Carmen looking after my bills, letters etc. Elena ringing me from Spain twice a week. Going out with Tom, Mu and Ian each week. Going to the hairdresser myself every week. Watching my DVDs. Going to the village shopping on my own. Jean and Brian being my neighbours Going to church with Jean and Brian. Baking, making soup, cooking generally. Checking my blood sugars myself each day. Ian looking after the garden	Can't have cakes and sweets. Everybody mythering me not to go out on my own; I am alright. People borrowing my DVDs – I don't like it. People I don't know coming in to my house like cleaners or workmen (or women I guess!). The chiropody clinic's moved and I have to get two buses. I get a bit confused and mixed up sometimes.

Leonora's family in the UK

What's working?	What's not working?
Staying over with Leonora. Sorting out her bills and correspondence with her. Going into Clevelys shopping and having a coffee. Watching DVDs together. Going out for tea with Leonora. Contact with Elena. Having a gardener. Knowing that Brian and Jean are nearby. Jean and Brian taking Leonora to hospital appointments in their car. That Leonora is baking and cooking.	Leonora has lots of cakes and chocolates. Crossing roads is a real worry. Leonora won't use her white stick and often walks out without seeing cars. Cleaning the house. Leonora's belief she can walk straight out on to a zebra crossing and cars have to stop. Fear of her falling in the house when she is alone. Leonora cannot see if food is mouldy and would eat it unknowingly. Leonora struggles to climb into the bath to shower. Going up and downstairs.

Elena (Leonora's daughter in Spain)

What's working?	What's not working?
Knowing that Theresa and Carmen are there for Mum. That Mum is surrounded by friends who help out when necessary. Mum's joy of life, her DVDs, friends and wonderful attitude to living.	That Mum is so far away. Mum is reluctant to come over to Spain due to the flight. Mum's health is a worry. Mum not being able to see when the house needs cleaning. Mum not being able to see when crossing the roads. Mum frequently falling over when she goes out.

Figure 18.2a Leonora's working and not working from different perspectives

Action plan

What	Who	By when
Discuss with Leonora further and arrange for a cleaning agency to come in once a month to clean the house top to bottom.	Carmen	15 July 2010
Contact RNIB for a catalogue to show Leonora other white sticks she may be more likely to use.	Theresa	10 July 2010
Contact Social Services for contact to arrange Leonora having a pendant alarm system fitted.	Carmen	10 July 2010
Clear the fridge and cupboards of any food which is out of date. Carmen every Sunday, Theresa every Tuesday.	Theresa and Carmen	Each Tuesday and Sunday as from 6 July 2010
Let Joan know that Elena, Theresa or Carmen will fly to and from Spain with Leonora so that she can continue to visit them there.	Carmen	15 July 2010
Make arrangements for Leonora's bathroom to be adapted and fitted with a walk-in shower handrail and shower chair.	Theresa	20 August 2010
Arrange to have a handrail fitted on the wall going upstairs and at the front door.	Carmen	20 August 2010
Have a downstairs toilet fitted.	Theresa	20 August 2010
Arrange a taxi for Leonora's podiatry appointments every three months.	Carmen	29 August 2010

Figure 18.2b Leonora's action plan

Support at home: domiciliary care

Typically, domiciliary care is provided in units of 15 minutes. How can you personalise a service when all you have is 15 minutes to get someone out of bed in the morning? Here are two very different experiences of 15 minutes of support:

- Someone arrives at your door whom you have only met once before; she is one of the eight different people who help you get up.

- You have no choice about what time she comes; it is all down to what is on her rota. You don't know who is coming in advance.

- She doesn't know anything about you or you about her.

- She doesn't know how you like to be got out of bed, so you either repeat what you want as you seem to do every time someone comes, or you stay quiet and let her get on with it.

This is how the experience could be different with some investment in person-centred thinking and determination to ensure that people have as much choice and control in that 15 minutes. As the manager you could:

- ensure that everyone had a one page profile which clearly describes how they want to be supported to get out of bed, as well as what is important to them.

- use the 'matching' person-centred thinking tool, based on the information in the one page profile, to work out with staff who the best match would be. It may be impossible to have the same person each time, but you may be able to guarantee the same three people, who are the best match for the person. Ideally, the person would be making that decision with you, by looking together at the one page profiles of staff.

- negotiate with the person the optimum time of day, for her, and if that is not possible every day, you negotiate on what is possible and acceptable.

- regularly ask people what is working and not working about their support, and act on what you learn from this.

This could mean a different experience of 15 minutes:

- One of the three people who help you in the morning arrives.

- You knew what time to expect her, and you know when she will be coming again, and who is supporting you tomorrow.

- You both love watching sport on TV, so the conversation is about the match last night and the fixtures at the weekend.

- You are supported in exactly the way you want to be – it is these 'little things' that really matter to you.

Arthur's domiciliary care support was not working for him or his family, but using person-centred practice like a one page profile and a person-centred review made a significant difference.

Arthur's story

Arthur, 86, is a charming man and a real gent. He has lived in his own flat in an inner-city area for 35 years. He lost his wife, Madge, 20 years ago and treasures her wedding ring that he wears on his little finger. He loves talking to people and is an amazing storyteller. Sometimes, he likes to talk about his time driving tanks during the war, but only when he is in the mood. He also likes to talk about the old boxers, especially Cassius Clay, but would never call him Muhammad Ali.

Arthur is supported by the local domiciliary care services. His district nurse, Marie, was concerned that Arthur may need residential care. Arthur is terrified of being 'put in a home', so Marie spoke with Gill, the local person-centred planning coordinator. Gill spent an hour with Arthur. She asked him about things like his past and what makes up a good or bad day. She found out how he'd like to be supported and what kind of routine he likes. She used this to develop a one page profile, which described all this information. Gill then organised a person-centred review with Arthur, his nephew, Stephen, and wife, Sally, the manager of the domiciliary service and a staff member. Together they looked at the one page profile and talked about what was working and not working in Arthur's life from each of their perspectives.

From Arthur's perspective, the highlight of his week was spending Friday evenings with Stephen, Sally, and their three children, whom he loves dearly. Stephen also phoned him at 5 p.m. every day. Arthur felt both of these actions worked well for him. He also said it was important to have someone to talk to, especially at meal times. His staff spent their time making his evening meal and left it with him, but did not have time to sit and chat. He also said it was important that his meals were served piping hot. It didn't work for him when the staff gave him his dinner lukewarm and left him just a sandwich for lunch. Arthur usually threw both meals into his back yard. This caused problems with his neighbours and a rat infestation. Arthur also said he was sick and tired of people telling him to take off his wool bob hat.

From the staff's perspective, it did not work when Arthur sometimes hit out with his walking stick when they came to wake him in the morning. As he can't see well, he had assumed they were burglars. Arthur's poor eyesight means that good support would be for staff call to him from the bedroom door to wake him up and to never approach him and shake him while he sleeps. Staff were also concerned he sometimes wandered out late at night, which was not safe. Arthur makes sense of his days by sticking to his routines. He needs to be reminded daily if something out of the ordinary is happening; otherwise, he becomes disoriented, confused and likely to go outdoors in search of help.

Stephen said that something that did not work for him was Arthur's late night phone calls when he couldn't find the £10 note he usually kept in his pocket at all times 'in case he needs it'. Some of the staff had taken this out for 'safekeeping' and put it away in a drawer, but Arthur would become distressed looking for it, sometimes struggling on his hands and knees for hours.

Together, Arthur, his family and staff agreed some simple actions that meant that Arthur could stay living in his own home and address what was not working for him. Staff agreed to use the one page profile as the way to support Arthur – particularly around how to help him wake up in the morning (by calling from the door) and never taking his £10 out of his pocket. The family suggested that Sally provide frozen meals for Arthur, so that the staff simply heated these until they were piping hot. They could then use their time to stay and talk to Arthur while he ate. This made life better for Arthur; he started to eat well, had company and no longer had problems with his neighbours.

These small, but significant changes meant that Arthur's life improved and he was able to stay at home longer. When he was receiving domiciliary support that was not personalised to what was important to him, and how he wanted to be supported, his health suffered (he was not eating) and his relationships with his neighbours suffered (due to the rat infestation). Arthur was miserable and this had an impact on his family as well. It took a person-centred planning coordinator, Gill, little more than an hour to learn enough about him to put together a one page profile, and then another hour for the person-centred review. The changes that resulted from this meant that Arthur stayed in his own home.

In this situation there was a person-centred planning facilitator who could work with Arthur; in other situations professionals who are trained in person-centred thinking could take this role (developing the one page profile, and facilitating a person-centred review). Sometimes family members or volunteers could work with people to develop one page profiles and use person-centred thinking tools to figure out how people's lives could be different.

Person-centred thinking and residential care

One of the biggest challenges in delivering personalisation for everyone using health and social services is making choice and control a reality for people in residential care. It is easy for people to lose their individuality, as they become one of many to be got up and dressed in the morning. People can be seen as problems or conditions rather than people with a rich history, talents and abilities.

Some people may think that this is impossible but any move towards more personalised services has to begin with seeing people as individuals, learning what is important to each person and how to provide support in the way that person wants.

APPRECIATIONS

In Part II, we explained how one page profiles can begin with an appreciation of the person. It can be powerful just to capture and share what people appreciate about someone, as Sue, a volunteer, did with Florrie (see Figure 18.3).

Florrie, 98, has lived for 21 years in a residential care home. Sue was trained in using person-centred thinking and had volunteered to work there. The manager asked her to work with Florrie which led to some valuable insights from Sue.

When we first met, I noticed how isolated she appeared. The staff at the care home rarely talked to her. When I asked staff to tell me a little about Florrie, they did not seem to know who she was as an individual. She was another mouth to feed, someone else to clean and dress. The fact that she sat quietly in the lounge gave staff time to attend to other people.

After spending time with Florrie and getting to know her, I discovered a gem of a woman: full of wonderful stories and humour. She captivated me with her tales about her life in service from 1920 to 1970.

Cooking and baking have given Florrie great joy over the years. She loved nothing more than to cook slap-up meals and bake delicious cakes for the household where she worked. She will tell you she was 'married to her job' but had to give it up when 'her legs gave up on her'.

I began to gather information about what mattered to Florrie and how she wanted staff to support her. I worked with the staff team on this and we wrote the information on one page (a one page profile). This helped staff see Florrie differently. Six months later, to develop the information further, I asked the team what they liked and admired about Florrie.

Florrie does not have any family, so the list reflects solely staff perceptions. We wrote this on a separate page, with a photo of Florrie and it hangs in her bedroom. I was amazed at how the responses differed from those of six months ago. As a result of knowing what is important to her and how best to support her, staff now truly see Florrie for who she is.

One staff member said, 'I was really upset that after working at the care home for nine years, I didn't even know that Florrie had led such an interesting life or worked as a housekeeper. We never get the chance to talk because we would get in trouble if the chores don't get done.'

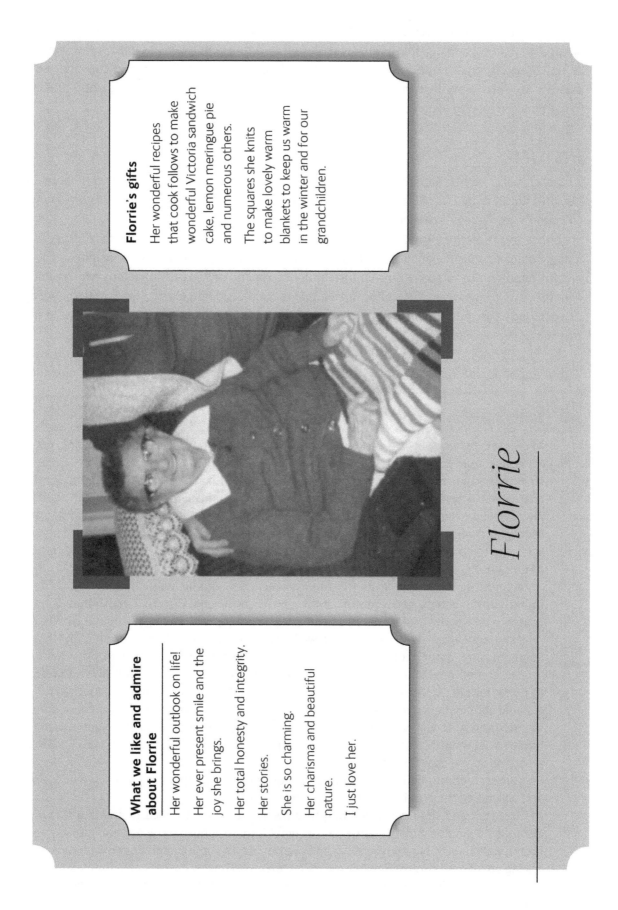

Florrie's gifts

Her wonderful recipes that cook follows to make wonderful Victoria sandwich cake, lemon meringue pie and numerous others.

The squares she knits to make lovely warm blankets to keep us warm in the winter and for our grandchildren.

What we like and admire about Florrie

Her wonderful outlook on life!

Her ever present smile and the joy she brings.

Her total honesty and integrity.

Her stories.

She is so charming.

Her charisma and beautiful nature.

I just love her.

Florrie

Figure 18.3 Florrie appreciation

Older people in residential care can easily lose their individual identity. Focusing on appreciations sends a very strong message that 'You are important; staff care about you and knowing you matters to us.' Appreciations can be a way in to start thinking about contribution and connections, by asking: 'Are there ways that these gifts and skills could contribute to the lives of other people? What would it take to explore this?'

HISTORIES

Knowing what we like and admire about someone can easily lead on to discussions about that person's life story and what has shaped and influenced her. Knowing someone's history is a way to connect, develop and deepen relationships.

Life story or biography work has had a very positive benefit for people with dementia and many homes develop detailed 'life history books'.[198] Histories can also offer insights into *why* what is important to someone is so important in her life and provide insights into why particular activities may trigger powerful feelings that could relate to a painful event. Sometimes knowledge of someone's past provides insight into particular mannerisms or behaviours, which could help provide possible solutions.

Knowledge of histories can also provide clues about activities that the person may still enjoy. This is important information for providing person-centred care for people who have dementia.[199]

Alice's story

Alice used to work in the residential home where she now lives. The imposing house, Millbrook, used to belong to a mill owner and Alice was the nanny to his children. Once the children had grown, she became the housekeeper and cook. She was a well-known local character, always at the heart of the local church community. She is great company and has always loved to chat with other people, showing a real interest in what they have to say. Alice is delighted when staff, visitors and the people she lives with at the home chat with her and she loves to be acknowledged as people walk by, even if that means saying 'hello' a number of times as Alice will forget that you have already spoken to her.

Alice looks forward to visits from her brother, Jim, and his wife, Agnes. June, a friend, brings her the church newsletter each month. As she struggles to read more than the odd sentence on her own, she loves to sit and listen to somebody reading it through with her.

Now and again Alice takes short walks with her Zimmer frame, around the home. Sometimes the other people she lives with tell her to sit down, which really upsets her.

She sometimes becomes very anxious, believing that her mother is still alive and waiting at home for her. At these times, Alice gets very agitated, as she thinks her mother will be worried about where she is and vexed with Alice when she gets home. During these periods of confusion Alice will wander about the home trying to open the doors to get out and go home to her mum. Staff try to calm Alice by asking if she would like to go out for a walk, have a bath or sit and chat for a while.

Alice sometimes believes that the other residents are people she has known in the past and will talk to them as if they are. This seems to reassure Alice.

The staff and someone who enjoyed drawing worked with Alice to create a picture of her past – a graphic history – and some of what is important to her (see Figure 18.4). It's up on the wall now. 'It brightens my day to have people sit and ask me about my picture. I love talking about Millbrook and telling my many tales,' says Alice.

The picture gives people clues about her past, so that they can talk with Alice and ask her about it.

A staff member said, 'We knew so little of this information – especially about Alice's past. Who would have thought Alice was a keen birdwatcher and rambler? She has lived here almost six years and all that time we didn't know. I've learnt so much about her by using this approach. It's just brilliant. It has given us a chance to step aside, learn real things about people and what changes they want to make in how they live.'

Figure 18.4 Alice's history

Moving to a care home can be a traumatic experience for many different reasons. Histories can help staff and others working in or visiting that home to get to know someone well. Using visual aids and prompts can bring these life stories alive. Having framed photos, pictures, framed family trees or scrapbooks to share are great ways to personalise people's living areas. People could use these to introduce themselves to new members of staff. Their past can also offer clues about what may be important to the person now. Involving family members and friends in sharing these stories, and providing photos and mementos to build this bigger picture, is also a good way of ensuring that they continue to have strong and positive relationships with the person who has moved to the home. Asking different family members to share their versions of family history can also bring people closer together in order to support someone through this transition.

KNOWING WHAT IS IMPORTANT TO PEOPLE AND HOW THEY WANT TO BE SUPPORTED

Recognising and valuing individuality and history needs to be extended to delivering a service that reflects what matters to people and to providing support in the way which works for the person.

Nora's story

Nora, 87, lives in a residential home. She has a beautiful dress sense. She loves to see her sons and daughters, Tony, Jim, Margaret and Irene. The managers of the residential home wanted to start to 'personalise' the service. They thought that one thing which they could change that would improve the quality of everyone's lives would be to look at the evening routine at the home. They worked with all the staff at the home to give them an understanding of and confidence in person-centred thinking skills. The staff worked with a person-centred planning coordinator and developed, with each individual in the home, a description of what was important to each person about her night time routine, and what support each person needed (what was important for her). The managers then worked at making sure that what was important to each individual was happening so that people were getting support in the way that they wanted it.

What is important to Nora

Nora needs her routines to run like clockwork: everything has to happen at a certain time, otherwise this will develop into a bad evening and night for her. It is really important to Nora that other people living at the care home do not go into her bedroom, although she is happy for staff to enter her bedroom. Nora must begin getting ready for bed at 7.30 p.m. As soon as the music comes on at the end of *Emmerdale*, Nora's favourite soap opera, she will take her feet off her footstool, remove the rug from her knee and look in an obvious way at the clock.

Nora washes her face herself using Dove soap. She loves to wear clean clothes each night for bed and must choose which nightie to wear. Nora also chooses the clothes she will wear the following day while getting ready for bed. Nora must have a body wash each evening in order to feel comfortable and clean for bed. She has talc on after her wash: no particular favourite but usually scented. Nora loves her four pillows to be arranged comfortably once in bed. She is only comfy with lightweight covers and must have cotton sheets and a bedspread. She must not have a duvet! Nora loves her small lamp by the bed to stay on all night and the bedroom door to remain open.

What is important for Nora – how she wants to be supported

Staff should acknowledge Nora's wishes around other people living at the care home not going into her bedroom and support her with this respectfully, by speaking to the other people living there when necessary.

Nora's reliance on routine are central to her happiness and staff need to be aware of Nora's cues when she is ready to go to bed and respond – this will invariably be at 7.30 p.m. Two staff should support Nora from her armchair into her wheelchair in order to go and get ready for bed in her room. Nora needs support to use the toilet; she will then have a wash. Nora needs support in filling the sink with warm water. Nora's flannel then needs to be soaped up with her Dove soap so that she can wash her face; the cloth then needs to be rinsed and handed back to Nora so that she can rinse her face, she will then dry her face herself.

Nora chooses from three nightdresses, which staff hold up and Nora will fix her eyes and say 'yes' to the one she wishes to wear for bed. Two staff should support Nora into bed and then arrange her four pillows comfortably around her. Nora's bedroom should always be warm enough for her to sleep comfortably, with just a cotton sheet and bedspread; if it is very cold Nora may like a blanket. Nora's small lamp must be left on and her door open.

Balancing what is important to, with what is important for, Nora

It is important to Nora that, when she goes to bed, she can look at the long mirror on her wardrobe. She can then see whether there were people in the corridor. This helped Nora to feel safe and secure. Nora would become upset and anxious when the night staff shut the door. The door was a fire door and regulations dictated that it had to be closed. Nora would sometimes struggle to get out of bed to open the door again, only for night staff to close it again as they did their round.

Although what was important *for* Nora was being met, as she was safer from fire by having a fire door, this was not in balance with what is important *to* her. It is important to her to look through the mirror out into the corridor.

The manager had a magnetic smoke detector fitted to the bottom of the door. This means that Nora is still safe from fire (important for her) and has what is important to her, as the door stays open and she can look through the mirror into the corridor. This means that Nora can now sleep through the night, rather then being anxious that somebody may be out in the corridor.

The stories about Florrie, Alice and Nora illustrate the changes that can happen when using person-centred thinking with individuals. Another approach is to using person-centred thinking to look at a routine or specific area of life at the home and find out what is working and not working for people. This is what the managers at Oakwood House did. We met the managers Steve and Sheila in Chapter 9 and described how they introduced person-centred reviews as one way to introduce person-centred change. They both thought that there had long been a need for a change in cultural practice in many care homes for older people. Historically, there is a great emphasis on operational routines, rigid systems and care within restrictive boundaries. They think that the traditional and somewhat negative views and public portrayal of care homes for older people will become a thing of the past if people start to work in a person-centred way: 'At Oakwood House we want to help break down traditional cultures of residential and nursing care settings. We want to use person-centred approaches to look closely at the individual wants, needs and wishes of the people using our service, and ultimately, to find out what's really important to them.'

Like many other care homes, Oakwood House encourages people living there to create their own lifestyles and have a strong voice in how their services are provided in the future. 'We don't want people living here to have to fit in with organisational routines, and person-centred thinking is helping us to scrutinise our own practice by listening to people's real experiences of living at Oakwood House.'

They started by taking a detailed look at one area which they want to make more personalised and by starting with something specific, they could make changes at a pace with which they could cope. They decided to use the person-centred thinking tool 'working and not working' to look at the evening routine because the owners felt that it was not person-centred.

The tea trolley came along at 4 p.m., with the tea already brewed in a pot and one type of biscuit for everyone. Using the person-centred thinking tool clearly showed that this routine was not working for most residents. Now teatime is whenever residents want it, rather than when it suits staff rotas. Residents can choose how they take their tea and there is a selection of biscuits. One resident who used to be unhappy with the old system is delighted that she can now have a Wagon Wheel and a nip of whisky in her tea. Next, the managers focused on suppertime, and asked people what was working and not working for them. Table 18.1 shows what people said.

Table 18.1 *What's working and not working at Oakwood House about suppertime from various perspectives*

Perspective	What's working	What's not working
People who live at the care home	Drinks at 7 p.m. Having a choice of drinks – coffee made with milk or water, tea, peppermint tea, a tot of whisky, hot chocolate, Horlicks. Having own cup – china cup, pint mug. Occasionally having cake, toast, jam sandwiches, hot cross buns or fruitcake.	No choice of snack – plain biscuits.
Staff team	Drinks at 7 p.m.	People not drinking: this may adversely affect their health. Limited snacks at suppertime. Nothing to offer people with diabetes at suppertime. Having to bring cakes, snacks in themselves to give people choice at supper.
Managers	Cook does not require more hours to provide extra food at suppertime.	Staff and people who live there are unhappy with choice of snack at supper.

Sheila and Steve are now working to extend the range of snacks at suppertime on a daily basis. Their first action is to find out exactly what people would like, or find other creative ways to make this happen – including some people cooking the snacks themselves.

Another residential care home took a different approach to increasing the choice and control that people have. The manager, Sue, and many of the staff, had training in person-centred thinking tools. Sue had a real belief that things should and could change, but she also knew that it required a huge shift in culture. This shift began with uniforms no longer being worn, to create a 'family feel', thus avoiding a 'them and us' culture. Toilets became communal – there were no separate staff toilets, and no staff mugs – sitting and eating with people who lived there became the way things were done.

Sue, manager of a residential care home

Sue was concerned that inspecting on quality of life does not happen enough and that there was too much emphasis on the quality of the records, which didn't have any impact on people's lives. Sue organised for each member of staff to be taken off rota for two hours and asked to simply sit in the lounge in order to feel, hear and see the 'lived experience' of the people whom they supported. They were then asked 'Is this social care with which you would be happy?' The resounding answer was 'no' and so the desire for real change began in earnest. Sue decided that one way to give people choice and control was for each person to have four individual hours a month of one-to-one support, and that the person could determine exactly how that was spent. Sue started with Sam, who lives there, before offering it to more people in the home.

Sue developed a history time line with Sam, and they also spent time doing a one page profile, relationship circle and thinking about what was working and not working. All of this information led to Sam deciding that he wanted to spend his time reconnecting with friends at Crown Green bowling. Sam was supported to write to some of his old friends, and as they responded. Sam now meets up with them at the Crown Green Bowling Club.[200] Sam has also started playing dominoes at the same club. Sam now writes the monthly newsletter for the bowling club. Prior to retiring, Sam was a keen writer and produced the church newsletter each week, so he feels that he is giving something back.

Sam's life feels very different now and as he said recently, 'I've got something to get up for, meeting the lads and I'm working on a newsletter.'

These are just two of the ways that person-centred thinking could start to be introduced into residential care to enable people to have more choice and control – by systematically looking at what is working and not working for people, or by finding a way for people to have dedicated individual time and decide how they want to use it.

In this chapter we have shown the contribution which person-centred practice can make when people need ongoing support. Carers may find person-centred thinking tools helpful in their role supporting loved ones – they help to ensure all perspectives are included and can ensure that carers have their own support needs acknowledged. Investment in person-centred thinking and determination to ensure that people have as much choice and control over their support as possible means that even in only 15 minutes, people can experience more personalised domiciliary care. It is also a way for people to keep their individuality in residential care settings and can be introduced with relative ease by using person-centred thinking tools like appreciations, histories and one page profiles. In the next chapter we look at how to provide people with as much choice and control as possible as they approach the end of their life.

Chapter 19

Person-Centred Thinking and End-of-Life Care

I felt in control; using Living Well ensured that my voice was heard not ignored in such a new and overwhelming medical world.

Jane, a woman living with a life-limiting illness
and approaching the end of life

In this chapter, we explain how person-centred thinking can help people at the end of life. We explain the different processes which can be employed to support people, and illustrate them through Madge's story.

There are different processes to support people at the end of their life. These include the end-of-life care pathway, Gold Standards Framework, advanced care planning and Liverpool Care Pathway. Person-centred thinking tools can be used with each of these to provide additional information or another way to have the conversation during assessment, care planning or reviewing.

Preferred priorities for care

The preferred priorities for care[201] document is designed to help people prepare for the future. It gives them an opportunity to think about, talk about and write down their preferences and priorities for care at the end of life.

Gold Standards Framework

The Gold Standards Framework[202] (GSF) is a systematic-evidence based approach to optimising the care for patients nearing the end of life delivered by generalist providers. It helps people to live well until the end of life and includes care in the final years of life for people with any end-stage illness in any setting.

Advanced care planning

The is a process for indentifying future individual wishes and care preferences. This may or may not result in recording these discussions in the form of an 'advance care plan'.

Liverpool Care Pathway

This is an integrated care pathway that is used at the bedside to drive up sustained quality of dying in the last hours and days of life. It is recommended as a best practice model, most recently by the Department of Health in the UK.

Figure 19.1 is a summary of the similarities and differences between general care planning, advance care planning and using person-centred thinking at the end of life. 'Living Well'[203] is a workbook that people can use at the end of their life with the person-centred thinking tools that Madge and her family used.

	General care planning	Advance care planning	Living Well – using person-centred thinking at end of life
What is covered?	Can cover any aspect of current health and social care.	Can cover any aspect of future health and social care.	Can cover all areas of the person's life both now and in the future.
Who completes it?	Can be written in discussion with the individual who has capacity for those decisions. Or Can be completed for an individual who lacks capacity in his best interests.	Is written by the individual who has capacity to make these statements. May be written with support from professionals and relatives or carers. Cannot be written if the individual lacks capacity to make these statements.	The individual, with friends and family as he chooses. Can also be written with support from care staff or professionals. Cannot be written without the person's involvement.
What does it provide?	Provides a plan for current and continuing health and social care that contains achievable goals and the actions required.	Covers an individual's preferences, wishes, beliefs and values about future care to guide future best interest decisions in the event that an individual has lost capacity to make decisions.	Information about what is important to the person and the support he wants and needs. Specific actions to improve the quality of life and services received. Information about the person's preferences for the future and how he wants to be involved in decisions.
Is it legally binding?	No – advisory only.	No, but must be taken into account when acting in an individual's best interest.	No – advisory.
How does it help?	Provides the multidisciplinary team with a plan of action.	Makes the multidisciplinary team aware of an individual's wishes and preferences in the event that the patient loses capacity.	Provides information for family, friends and everyone supporting the person and professionals. The actions improve the quality of life now. Provides direction for the future. Information can be used to build into agreements and contracts with service providers. Can be the basis of a personal care plan for a personal budget.
Does it need to be signed and witnessed?	Does not need to be signed or witnessed.	A signature is not a requirement, but its presence makes clear whose views are documented.	A signature is not a requirement, but its presence makes clear whose views are documented.
Who should see it?	The multidisciplinary team as an aid to care.	Patient is supported in its distribution, but has the final say on who sees it.	Individual makes these decisions and usually this involves everyone who needs to know how best to support the person and what is important to him.

Figure 19.1 The differences between general care planning, advance care planning and 'Living Well' in end-of-life care

Person-centred thinking tools helped Madge and her family to remain cheerful and for Madge to get as much enjoyment from her family and friends towards the end of her life.

Madge

Madge, 67, lives on the Fylde Coast. She is full of fun, a great storyteller and is comfortable talking with anybody. She has three children: Sally and Ian live nearby with their partners Stephen and Jane. Both couples have two children each. Sam is her other son who lives in Australia. Madge adores her grandchildren whose ages range from 6 to 11 years. Madge was diagnosed with cancer of the oesophagus one year ago and had major surgery ten months ago. She is doing her best to remain cheerful and get as much enjoyment as she can with her family and friends.

The person-centred thinking tool 'good days, bad days' was used to learn more about Madge's days, and what would make them better (see Figure 19.2).

The good day and bad day information was developed into a one page profile, a great summary of who Madge is and how to support her (see Figure 19.3).

Madge loves having a tea or a coffee with Sally who calls at Madge's house each day to hear about how the children are doing. Sally knows not to push Madge to talk about her health – she respects that if Madge says she is OK, she doesn't want to talk about it. Another highlight for Madge is having Ian and his family coming to her place for tea on Saturday and Sunday; and going down to the sea front with Sally, Ian and the children on a Sunday. They often go for Sunday lunch to Madge's favourite restaurant, the Blue Anchor.

Madge would never miss chatting with Sam in Australia on Skype each Saturday evening. Sally or Ian always dials through for her as Madge openly says that she struggles with technology. This mustn't clash with *X Factor*! Family and friends are the greatest joy in Madge's life. Her sister, Ann, calls most days. If the weather is fine they have a wander down to the village. Madge looks forward to calling into Betty's cafe for a coffee and catch-up. If Madge is tired, Ann will push her in her wheelchair, although Madge is quite embarrassed about using it.

The people supporting Madge, including her family, used the one page profile to look at what was working and not working for Madge, and what they learned is shown in Figure 19.4.

Madge will really push herself to get to the luncheon club on Wednesdays to see Jane and Jim. They are her oldest friends. Barbara, Stan and Ron are other old friends of Madge and her late husband, Jim. They often call on a Sunday evening and all enjoy a night in, playing cards – gin rummy is a favourite.

Madge is irritated when people tell her it will be OK; the stark truth is we know it won't be OK and it is not helpful to pretend. Madge is taking things in her stride. What really makes Madge smile is the great things happening in people's lives. She would not want people to avoid telling her about great things in their life because they feel awkward.

What does a good day and a bad day look like for Madge?

 Good day

 Bad day

Good day

Lots of family noise in the house.

Speaking to Sam.

Seeing or speaking on the phone with my grandchildren.

I get a picture my grandchildren have made at school.

The sun is shining!

I have a meal I enjoy – favourite foods fluctuate often.

I enjoy my cups of tea – at least 5 a day.

I go to sleep quickly and have a good night.

Enjoying peeled grapes – especially when lovingly peeled by any of my grandchildren.

I get outdoors and feel up to walking.

I spend an evening playing cards with friends or go to meet them at luncheon club or the tea dance, having fun with friends or just having good conversations. I love to talk.

Bad day

I have a restless night.

I cannot face drinks or food.

Any day where I have a medical appointment especially endoscopies and having to wait for results.

I don't feel right and jump into panic mode that something is going badly wrong with me.

I do not see any of my family or friends.

Not having the energy to do the things I want to do – such as tidying the house.

Having to take my PRN medication due to discomfort – it makes me feel very groggy.

Having to have nutrient drinks because I cannot manage a meal.

I cannot face a cup of tea.

Figure 19.2 Madge's good days, bad days

What is important to Madge, and how she wants to be supported

What Madge's family appreciate about her

Her unconditional love, her cuddles, she is always there for me, she goes the extra mile every day, I just love her – everything about her, her kindness.

How best to support Madge

Ask me how I am and if I say I am ok, respect I do not want an in-depth conversation. I will talk about my health when I need or want to, please do not push me on it.

Know that when I have examinations or treatment it is so irritating if you don't tell me what you are going to do with me before you try and do it.

Don't tell me it will all come out in the wash, we know it won't. I want no elephants in the room, let's just make the most of the time we have, and be as 'normal' as we can.

Give me clear and simple information. Do not talk over me as though I am not there; I am an intelligent woman. Give any detail to Sally she will remember better than me. It works best for me if any correspondence about my condition comes to me through Sally.

Know that I am aware of the need to eat and will do so when I can. Do not make mealtimes a nightmare by watching my every mouthful or commenting if I don't eat much.

Do not make a fuss and cheer me on if I clear my plate. I want this focus on what I eat to stop – the medics will monitor this not family and friends.

Know that I cannot work Skype to speak with Sam on my own. I need Sally or Ian to set it up for me.

Know that I detest the hospital appointments and will be very quiet on the days they are due. Leave me be – I will talk if I want to.

Know that I use a wheelchair to get around if I am not up to walking but it embarrasses me terribly.

Work out between you who is coming with me to each appointment, then just let me know who is calling for me.

Know that I detest being late and get anxious – the earlier the better for me. I must never be late!

What is important to Madge

- Sally, my daughter who comes to see me at my house after work each day, our coffee and chats together, hearing how the children are doing at school.

- Ian, my son who comes for his tea Saturday and Sunday with my grandchildren whom I adore; Mark and Kim.

- Staying healthy and out of hospital.

- Sally and her husband Stephen taking me out to the seaside on a Sunday morning with Jess and Jon my beautiful grandchildren. Having our Sunday lunch out – the Blue Anchor is a favourite.

- Speaking on Skype with Sam every Saturday.

- That you share with me the great things that are happening in your life – I want to hear it, it cheers me.

- My sister Ann popping in each day and having a walk into the village together – we sometimes go to Betty's cafe for coffee which is lovely.

- Meeting up with Jane and Jim at the luncheon club on Wednesdays.

- Barbara, Stan and Ron coming round for an evening in and a game of cards – gin rummy is a favourite.

- That I always take my yellow bed socks Sam bought me if I have to go into hospital for a stay – they are my comfort blanket.

- I love grapes with the skin peeled off.

Figure 19.3 How best to support Madge

What is working and not working in my life and what do I want to change?

Madge

Seeing lots of Sally, Ian and their families.	More frequent off days. Having to spend more and more time in bed.
Having Sunday lunch at the Blue Anchor with Sally and the family. The noisy, busy atmosphere works so well for Madge.	Having to use her wheelchair when she feels jittery.
	Not getting outdoors as often as she would like.
Going to luncheon club and the tea dance with friends.	Not being able to look after the garden.
Having evenings in with old friends playing cards, watching TV.	Too many telephone calls from friends.
Speaking with Sam on Skype.	Too many hospital appointments and having to continually repeat the same information to different people.
Having a big screen TV is wonderful.	
Busy weekends with family and friends.	The long waits in the waiting area for some of her appointments.
Eating peeled grapes, drinking tea and coffee.	Seeing Sally so tired out as she is doing so much for her.
Family and friends sorting out her hospital appointments and taking her to them.	The struggle to find food she can enjoy.
	Mealtimes are uncomfortable; Madge feels she is being watched by everybody.
Dr Prakesh, Madge's GP	Weight loss. Madge has lost 3 stone in the last 5 months.
Sal, the community nurse, calling every few weeks.	Looking gaunt.
	Nutrient drinks.
	Hospital admissions due to severe abdominal pain.
	Not being able to go on holiday.
	PRN meds making Madge groggy.
	Seeing how unhappy her family are and not being able to tell them everything is ok.
	Not sleeping.
	Not seeing John and Kate, her old friends.

Figure 19.4 Madge's working and not working

Madge knows that her friends and family are aware of her sensitivity around food. They know not to fuss when she is eating or not eating and mostly respect this, though rows still occur occasionally if Madge feels that they are watching her too closely. She hates it when she is cheered on through every mouthful or for clearing her plate – she is clear that she is aware of the need to eat and will do so when she can. She has told family and friends that they make mealtimes a nightmare when they comment that she hasn't eaten much. Madge is clear that it is for the medics to monitor her food and wants no comments from family and friends around how much or little she eats.

Madge does her best to stay out of hospital. She really fears having to be admitted. If she does have to go in she always takes her yellow bed socks. She describes them as her comfort blanket.

Madge becomes anxious about hospital appointments and asks that people leave her be if she is quiet when they are due. She is clear that if she wants to talk about it she will do. She appreciates medical staff giving her clear simple information and will become upset if she is talked over as though she is not there. Madge is an intelligent, forthright woman, but finds it difficult to be assertive when in the company of medical professionals. Sally, Ian or Jane and Jim run Madge to the hospital appointments. She prefers them to sort out between themselves and just let her know who is picking her up and when. They are always at least an hour early otherwise Madge's anxiety goes through the roof. The less conversation about appointments and tests the better as far as Madge is concerned. Sally is seen as the main contact, with Madge's consent, for the health practitioners.

One of the things Madge really wanted to do when we explored the 'If I could, I would' question was to have a mini-break in London and go to see a show in the West End (see Figure 19.5).

From this information they developed an action plan together (see Figure 19.6).

Madge loved going to London and happily reported; 'I had a ball. Sally and I went to see *The 39 Steps* at the Criterion. It was wonderful'. Another highlight was a cream tea at Harrods. 'I had a cup of tea and a mousse, unusually for me I really enjoyed sitting down to eat with Sally, I never thought we would make this trip happen, but by taking a step back and thinking this through at my person-centred review we did it – it was fantastic.'

Barbara, Madge's neighbour, arranged for someone from the Macmillan support service to come and talk with Madge and Barbara about the benefits Madge was entitled to and as a result they found that she wasn't claiming everything that she was entitled to. This means that she is now in a position to pay a cleaner, so a family friend whose company Madge really enjoys is now cleaning for three hours each week.

This means that Sally and Ian can spend more time with Madge when they visit without having to try and keep on top of household chores as well. This has made a huge difference to Madge as she had felt she was asking too much of Sally and Ian which made her feel very guilty, but she can now relax and chat with them.

Another difference is that Sally spoke with her line manager at work and is now working reduced hours (three days a week instead of five). This has a huge impact on the opportunities for Sally and Madge to get out and do things together. It has also eased the pressure on Sally which in turn delights Madge.

The dietician has visited Madge at home and taken her a number of options to increase her intake of nutrients – smooth soups, smooth cereals and enriched yoghurt drinks rather than the nutrient drinks which were delivered as a block.

The family started to think together with Madge what she wanted to do as she got closer to the end of her life. Madge was very clear about how she wanted to be remembered (see Figure 19.7).

If I could, I would...Madge

Go on holiday in a log cabin by the Lake in Windermere.

Visit Sam in Australia.

Go to a show in London.

Go on a cruise with the children and grandchildren.

Figure 19.5 Madge's If I could, I would...

Making changes to my life – Madge's action plan

Who	What	By when
Sally	Will speak to Dr Prakesh about Madge's PRN meds.	8 September 2010
Ian	Will arrange a weekend break for Sally and Madge to London taking in a trip to a show in the West End.	15 September 2010
Ian and Jane	Have Sally's children stay over with them when Sally and Madge go away.	On the weekend they go away
Sally	Will speak to her husband, Stephen, about working away less for a while.	6 September 2010
Barbara, Madge's neighbour	Will make enquiries to look at what benefits, such as attendance allowance, Madge is entitled to – with a view to paying a cleaner.	15 September 2010
Madge and Ian	Will contact the bank to look at her financial situation to see if she can afford a cleaner for herself and Sally.	15 September 2010
Ian	Will speak with Sam to work out if he can visit and stay with Ian for a few weeks.	8 September 2010
Sally	Will contact John and Kate (Madge's old friends in London) to arrange to visit with Ian and Mum and go to see a show in the West End.	28 September 2010
Tracey (community nurse)	Will contact the consultant Mr John and the social worker to arrange a meeting about Madge's deteriorating health and options for additional support for the family, options to the nutritional drinks and insomnia.	8 September 2010
Sally and Ian	Will look at what resources are out there to support Madge to get out more.	30 September 2010
Sally	Will arrange a meeting with her supervisor to take a period of leave from her post.	8 September 2010

Figure 19.6 Madge's action plan

How would I like to be remembered? Madge

Do not dwell on my frailty when you think of me. Remember the fun and laughter we shared.

Madge would like her three children to meet on Blackpool pier and scatter her ashes in the sea together.

Go to the illuminations some years and walk along the front and talk about the wonderful times we knew.

Figure 19.7 How Madge would like to be remembered

They also thought together about how Madge could stay in control, and what decisions would need to be made (see Figure 19.8).

Madge also talked to Sally and Ian about her final arrangements (see Figure 19.9).

Madge died quietly at home. Here are her thoughts on how she had thought about her life, what was working and not working for her, what she still wanted to do and how she wanted to die:

Living Well...has helped me and mine work through things and chat more easily about what we all wanted, it gave me hope and things to look forward to as well - I hope by sharing the things we talked about and worked out, I can leave a legacy which will help other people.

Madge, February 2011

When a person is approaching the end of his life, person-centred thinking tools and plans can help him and his family and carers to better manage this and experience things in a way which makes most sense to them all. It is the final stage in our journey of support through adulthood. The common thread that runs right the way through all of this support is managing risk in a way that still means that people achieve their desired outcomes. This is the focus of the next and final chapter.

End of life decision making agreement – Madge

Decisions to be made	How Madge is involved and who else is involved	How the decision is made and who makes the final decision
Around my treatments and my condition.	I want to be fully involved but it makes more sense if information comes to me through Sally. She knows how to put things across to me and helps me come to decisions. I cannot follow some of the consultants.	Madge.
Where will I be looked after if I become very dependent?	I want Sally and Ian to be OK. I would want to stay at home but know they will do what is best if it gets to the point where they find it too difficult.	Sally and Ian.
Where to die.	Madge talks through with her son Ian and daughter Sally.	Madge – her preferred place for her end of life is at home but she is comfortable for Sally and Ian to ultimately control this decision given that she trusts them completely.
How I want to be remembered.	Madge, Sally and Ian (daughter and son) will discuss. Madge will also talk to Sam her other son who lives in Australia. Alison from the long-term condition team also has some ideas for Madge.	Madge.
Whether to be resuscitated.	Madge, the district nurse, her consultant and his medical team.	Madge has decided she does not want to be. Her decision to be respected by medical team.
Which funeral directors.	Madge, Sally and Ian.	Madge.

Figure 19.8 Madge's end of life decision making agreement

What do I want to add as I think about the end of my life?

	What I want	What I don't want	My family's view
Where I want to die	At home.	To be in hospital on my own.	Sally, Ian and Sam want to be with me.
About my funeral (music, readings, flowers etc)	I would like my funeral to be quick with just two hymns and one reading – at the crem. at Carlton. No flowers – a donation to charity of people's own choice if they wish. Donation made by them – I don't want Sally to have anything to worry about.	Black clothes.	My family are happy with this.
About being buried or cremated (clothes, hair, jewellery)	I want to be cremated Sally and I have chosen the clothes I will wear. I want my glasses on.	A shroud.	I would want to lie in rest at the funeral directors, not at home.
About the scattering of my ashes	Sally, Ian and Sam scatter my ashes together at the end of Blackpool pier into the sea. At least if I go suddenly and Sam does not get back in time from Australia the three of them can do this together which matters so much to me.	My ashes standing about in a pot.	The children have promised me they will do this together.
About what people do after my funeral (food, drink, a celebration, memorial)	My family and friends to go back to Sally's with a buffet I have ordered from Marks and Spencer's and remember with happiness the time we spent together.		The family will do what Madge wants.
About a gravestone or marker for my ashes or burial place	I just want those who love me to carry me in their heart. They will always feel close to me if they are by the sea – any sea. I just love the sea.	A physical memorial.	Sally would like a grave to visit but accepts my wishes. We have agreed to have a bench on Abbey Hill where the sea runs by but no plaque. She can go and sit there and think of me.
What else is important to me?	Sally and Ian know the things they can give to charity and who I want to have my remaining possessions.	Only Sally to sort my stuff out.	My family have agreed to this.

Figure 19.9 What does Madge want to add as she thinks about the end of her life?

Chapter 20

A Person-Centred Approach to Risk

People's autonomy used to be compromised by institution walls, now it's too often our risk management practices.

John O'Brien[204]

Part IV has taken us through the journey of support through adulthood using person-centred practice. One issue in common to every stage of support is risk. It is relevant to, and must be addressed in the support of, every person, in every situation and every setting. Many of the debates we have seen in the sector press, events and online have focused on the issue of managing risk and the fear of potential liability to a providing or commissioning organisation if they let a person take control of her own care (either financially, personally or in terms of publicity). This chapter explains how to take a person-centred approach to risk so that a person can still be supported to achieve the outcomes she wants.

Consider Kaarina Elisabeth's point made in a recent blog for *Community Care* magazine:

> Personalisation, I am in no doubt, would transform the lives of mental health service users and lead to better outcomes. Before I had even heard of self directed support, I was lobbying for it. Why, I wondered, does nobody listen to my assessment of my needs? There is one reason that appears to pre-occupy the minds of everyone I've met in commissioning services: that of risk. So while service users desperately long to regain control of their recovery, fear of risk stops personalisation in mental health moving forward.[205]

However, if we are to enable people to exercise more choice and control in managing their health and well-being through personalised care plans or person-centred support plans, then the issue of risk must be tackled head-on. Max Neill and colleagues[206] say that any positive approach to risk must include the basic tenets of all person-centred approaches, and be prepared to go beyond conventional service options. This means keeping the person at the centre, treating family and friends as partners in finding solutions, focusing on what is important to the person and building connections with the community.

This chapter looks at the issues and existing approaches used in risk management and introduces a person-centred approach to enabling risk.

Darius's story

Darius wanted to do some education courses to improve his employment prospects, so he was able to purchase a laptop and broadband with his recovery budget. However, a few months later, the nature of his fluctuating mental health condition meant that he began to show signs of a relapse. His supporters in the early intervention team were concerned that he was isolating himself by retreating into his room and distancing himself socially. In the past, this was a clear sign that things were getting bad for him.

He had previously been compulsorily admitted to hospital under the Mental Health Act, which his psychiatrist and nursing clinician hoped to avoid, as much of his paranoia focused on him being observed and monitored – something that would clearly have to happen if he was admitted to hospital.

When they went to visit Darius, they found that, although it appeared he was withdrawn and not going out of his room, the laptop in the corner was flashing instant messages on the screen. This was taken as evidence that Darius was still in contact with the outside world, even if it was through cyberspace. He had also been texting one of his supporters in the early intervention team – another sign he was still communicating with people. Both became part of the contributing factors that led the clinician to decide not to compulsorily admit Darius to hospital.

While those involved agreed that making this decision was difficult as the type of evidence was unusual in mental health services, it was considered to be positive risk enablement. It meant that Darius could continue his recovery process, and he is now on a course gaining qualifications in translation, which he hopes will eventually lead to a job.

The issue of risk

> Whilst positive risk-taking was part of the philosophy and a central benefit of Individual Budgets, it was also seen as a difficult culture shift for care co-ordinators in light of their responsibilities for safeguarding… Many staff interviewed voiced concerns about risks of poorer quality services, misuse of funds, financial abuse, neglect, and physical harm.
>
> *Caroline Glendinning* et al.[207]

Everyone takes risks in daily life – when using a car or cycling, for example. Yet in health and social services, risk has come to be seen as dangerous.[208] Almost all services have a blame culture. When something bad happens, they look for the person who failed to properly assess and act on the risk.

This has been described by some in the sector as the '*Daily Mail* factor'. No one wants to be the person whose lack of attention to risk resulted in something awful that ended up on the front page of a tabloid newspaper. When a story broke about a young disabled man using his personal budget to be supported in visiting a prostitute, there was initially a lot of negative coverage in the *Daily Telegraph*[209] and *Daily Mail*, but what eventually ensued across the media spectrum was a helpful and thought-provoking debate about risk.

As Kaarina Elisabeth points out, the experience of many people who have to rely on human services for their support is that 'risk' is the reason given to them by services as to why they cannot do the things that other people are doing every day. She argues that risk already exists and that asking people what they need to keep well and then meeting those needs can only result in an overall reduction of risk.

> Risk is my friend with severe needs, who receives no services at all, because she does not want other people to control her life…or another friend who asked for help, but only became eligible for it after making a suicide attempt and becoming too ill to work again… (or) when agencies don't talk to each other.
>
> It's the breakdown I had when all my services were cut off because I was suddenly re-housed outside the borough. To be housed far from friends and family, with no money

for food or the tube, and nobody to visit or help cook. That is risk. To have those needs listened to and met at that difficult time would have cost fifty quid a week. Not to have those met means I now cost £500.[210]

Making decisions about risk is often complicated by the fact that the person or group taking the decision is not always the person or group affected by the risk. Differences in power and status can affect the extent to which people influence risk decision making. For example, the views of developers wishing to build a dam across a river may be given more weight than those of people living near that river. Where a person with less power and status might wish to take a risk, and the consequences of that risk would affect more powerful people, it is more likely that she will be prevented from taking it. This is the problem faced by people supported by services and professionals, where those services and professionals fear various real and imagined consequences to them of the risk taking of the people whom they support.

This problem is deepened in modern society as the power of the news media can mean that the unpredictable actions of an individual can now have an amplified impact on the reputation of services, and on political and corporate institutions. Services that are now becoming increasingly concerned with 'reputational risk management' find that this demands 'the risk management of everything'.[211] In the case of human services, this means an ever more intrusive and obsessive focus on every aspect of the lives, behaviours and potential behaviours of the people whom they support. It can also mean the increasing 'proceduralisation' of work as defensive practice and blame avoidance[212] become more important than the particular lives of individual people receiving care and support.

Self-determination naturally involves risks and this needs to be recognised, understood and minimised whenever possible, but that does not mean avoiding risk at all cost.[213]

Another way to think of risk is balancing the possibility of good outcomes against bad outcomes and taking an approach that is 'thorough, professional, and personalised'[214] in recognising that life and risk are inseparable. It is important to look at risk from the point of view of the person, her family and friends and the wider community, rather than solely from the point of view of the service provider.

Providing that services are prepared to face the challenge, person-centred practices and the way they build an alliance of supporters around an individual can cut across this issue and generate new and creative ways of support. This is increasingly recognised by government which has started to commend person-centred approaches for everyone because they 'identify what is important to a person from his or her own perspective and find appropriate solutions.'[215]

EXISTING APPROACHES TO RISK ASSESSMENT

> They tell you what to do all the time and most importantly what you can and can't do. They say it is for your own safety. But it is my choice and my risk and my life.
>
> *Older person[216]*

The way in which risk is considered and operated is often defensive and concerned with safety – not of the individual or the public, but the organisation and the professionals themselves, meaning its management is negative, narrow and uncreative.[217]

The Health and Safety Executive's *Principles of Sensible Risk Management* defines sensible risk management as enabling innovation and learning, not stifling them, and focusing on reducing real risks, both those which arise more often and those with serious consequences.[218]

Let's look at the assumption behind a risk assessment. These detailed forms or checklists are assumed to demonstrate that the professional has assessed any risks and has taken steps to prevent bad outcomes, for the individual, the community, the professional and the organisation. They are more likely to come from a place of 'power over' than 'power with', more in the professional's interests than the person's, and are 'defensive' in nature. They reduce complex situations to a set of criteria leading to actions and 'lose the person'. Philosophically, they treat the person as an object to be assessed by the 'experts' rather than as an agent in her own life, as part of a family, community and society, with legal rights and choices. They focus on what is wrong with the person, often treating her as a problem to be managed rather than as a person to be enabled to fulfil her ambitions and offer a contribution to society.

We need an entirely different approach from the methods that services use to 'risk assess' their hoists, fridges and kettles and instead focus on 'working with people to achieve their potential without compromising their safety'.[219] We need a process that is sustainable and emphasises 'resilience, self reliance, freedom, innovation and a spirit of adventure'.[220]

There are seven criteria that can help staff and professionals find the 'holy grail' of balancing 'positive risk taking' and minimising harm:[221]

1. involvement of service users and relatives in risk assessment

2. positive and informed risk taking

3. proportionality

4. contextualising behaviour

5. defensible decision making

6. a learning culture

7. tolerable risks.

Introducing a person-centred approach to risk

> Safeguarding must be built on empowerment – or listening to the person's voice. Without this, safeguarding is experienced as safety at the expense of other qualities of life, such as self determination and the right to family life.
>
> *Department of Health[222]*

A person-centred approach to risk does not lose the person in a sea of tick-boxes and charts. It has a more balanced approach with an inbuilt assumption that the purpose of any risk assessment is just as much about the happiness of the person, her family and the community, as it is about her safety.[223]

Practitioners of person-centred approaches who were unsatisfied with the traditional repertoire of risk management tools have begun to recombine these with person-centred thinking tools in innovative and creative ways. They applied them to thinking, acting and learning around real risk situations and developed a process involving people who use services and their supporters to manage risk, make decisions, take actions and learn together. This process is known as a 'person-centred approach to risk'.[224]

> When asked whose responsibility it was to 'keep people safe', many people said it was their own responsibility. They explained that no-one else could do it, because understanding what made them safe required understanding them as people – understanding their personalities, their experiences, their family relationships, their wishes for the future and their past history of choices. Safeguarding could not be an activity that was delegated to anyone else – although it could be a shared or supported activity.[225]

The person-centred approach to risk uses questions around a framework of purpose, people, process and progress. Right from the beginning, we must think seriously about what it is that we are trying to achieve. The way we think about the process and the way it will help someone become a citizen in her community with choice and control in her life, will influence who the people are that are called to participate in the process.

Anne's story describes how the person-centred approach to risk works in practice.

Anne's story

Staff support Anne to be as independent as possible. The first stage of this process involved Anne travelling by herself on trains. Anne and the staff team looked at potential risks and how to limit them as well as the benefits of independent travel. Anne purchased and learned how to use a mobile phone and was initially shadowed to ensure that she was OK travelling on her own. The result of this process was that Anne's self-esteem grew and she no longer needed staff to go with her on a train. She could travel where and when she wanted. Later, this independence allowed Anne the opportunity to find herself a job in a nearby town.

This early success meant that Anne could take more control over other parts of her life. She was supported, gradually, to cook all her own meals, use a weekly budget to purchase her own food and plan menus to ensure that she would have the right ingredients and eat healthily.

As Anne became used to this process, staff support became less necessary to the point that she budgets, plans her menu, shops for food and cooks independently.

With initial staff support Anne is now independent in administering her own medication. She knows what she needs and at what time; she uses a bubble pack system of administration and records what she has taken on a balance sheet. Together, Anne and her support staff considered the risks, but they were outweighed by the benefit of Anne being given the respect and responsibility she deserved and not having to wait for staff to administer her medication.

In the last five years, Anne has not made one medication error, which is a better track record than many staff can claim. As a result of this success, the staff team agreed to stop doing a weekly medication check for her medication and, although this was challenging for staff used to working a certain way, it meant that Anne didn't have to wait around for staff to enter her bedroom and carry out what had effectively become a pointless exercise.

The most recent development in terms of Anne's increased independence concerns how she manages her finances. Although she goes to the bank on her own and has had sole access to her money for several years, Anne still used the audit book system which was seen as a means to reduce the risk of financial abuse and to account for her income and expenditure. The problem with this system was that Anne found it difficult to use, was constantly thinking about what her next receipt number would be and was often anxious about staff being available to check her audit book. Consequently, with Anne's approval, the staff team no longer uses the audit book. After the initial shock of changing a long-standing practice, it became apparent that the risk of financial mismanagement or abuse was not increased by abandoning the long-standing system. Anne alone has access to her money and she still receives a monthly bank statement which records all transactions. There is, however, a real reduction in her anxiety and improvement in her quality of life. She no longer worries about recording purchases in her audit book every time she gets home from a shopping trip.

The result of all these changes means that Anne lives a life which allows her to enjoy the sort of freedoms and choices many of us take for granted. Anne is more self-confident and less reliant on staff meeting her basic needs. Many of these developments came about because it was recognised that what was important to Anne outweighed any perceived risk. There is always the possibility that harm could occur through independent travelling, the self-administration of medication or cooking meals without support, but these risks in Anne's case are minimal, managed and are outweighed by the greater risk of a life that is restricted from achieving its full potential.

The following process is a step-by-step explanation of taking a person-centred approach to risk, covering who the person is, where she is now and where she wants to be, what has been tried and learned already and what should be done next (see Figure 20.1).

WHO IS THE PERSON?

Once the purpose is understood and people are gathered together, the first and biggest priority of the process is to gain an understanding of *who the person is*. The ultimate success of any strategies or solutions will depend on how well we listen for the person's capacities, gifts and skills, and to what is important to the person, as well as our understanding of what makes the best support for that person.

The best support is what keeps the person healthy and safe in a way that is congruent with how she wishes to live now, and what she wishes to achieve in the future. Tools to explore this include a full person-centred plan. If the person does not have such a plan, then a one page profile is used.

WHERE ARE WE NOW?

A picture of what is working and not working now, from the perspective of the person and from the perspectives of others, is built up, and the risk issue is clearly defined. It's important to know what is working now, so that when strategies are developed, they do not conflict with what we know already works well.

WHERE DO WE WANT TO BE?

Traditional risk assessments lack any sense of vision about how things could be different or better for the person. In the person-centred approach, it is central that a vision of what success could look like is put together, beginning with the person's perspective, then adding in others.

This vision, coupled with a picture of who the person is, can generate the energy and commitment within the group to work toward real and lasting changes.

WHAT HAVE WE TRIED AND LEARNED ALREADY?

A huge amount of people's learning and knowledge around risk issues is wasted when new strategies are tried without reference to what has gone before.

A Person-Centred Approach To Risk

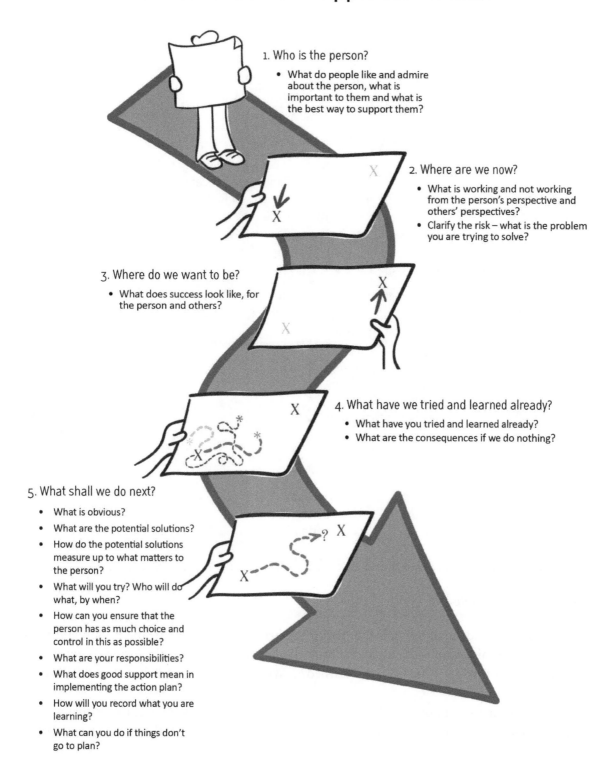

1. Who is the person?
- What do people like and admire about the person, what is important to them and what is the best way to support them?

2. Where are we now?
- What is working and not working from the person's perspective and others' perspectives?
- Clarify the risk – what is the problem you are trying to solve?

3. Where do we want to be?
- What does success look like, for the person and others?

4. What have we tried and learned already?
- What have you tried and learned already?
- What are the consequences if we do nothing?

5. What shall we do next?
- What is obvious?
- What are the potential solutions?
- How do the potential solutions measure up to what matters to the person?
- What will you try? Who will do what, by when?
- How can you ensure that the person has as much choice and control in this as possible?
- What are your responsibilities?
- What does good support mean in implementing the action plan?
- How will you record what you are learning?
- What can you do if things don't go to plan?

Figure 20.1 A person-centred approach to risk

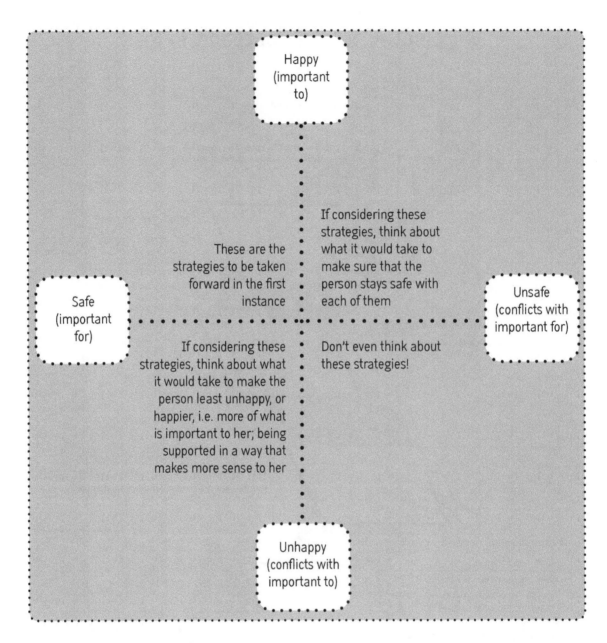

Figure 20.2 Happy/safe grid

Here person-centred thinking tools are used to gather the knowledge of the person and their allies around the history of the issue, and to bring all the information together using the questions, 'What have you tried?', 'What have you learned?', 'What are you pleased about?' and 'What are you concerned about?'

The consequences of doing nothing are considered, including the opportunities that will be lost if we don't support the person to take the risk. What the law says on the issue is also thought about.

WHAT SHALL WE DO NEXT?

Obvious solutions are considered first, then more creative 'blue sky' thinking techniques are used to generate a wider range of solutions – good, bad and indifferent. All the various solutions are mapped onto a 'happy/safe' grid, depending on how happy they make the person, and how safe they keep the person and the community. This clear mapping enables action planning and gives a clear rationale for why some strategies have been adopted and others rejected (see Figure 20.2).[226]

Strategies for ensuring that the person has as much choice and control within this are developed using the 'decision making agreement' and people's responsibilities are made clearer using the 'doughnut' tool. Contingency plans are developed in case the agreed strategies don't go to plan.

Finally, methods of reviewing progress are agreed, including a clear picture of how we will know things are not working.

Matching the person-centred approach to risk to the seven key criteria in the 'holy grail'

Here we look at the 'holy grail' referred to earlier in this chapter and show how we believe the person-centred approach to risk fulfils these criteria.

1) INVOLVEMENT OF SERVICE USERS AND RELATIVES IN RISK ASSESSMENT

This is one of the most fundamental tenets of any person-centred approach. The process we have put together considers carefully the people that need to be involved, using the 'relationship circle' to help the person and their allies identify key people who could form the person's 'circle of support'.

This group of people is involved from the outset: from the initial gathering of information, framing the risk discussion and generating ideas and solutions to making decisions around the risk, implementing the actions and learning what takes place during these actions.

Staff must understand what service users and others want, how they view their own risks and what responsibilities each person has in managing risks effectively.[227] The person-centred approach meets because it asks what the person wishes to achieve, why this is important, and what success looks like, and compiles a history of the risk and uses the doughnut and decision making agreement tools to determine staff roles and responsibilities for different important decisions in relation to the risk.

2) POSITIVE AND INFORMED RISK TAKING

The person-centred approach to risk is built around a positive view of the person – it seeks to learn what the person's gifts and skills are, what people like and admire about her, as well as investigating what would be necessary to keep her and others safe while taking the risk. The process is based on finding creative solutions rather than simply ruling things out. Bates and Silberman argue that quality of life should be 'maximised while people and communities are kept as safe as can be reasonably expected within a free society'.[228]

Thinking around what it takes to keep a person and others safe while taking the risk is a key part of the 'positive and productive process', as is the use of the 'happy/safe' grid. This looks at how solutions can make the person happy by meeting what is important *to* her and how they keep them and others safe by meeting what is important *for* her. One section of the process includes a question, 'What does the law say?'[229] enabling the process to be informed by the current law, including legislation such as the Human Rights Act.

3) PROPORTIONALITY

'The management of the risk must match the gravity of potential harm.'[230] Using the person-centred thinking tools provides flexibility. The more serious the issue, the more people and the more time can be spent considering it in greater detail. Unlike conventional risk assessment, the approach explores the consequences of *not* taking the risk to the person, her family, community and services, and balances these against the potential consequences of taking the risk.

4) CONTEXTUALISING BEHAVIOUR

Why did the person behave in this way? At this time? In this situation?[231] Part of the person-centred approach involves gathering previous personal information, including a history of her experience of the risk issue from her own perspective and information from person-centred thinking tools like 'learning logs', 'communication charts' and the '4 plus 1' questions. This provides an understanding of a person's behaviour in different contexts and builds a picture of what best support for that person would look like.

5) DEFENSIBLE DECISION MAKING

There needs to be an explicit and justifiable rationale for the risk management decisions.[232] Following the person-centred approach generates a clear trail of written records of what has been discussed and the different perspectives, issues, solutions and legal implications that have been considered. The paperwork generated during the process provides a clear rationale for why some decisions have been taken and others rejected. The rationale for decision making is also more clearly expounded and recorded than in traditional and common risk assessment forms.

6) A LEARNING CULTURE

The person-centred approach emphasises the importance of learning through the use of learning and reflective tools like the 'learning log', '4 plus 1' questions and what's 'working and not working'. It also clearly defines staff core duties and when they can use their judgement and creativity in relation to the risk. The approach can significantly contribute to the building of a learning culture in organisations if it is part of a serious and concerted attempt by services to change their philosophy and practice in a person-centred direction.

7) TOLERABLE RISKS

A key aspect of the person-centred approach to risk is that it uses creative methods to help a person move from happy but unsafe situations to ones where she and the community are safer, and from being safe but unhappy to where she can be happier. Participants can take a more balanced and rational approach to risk, helping the person achieve what is important to her as well as making sense for her, while considering what keeps everyone safe.

Services are good at highlighting the downside of risk – but poor at thinking about the great opportunities that facing up to risk and finding positive solutions in a creative and mindful way could mean for people, their families and their communities. Traditional methods of risk assessment are full of charts and scoring systems but tick-boxes 'lose' the humanity of the person – her objectives, dreams and life.

It is important to remember people's rights, including the right to make unwise decisions. We need to gather the fullest information and evidence available to demonstrate that we have thought deeply about all the issues involved and made decisions together based on what is important to the person, what is needed to keep her healthy and safe and on what the law tells us.

Current national policy says that 'it should be possible for a person to have a support plan which enables them to manage identified risks and to live their lives in ways which best suit them'.[233] In order to achieve this, a person-centred approach is required, based on the use of person-centred thinking tools. This will help people and those who care about them think in a positive and productive way about achieving the changes they want to see while keeping risk in its place.

Conclusion

Vale House was set up almost twenty years ago to look after people who had profound mental health needs due to their dementia. At that time in Oxfordshire, receiving that sort of care meant going to a general care home, or into hospital. Last summer, a woman called Marjorie came to live with us. When I went to assess her in her previous care home, I saw someone who was sitting quietly in her own room. She didn't engage much with me in conversation.

Her son had told us that she used to play the organ in the local church and had a lot of pleasure from that – music had been a very important part of her life. We then decided that we would try and sit with her for a very short period each day and see if she could pick up tunes again. So we would sing a hymn to her, and she started to pick them up again and play some of them. It's given her back some dignity. And this afternoon, she's actually going out to a concert with a volunteer. We think that she'll really enjoy that.

Because we're having to care for people, it would be very easy for us to forget that our residents are individuals with their own personal history, background, things they like to do and things they've been proud of. We're having to help bathe them, dress them, and help them have their meals...in a day's work. The easy way to do it would be just to treat everyone the same, to presume that all people over the age of sixty like to sit in a chair in front of the television for most part of the day, or that they all like the same food. It would be very easy to get in to the wrong way of doing it, but that wouldn't be to give good person-centred care.

If my mother was ill, I would want people to remember who she was, what her background was, the things that she used to like to do, and that's very important to us here at Vale House. Indeed, the whole process goes much more smoothly if we treat people as individuals.

Every day and every moment in someone's life is as important as the moment before. A moment in one of my residents' lives is no less important than a moment in mine. I don't throw away moments or days in my life, and we shouldn't do that for people who have dementia. So, it really matters that we find out (for example) that a man worked on the railways, that he liked football, and who his favourite football team were.

Even when people are very mentally disabled, if you say something that resonates with them and they remember, you will get a smile. You'll get some feedback. They'll start to feel better. They will be calmer. It's about their well-being. That's what we're striving for.

Tricia[234]

What could the future be like?

The government's vision for the future of health and adult social care requires that person-centred approaches and self-directed support become mainstream activities in order to deliver personalisation[235] and that must be achieved by handing over financial control. In order to achieve this, disabled and older adults, and their families and carers, need to be truly empowered. So we believe that the future must be one where older and disabled people, across all services, and alongside their families and carers, are supported in the way that makes most sense to them, with the maximum amount of choice available on a day-to-day basis.

This means a future where services take into account people's whole lives, builds their capacity and acknowledges the contributions they can make, as individuals and as part of a community, to solving problems.

This is a future where health and social care staff are passionately delivering personalised services through listening and working with people as equal partners to find out what it important to them, in the same way that Tricia does in the story about Vale House. People are seen beyond their label or condition and the staff supporting them are enjoying their jobs and getting increased satisfaction out of seeing the positive changes that they are making to people's lives.

Finally, this is a future where the health and social care services provided by statutory agencies and providers are commissioned, designed and delivered in a way that is truly 'co-produced'. That is, people have been enabled and encouraged to shape those services and make their own decisions about how they want to spend the budget they have available to them.

Person-centred practice is a way to achieve this future. It provides a basis for understanding and acting on what matters to people, how they want to be supported, builds on their assets and enables them to become full members of their community.

This book has shown the following:

- Using person-centred practice can assist in delivering the national policy priorities for personalisation and prevention – key components of the vision for adult social care, the NHS next stage review and the cross-sector partnership agreement *Think Local, Act Personal*. It goes beyond handing over financial control of the resources available for a person's support by providing real choice on a day-to-day basis. Person-centred practice is a crucial component in the effective roll-out of personal budgets because it can aid in the development of person-centred plans and support plans that are more likely to achieve people's desired outcomes.

- There is a long history of person-centred planning and thinking, which emerged from the continuing search by disabled people and their allies to find better ways of including people in society. Person-centred practice is not the latest 'fad' but has emerged naturally from the most progressive movements in the field of disability during the last 30 years. It is evidence-based practice, with research showing that it contributes to significant positive changes in the areas of social networks and levels of choice.[236]

- Person-centred practice is based on the values of independence and rights, co-production, choice and control and inclusive and competent communities. It assumes disabled and older people are ready to do whatever they want as long as they are adequately supported. Co-production increases people's well-being and there is overwhelming evidence that what people do for themselves and with others – not services – delivers the bulk of social outcomes.[237]

- Person-centred thinking helps to discover what is important to a person, so that support can be built around what matters to him as an individual; shows how, when and where a person wants support rather than offering a 'one size fits all' approach; and enables a person to communicate the way in which he wants his support.

- Health and social care workers, support workers and other professionals need to understand person-centred thinking tools and person-centred plans – and coach their staff and colleagues in using them – to deliver self-directed support. The tools offer a way of learning and understanding the balance between what is important to and for a person; to enhance voice, choice and control; to clarify roles and responsibilities; and to provide analysis and action. By looking at what's working and not working in someone's life, you can determine which person-centred thinking tools to use and build a person-centred description to inform a person-centred plan or support plan.

- There is a process for making statutory reviews person-centred. This is called a person-centred review or an outcome-focused review (where the person has a personal budget). These create shared actions for change, based on a reflection and analysis of what is working and not working for the person, and others. They can be used across services, including mental health services, and can change a typical CPA for the better.

- Implementing person-centred reviews and person-centred thinking are two ways to get started with person-centred plans across services. They can contribute to ensuring 'service competence' (services are personalised to reflect what matters to people) and 'community competence' (creating communities where everyone belongs and contributes). Support plans can be built from a person-centred description or person-centred plan to show how a person intends to spend his personal budget. They are crucial to the successful handing over of financial control to people who need support.

- Person-centred practice contributes to every stage of a person's journey of support through adulthood. Improving an individual's connection with the community by making him feel 'good' and improving his well-being is one way of meeting the prevention agenda and potentially reduces the need for unnecessary support.

- When people have long term-conditions, person-centred thinking tools can help in the development of personalised care plans which, when done in partnership with healthcare practitioners, meets a person's support needs in a way that suits his 'whole life'. This extends to dementia when care mapping in residential homes is undertaken.

- Person-centred practice can provide a different approach to recovery – based on partnership – that asks people what they would like to achieve and then helps them to do that. It means doing things *with* people rather than *to* them.

- Person-centred thinking can help the reablement journey as the way people maximise their independence will be unique to them. It allows for people to be involved in all discussion and decisions about their support and strengthens natural support networks and community involvement.

- When people need ongoing support, carers may find person-centred thinking tools helpful in ensuring that their own support needs are acknowledged. Investment in person-centred thinking and determination to ensure that people have as much choice and control over their support means that it is possible to personalise domiciliary care even if only 15 minutes are available; and it ensures that people keep their individuality in residential care settings.

- When a person is approaching the end of their life, person-centred thinking tools and plans can help a person, his family and carers to manage this better and to experience things in a way that makes most sense to them all.

- It should be possible for a person to support another in a way that enables him to manage identified risks and for them both to live their lives in ways which best suit them. In order to achieve this, a person-centred approach is required, based on the use of person-centred thinking tools. This will help people and those who care about them think in a positive and productive way about achieving the changes they want to see while keeping risk in its place.

As we mentioned in the first part of this book, the delivery of personalisation is at risk of being undermined given the challenges of the current financial climate. People are asking whether person-centred approaches are a 'luxury' we cannot afford.

If people need any convincing, then perhaps they could consider this anecdote from a colleague involved in shaping the future of older people's services in England.

> *Visiting a service supporting people living with dementia recently I learned that nobody owned a pair of shoes! Even worse, this isn't uncommon - they are places where people stay in. Who is going to listen and act on the voices of people rarely heard! The need for person-centred planning is more crucial than ever — warehousing people is alive and well!*
>
> *Gill Bailey*[238]

In our view, person-centred approaches are neither a luxury nor unaffordable.

Person-centred thinking and planning helps people think about all the resources available to them – and then helps them and the people who support them use those resources to their full effect. It makes every penny of funds they receive, either from public or private sources, stretch so much further. When money is tight, it is even more important to use resources as effectively as possible. And what better resource is there than what a person (or those close to him) thinks, knows and feels about what is important to him, works well for him and what he wants for his life. We can't afford not to listen well to people and act on this information. 'It's better to spend a couple of hours thinking about how to support someone well than to continue to support them in a way that causes anxiety, distress, depression and results in much more expensive supports in the future.'[239]

Person-centred practice can also greatly assist in changing a culture from one where the power is over people to power with people. People want lives not services. Person-centred approaches support this journey and are the embodiment of all that is essential to our role as enablers and promoters of social justice.

This book has shown what the future could be like. And we hope it will change the way you think, plan and do your job. Some readers will find it challenging, with the attempt to shift power, from being the person who has a certain degree of control over the process, to really sharing and empowering a person who needs care and support to be completely at the centre.

But we see this as an opportunity to support you in doing what you have always wanted to do, rather than providing another way to create yet more paperwork.

We must continue in our efforts to embed a culture of person-centred thinking as a habit among health and social care workers, and we need to grow person-centred plans for individuals, their families and carers.

Person-centred thinking and planning are required if we are serious about making choice and control a reality and must be at the centre of all our personalisation effort. If we continue to think about the individuals – and with their help, or the help of those closest to them – understand their hopes, needs, dreams and aspirations, then we will have the best chance yet of delivering personalisation, and helping more people to live full, independent lives as equal citizens in the community.

Endnotes

1. Social Care Institute for Excellence (2010) *Personalisation for Someone with a Physical Disability*. SCIE TV. Available at www.scie.org.uk/socialcaretv/video-player.asp?guid=91834b9d-26ef-44ba-9055-c9720606edf9, accessed on 10 May 2011.

2. Social Care Institute for Excellence (2010) *Personalisation –Making It Happen: The Social Worker's Perspective*. SCIE TV. Available at www.scie.org.uk/socialcaretv/video-player.asp?guid=673c2b14-d004-45e1-98e8-86b69c22b90a, accessed on 10 May 2011.

3. Department of Health (2010) *Capable Communities and Active Citizens: A Vision for Adult Social Care*. London: DoH, p.15.

4. Robertson, J., Emerson, E., Hatton, C., Elliott, J. *et al.* (2005) *The Impact of Person Centred Planning*. Lancaster: Institute for Health Research, Lancaster University.

5. Department of Health (2010) *Capable Communities and Active Citizens*, p.15.

6. Department of Health (2008) *High Quality Care for All: NHS Next Stage Review, Final Report*. London: DoH.

7. Routledge, M. (2011) 'Cuts should not derail personal budgets.' *The Guardian*, 13 April. Available at http://bit.ly/hhbxPM, accessed on 19 May 2011.

8. Sanderson, H., Kennedy, J., Ritchie, P. and Goodwin, G. (1997) *People, Plans and Possibilities: Exploring Person Centred Planning*. Edinburgh: Scottish Human Services Trust.

9. Ritchie, P., Sanderson, H., Kilbane, J. and Routledge, M. (2003) *People, Plans and Practicalities: Achieving Change Through Person-Centred Planning*. Edinburgh: Scottish Human Services Trust.

10. Smull, M. and Sanderson, H. (2005) *Essential Lifestyle Planning for Everyone*. Stockport: Helen Sanderson Associates Press Ltd.

11. Department of Health (2010) *Personalisation Through Person-Centred Planning*. London: DoH.

12. Sanderson, H. *et al.* (1997) *People, Plans and Possibilities*.

13. Department of Health (2010) *Personalisation Through Person-Centred Planning*.

14. Social Care Institute for Excellence (2010) *Personalisation for Older People: Living at Home*. SCIE TV. Available at www.scie.org.uk/socialcaretv/video-player.asp?guid=957c57f1-8e4a-4651-a9c1-8efe43c3c514, accessed on 10 May 2011.

15. Think Local, Act Personal Partnership (2011) *Think Local, Act Personal: Next Steps for Transforming Adult Care*. January. London: Think Local, Act Personal Partnership. Available at www.thinklocalactpersonal.org.uk/_library/Resources/Personalisation/TLAP/THINK_LOCAL_ACT_PERSONAL_5_4_11.pdf, accessed on 10 May 2011.

16. Department of Health (2010) *Capable Communities and Active Citizens*, p.15.

17. Department of Health (2008) *High Quality Care for All*.

18. Department of Health (2010) *Capable Communities and Active Citizens*, p.16.

19. Think Local, Act Personal Partnership (2011) *Think Local, Act Personal*.

20. Department of Health (2011) *Anita and Trevor's Story*. Personal Health Budgets Learning Community. London: DoH.

21. Department of Health (2005) *Our Health, Our Care, Our Say: A New Direction for Community Services*. White Paper. London: DoH.

22. Department of Health (2007) *Putting People First: A Shared Vision and Commitment to the Transformation of Adult Social Care*. London: DoH.

23. Department of Health (2008) *High Quality Care for All*.

24. Cabinet Office (2010) *The Coalition: Our Programme for Government*. London: Cabinet Office.

25. HM Treasury (2010) *The Spending Review*. London: HM Treasury, p.34.

26. Department of Health (2010) *Capable Communities and Active Citizens*.

27. Think Local, Act Personal Partnership (2011) *Think Local, Act Personal*.

28. Office for Disability Issues (2010) *Right to Control Trailblazers*. Available at http://odi.dwp.gov.uk/odiprojects/right-to-control-trailblazers.php, accessed on 13 May 2011.

29. Think Local, Act Personal Partnership (2011) *Think Local, Act Personal*.

30. Bates (2004), cited in Coyle, D. (2009) *Recovery Budgets in a Mental Health Service. Evaluating Recovery Budgets for People Accessing an Early Intervention Service and the Impact of Working with Self-Directed Services on the Team Members within a North West of England NHS Trust*. Liverpool: Merseycare NHS Trust.

31. Glendinning, C., Challis, D., Fernández, J., Jacobs, S. *et al.* (2008) *Evaluation of the Individual Budgets Pilot Programme: Final Report*. York: Social Policy Research Unit (SPRU), University of York.

32. Glendinning, C., Challis, D., Fernández, J., Jacobs, S. et al. (2008) *Evaluation of the Individual Budgets Pilot Programme: Summary Report*. York: Social Policy Research Unit (SPRU), University of York, p.20.

33. Glendinning, C., Arksey, H., Jones, K., Moran, N., Netten, A. and Rabiee, P. (2009) *Individual Budgets: Impacts and Outcomes for Carers*. York: Social Policy Research Unit (SPRU), University of York.

34. Department of Health (2008) *Making Personal Budgets Work for Older People: Developing Experience*; (2010) *Personal Budgets for Older People: Making it Happen*. London: DoH.

35. Social Care Institute for Excellence (2011) *Personal Budgets Briefing: Learning from the Experiences of Older People and their Carers.* Available at www.scie.org.uk/publications/ataglance/ataglance40.pdf, accessed on 10 May 2011.

36. Ibid., p.2.

37. Alakeson, V. (2007) *Putting Patients in Control: The Case for Extending Self-Direction into the NHS.* London: Social Market Foundation.

38. Ibid., p.48.

39. Ibid., p.43.

40. Jones, K., Welch, E., Caiels, J., Windle, K. *et al.* (2010) *Experiences of Implementing Personal Health Budgets: Second Interim Report, PSSRU Discussion Paper* 2747/2. Canterbury: Personal Social Services Research Unit, University of Kent, p.2.

41. Department of Health (2010) *Liberating the NHS: Legislative Framework and Next Steps.* London: DoH.

42. Ritchie, P. (2002) 'A Turn for the Better.' In J. O'Brien and C. Lyle O'Brien (eds) *Implementing Person-Centred Planning,* Volume II. Toronto: Inclusion Press, p.21.

43. O'Brien, J. (undated) Personal communication.

44. For a more detailed account see O'Brien, J. and Lyle O'Brien, C. (2002) *Implementing Person-Centred Planning: Voices of Experience.* Toronto: Inclusion Press.

45. Hurst, R. (1994) 'Review of John Swain, Vic Finkelstein, Sally French and Mike Oliver, "Disabling Barriers – Enabling Environments."' *Journal of Social Policy* 23: 116–17, p.116.

46. Nirje, B. (1969) *The Normalization Principle and Its Human Management Implications.* Stockholm: Swedish Association for Retarded Children.

47. Wolfensberger, W. (1972) *Principle of Normalization in Human Services.* Canadian Association for the Mentally Retarded.

48. O'Brien, J. (1989) *What's Worth Working for? Leadership for Better Quality Human Services.* Syracuse, NY: The Center on Human Policy, Syracuse University for the Research and Training Centre on Community Living.

49. For more information on circles of support, please go to www.circlesnetwork.org.uk (last accessed on 28 June 2011).

50. Smull, M. and Sanderson, H. (2005) *Essential Lifestyle Planning for Everyone.*

51. Mount, B. (1992) *Person-Centered Planning: A Sourcebook of Values, Ideas, and Methods to Encourage Person-Centered Development.* New York: Graphic Futures.

52. Sanderson, H. *et al.* (1997) *People, Plans and Possibilities.*

53. Department of Health (2001) *Valuing People: A New Strategy for Learning Disability for the 21st Century.* White Paper. London: DoH.

54. Department of Health (2007) *Putting People First.*

55. O'Brien, J. and Lyle O'Brien, C. (2002) *Implementing Person Centred Planning,* p.1.

56. Robertson, J. *et al.* (2005) *The Impact of Person Centred Planning.*

57. Grant, G. and Ramcharan, P. (2007) *Valuing People and Research: The Learning Disability Research Initiative.* Overview Report. London: Department of Health, cited in Department of Health (2010) *Personalisation Through Person-Centred Planning,* p.13.

58. Think Local, Act Personal Partnership (2011) *Think Local, Act Personal.*

59. Sanderson, H. *et al.* (2007) *People, Plans and Possibilities,* p.13.

60. Office for Disability Issues (2008) *Independent Living: A Cross-Government Strategy about Independent Living for Disabled People.* London: ODI, p.11.

61. Department for Work and Pensions (2008) *The Independent Living Strategy.* London: DWP.

62. Corbett, J. (1997) in H. Sanderson *et al. People, Plans and Possibilities,* p.17.

63. Duffy, S. (2010) *Citizenship Theory.* Sheffield: The Centre for Welfare Reform.

64. Williams, S. for the New Economics Foundation/National Endowment for Science, Technology and the Arts (2010) *What is the Definition of Co-Production?* The Lab. Available at http://coproductionnetwork.com/forum/topics/what-is-the-definition-of, accessed on 10 May 2011.

65. Stevens, L. (2010) *Joining the Dots: How all the System Elements Can Connect to Drive Personalisation and Coproduction, Incorporating Individual Social and Community Capacity.* London: New Economics Foundation. Available at www.puttingpeoplefirst.org.uk/BCC/caseStudy/BuildingTheBigSociety/ThinkPieces/?parent=7821&child=8380, accessed on 28 June 2011.

66. Hunter, S. and Ritchie, P. (eds) (2008) *Co-Production and Personalisation in Social Care.* London: Jessica Kingsley Publishers, p.111.

67. Ibid.

68. Croydon Drug and Alcohol Action Team (2010) *Operational Policy for Personal Health Budgets Pilot.* London: CDAAT, p.9.

69. O'Brien, J. and Lyle O'Brien, C. (2007) *A Little Book About Person Centred Planning.* Toronto: Inclusion Press, Introduction, p.8.

70. Roberts, S. (2007) *Working Together for Better Diabetes Care: The Clinical Case for Change.* London: DoH, p.7.

71. Picker Institute Europe. Available at www.pickereurope.org/sharingdecisions, accessed on 28 June 2011.

72. Stevens, L. (2010) *Joining the Dots.*

73. Boyle, D., Slay, J. and Stephens, L. (2010) *Public Services Inside Out: Putting Co-Production into Practice.* London: National Endowment for Science, Technology and the Arts.

74. Stevens, L. (2010) *Joining the Dots*.

75. Roberts, S. (2007) *Working Together for Better Diabetes Care*, p.6.

76. Alakeson, V. (2011) *Active Patient: The Case for Self-Direction in Healthcare*. Sheffield: The Centre for Welfare Reform, p.37.

77. Think Local, Act Personal Partnership (2011) *Think Local, Act Personal*.

78. Department of Health (2010) *Personalisation Through Person-Centred Planning*, p.13.

79. Department of Health (2009) *Working Together for Change: Using Person-Centred Information for Commissioning*. London: DoH.

80. Leadbeater, C. (2004) *Personalisation Through Participation: A New Script for Public Services*. London: Demos, p.24.

81. Smale, G. (1993) *Empowerment, Assessment, Care Management and the Skilled Worker*. London: HMSO.

82. Ibid.

83. Lawson, M., quoted in Sanderson, H. *et al.* (1997) *People, Plans and Possibilities*, p.30.

84. Alakeson, V. (2011) *Active Patient*, p.36.

85. Glover, J. (1988) *I: The Philosophy and Psychology of Personal Identity*. Oxford: Allen Lane, p.16.

86. Routledge, M. and Wilton, C. (2010) *Improving the Lives of Disabled and Older People Through Building Stronger Communities*. London: DoH, p.8.

87. Routledge, M. and Wilton, C. (2010) *Improving the Lives of Disabled and Older People Through Building Stronger Communities*.

88. Innovations in Dementia (2011) *The Views of People with Dementia and their Supporters*. Exeter: Innovations in Dementia. Available at www.dementia.dh.gov.uk/_library/dementia_capable_communities_report.pdf, accessed on 10 May 2011.

89. Miller C. with Wilton, C., Wood, A. and Janjua, A. (2011) *Putting the Local into Think Local, Act Personal: A Practical Checklist and Planning Tool to Support Community Contribution*. London: Think Local, Act Personal Partnership. Available at www. thinklocalactpersonal.org.uk/BCC, accessed on 28 June 2011.

90. Crowther, C., Mumford, B. and McFadzean, G. (2011) *Great Interactions: It Ain't What You Do…It's the Way That You Do It*. Milton Keynes: MacIntyre.

91. Think Local, Act Personal Partnership (2011) *Think Local, Act Personal*, p.5.

92. Smull, M. and Sanderson, H. (2005) *Essential Lifestyle Planning for Everyone*, p.64.

93. Innes, A., Macpherson, S. and McCabe, L. (2006) *Promoting Person-centred Care at the Front Line*. York: Joseph Rowntree Foundation, p.ix.

94. Winney, F. and Care UK (2011) *Ping!* Stockport: Helen Sanderson Associates. Available at www. helensandersonassociates.co.uk/blogs/care-uk.aspx, accessed on 11 May 2011.

95. Smull, M. and Sanderson, H. (2005) *Essential Lifestyle Planning for Everyone*.

96. Handy, C. (1994) *The Empty Raincoat: Making Sense of the Future*. London: Hutchinson.

97. Mount, B. (1987) *Personal Futures Planning: Finding Directions for Change*. Doctoral dissertation, University of Georgia.

98. O' Brien, J. (1987) 'A Guide to Lifestyle Planning.' In B. Wilcox and G.T. Bellamy (eds) *The Activities Catalog: An Alternative Curriculum for Youth and Adults with Severe Disabilities*. Baltimore, MD: Brookes Publishing.

99. Duffy, S. (2004) *Keys to Citizenship: A Guide to Getting Good Support Services for People with Learning Difficulties*. Birkenhead: Paradigm Consultancy and Development Agency Ltd.

100. Smull, M. and Sanderson, H. (2005) *Essential Lifestyle Planning*, p.21.

101. Ibid.

102. Department of Health (2010) *Capable Communities and Active Citizens*, p.8.

103. Think Local, Act Personal Partnership (2011) *Think Local, Act Personal*.

104. Langer, E.J. (2009) *Counter Clockwise: Mindful Health and the Power of Possibility*. New York: Ballantine Books.

105. Smull, M. in M. Smull, H. Sanderson with B. Allen (2005) *Person Centred Thinking: Resource Guide*. Annapolis, MD: The Learning Community for Essential Lifestyle Planning, p.36.

106. Think Local, Act Personal Partnership (2011) *Think Local, Act Personal*.

107. Department of Health (2010) *Capable Communities and Active Citizens*.

108. Bogg, D. (2010) *Mental Health and Personalisation: Themes and Issues in Recovery-Based Mental Health Care and Support*. Brighton: Pavilion Publishing, p.9.

109. Poll, C., Kennedy, J. and Sanderson, H. (2009) *In Community: Practical Lessons in Supporting Isolated People to be Part of Community*. Stockport: Helen Sanderson Associates Press and In Control Publications. Chapter 11.

110. Smull, M. and Sanderson, H. (2005) *Essential Lifestyle Planning*, p.64.

111. Handy, C. (1994) *The Age of Paradox*. Boston, MA: Harvard Business School Press, p.70.

112. Handy, C. (1995) *The Empty Raincoat: New Thinking for a New World*. London: Random House, p.73.

113. Smull, M. and Sanderson, H. (2005) *Essential Lifestyle Planning*, p.28.

114. Ibid., p.47.

115. Ibid., p.50.

116. Ibid., p.55.

117. Yates, J. (1980) *Programme Design Sessions*. Carver, MA: Jack Yates, p.29.

118. Lovett, H. (1996) *Learning to Listen: Positive Approaches and People with Difficult Behaviour*. Baltimore, MD: Paul H. Brookes Publishing Co.

119. Ibid., p.43.

120. O'Brien, J., Pearpoint, J. and Kahn, L. (2010) *The PATH and MAPS Handbook: Person-Centered Ways to Build Community.* Toronto: Inclusion Press, p.102.

121. Department of Health (2010) *Personalisation Through Person-Centred Planning,* p.17.

122. Bailey, G., Sanderson, H., Sweeney, C. and Heaney, B. (2009) *Person Centred Reviews in Adult Services.* Stockport: Helen Sanderson Associates Press.

123. Department of Health and Bennet, T., Cattermole, M. and Sanderson, H. (2009) *Outcome Focused Reviews: A Practical Guide.* London: DoH.

124. George, A., Lepkowsky, M., Calderaro-Mendoza, T., Seaver, B. *et al.* (2010) *Person Centred Reviews: What Are We Learning?* Stockport: Helen Sanderson Associates Press, p.3.

125. Sanderson, H. and Mathieson, R. (2003) *From a Person Centred Review to a Person Centred Plan.* Stockport: Helen Sanderson Associates Press.

126. George, A. *et al.* (2010) *Person Centred Reviews.*

127. Wertheimer, A. (2007) *Person Centred Transition Reviews: A National Programme for Developing Person Centred Approaches to Transition Planning for Young People with Special Educational Needs.* London: Valuing People Support Team.

128. Bailey, G. *et al.* (2009) *Person Centred Reviews in Adult Services.*

129. Department of Health (2010) *Personalisation through Person-Centred Planning.*

130. Bailey, G. *et al.* (2009) *Person Centred Reviews in Adult Services.*

131. Valios, N. (2011) 'The personal touch.' *Mental Health Today,* January, p.35.

132. Ibid, p.35.

133. Ibid, p.35.

134. Department of Health (2010) *Personalisation Through Person-Centred Planning.*

135. Valios, N. (2011) *'The personal touch.'*

136. Ibid.

137. Personal correspondence with Helen Sanderson, May 2011.

138. Department of Health (2011) *No Health without Mental Health: A Cross Government Mental Health Outcomes Strategy for People of All Ages.* London: DoH.

139. Department of Health (2008) *Refocusing the Care Programme Approach: Policy and Positive Practice Guidance.* London: DoH.

140. Ritchie, P. (2002) 'A Turn for the Better.' In J. O'Brien and C. Lyle O'Brien (eds) *Implementing Person-Centred Planning,* p.11.

141. Department of Health (2010) *Personalisation Through Person-Centred Planning.*

142. Department of Health (2009) *Valuing People Now: A New Three-year Strategy for People with Learning Disabilities.* London: DoH.

143. Personal communication with Michael Smull. 17 May 2011.

144. The person-centred thinking tools 'presence to contribution' and 'community mapping', described in Part II, are examples of community connecting tools.

145. O'Brien, J., Pearpoint, J. and Khan, L. (2010) *The PATH & MAPS Handbook: Person-Centred Ways to Build Community.* Toronto: Inclusion Press.

146. New Economics Foundation (2010) *Ten Big Questions about the Big Society.* London: nef, p.2.

147. O'Brien, J. *et al.* (2010) *The PATH & MAPS Handbook,* p.20.

148. O'Brien, J. and Lyle O'Brien, C. (2006) *Implementing Person-Centred Planning,* p.11.

149. O'Brien, J. and Lyle O'Brien, C. (1988) *A Little Book of Person-Centred Planning.* Toronto: Inclusion Press, pp.8–9.

150. O'Brien, J., Forest, M. and Pearpoint, J. (1995) *PATH: A Workbook for Planning Positive Possible Futures* (2nd Edition). Toronto: Inclusion Press.

151. Ritchie, P. (2002) 'A Turn for the Better.' In J. O'Brien and C. Lyle O'Brien (eds) *Implementing Person-Centred Planning,* p.11.

152. Ibid.

153. O'Brien, J. *et al.* (1995) PATH.

154. Individual Budgets Evaluation Network (2008) *Individual Budgets Pilot Evaluation: Summary Report.* York: Social Policy Research Unit (SPRU), University of York. Available at http://php.york.ac.uk/inst/spru/research/summs/ibsen.php, accessed on 28 September 2011, p.49.

155. Bennet, T., Cattermole, M. and Sanderson, H. (2009) *Outcome-Focused Reviews: A Practical Guide.* London: DoH.

156. O'Brien, J. and Lyle O'Brien, C. (1988) *A Little Book of Person-Centred Planning,* p.8.

157. Ibid., p.37.

158. Department of Health (2010) *Capable Communities and Active Citizens,* p.9.

159. Department of Health (2010) *Capable Communities and Active Citizens.*

160. Aked, J., Marks, N., Cordon, C. and Thompson S. (2008) *Five Ways to Wellbeing Centre for Well-being.* London: The New Economics Foundation. Available at www.neweconomics.org/projects/five-ways-well-being, accessed on 19 May 2011.

161. Ibid.

162. Ibid.

163. Ibid.

164. Department of Health (2009) *Supporting People with Long Term Conditions: Commissioning Personalised Care Planning – A Guide for Commissioners.* London: DoH, p.4.

165. Department of Health (2011) *What Motivates People to Self Care: Improving Care for People with Long Term Conditions.* London: DoH, p.2.

166. Department of Health, Diabetes UK, NHS Diabetes and The Health Foundation (2011) *The Year of Care Partnership.* Available at www.diabetes.org.uk/Guide-to-diabetes/Support_for_managing_your_diabetes/Year-of-care, accessed on 19 May 2011.

167. Harvey, J. (2010) *Key Elements of Personalised Care Planning in Long Term Conditions and Personal Health Budgets.* Stockport: Helen Sanderson Associates. Written by Jo Harvey of Helen Sanderson Associates with the Department of Health's Personal Health Budgets Pilot programme.

168. Expert Patients Programme (2011) *Healthy Lives Equal Healthy Communities – The Social Impact of Self-Management.* London: Community Interest Company.

169. Harvey, J. (2010) *Key Elements of Personalised Care Planning.*

170. Morley, A., Redburn, D., Jennison, W., Mascall, J. *et al.* (2010) *Using Person-Centred Thinking to Implement Dementia Care Mapping.* Stockport: Helen Sanderson Associates.

171. DCM was developed by Professor Tom Kitwood and the Bradford Dementia Group at the University of Bradford (1992). Available at www.brad.ac.uk/health/dementia, accessed on 19 May 2011.

172. Coyle, D. (2009) Personal communication.

173. Buchanan-Barker, P. and Barker, P. J. (2008) 'The tidal commitments: extending the value base of mental health recovery.' *Journal of Psychiatric and Mental Health Nursing* 15, 2, 93–100.

174. Ibid.

175. Department of Health (2009) *New Horizons: Towards a Shared Vision for Mental Health Consultation.* London: DoH, p.24.

176. Buchanan-Barker, P. and Barker, P. J. (2008) 'The tidal commitments'.

177. Ibid., p.98.

178. Barker, P. and Buchanan-Barker, P.J. (2005) *The Tidal Model: A Guide for Mental Health Professionals.* London/New York: Routledge.

179. Buchanan-Barker, P. and Barker, P.J. (2008) 'The tidal commitments'.

180. Barker, P. and Buchanan-Barker, P.J. (2005) *The Tidal Model,* p.95.

181. Buchanan-Barker, P. and Barker, P.J. (2008) 'The tidal commitments', p.86.

182. Leadbeater, C. and Lownsbrough, H. (2005) *Personalisation and Participation: The Future of Social Care in Scotland.* Commissioned by Care 21 for the Social Work Review. London: Demos, p.4.

183. Copeland, M.E. (1997) *Wellness Recovery Action Plan.* Dummerston, VT: Peach Press.

184. MacKeith, J. and Burns, S. (2009) *Mental Health Recovery Star.* London: Mental Health Providers Forum.

185. Copeland, M.E. (1997) *Wellness Recovery Action Plan.*

186. See Fiona's example of a 'stay well plan' earlier in the chapter.

187. Department of Health (2011) *No Health without Mental Health.*

188. MacKeith, J. and Burns, S. (2009) *Mental Health Recovery Star.*

189. National Development Team for Inclusion (2008) *Inclusion Web.* Available at www.ndti.org.uk/what-we-do/community-inclusion/the-inclusion-web, accessed on 19 May 2011.

190. Pitts, J., Sanderson, H., Webster, A. and Skelhorn, L. (2011) *A New Reablement Journey.* Stockport: Helen Sanderson Associates.

191. Ibid.

192. Ibid.

193. Bowers, H., Clark, A., Crosby, G., Easterbrook, L. *et al.* (2009) *Older People's Vision for Long Term Care.* Available at www.jrf.org.uk/sites/files/jrf/older-people-vision-for-care-summary.pdf, accessed on 19 May 11, p.34.

194. Fox, A. (2009) *Putting People First Without Putting Carers Second.* Woodford Green: Princess Royal Trust for Carers.

195. Department of Health (2010) *Carers and Personalisation: Improving Outcomes.* London: DoH.

196. Ibid, p.7.

197. Fox, A. (2009) *Putting People First Without Putting Carers Second,* p.1.

198. Stokes, G. (2010) *And Still the Music Plays: Stories of People with Dementia.* London: Hawker Publications Ltd.

199. Brooker, D. (2006) *Person-Centred Dementia Care – Making Services Better.* London: Jessica Kingsley Publishers.

200. You can read about how Sue used the matching tool to find the best staff member to support Sam at Crown Green Bowling in Part II.

201. Lancashire and South Cumbria Cancer Network (2004) *Preferred Priorities for Care.* Available at www.endoflifecareforadults.nhs.uk/assets/downloads/PPC_document_v22_rev_20111.pdf, accessed on 19 May 2011.

202. National Gold Standards Framework Centre (2011) Available at www.goldstandardsframework.org.uk/About_GSF, accessed on 19 May 2011.

203. Helen Sanderson Associates (2010) *Living Well: Thinking and Planning for the End of Your Life*. Stockport: Helen Sanderson Associates Press.

204. Personal correspondence with John O'Brien, 12 April 2011.

205. Elisabeth, K. (2009) *Community Care Blog: The Progress Report. Risk Averse Agencies are the Enemy of Personalisation*. Available at www.communitycare.co.uk/blogs/progress-on-personalisation/2009/10/riskaverse-agencies-are-the-enemy-of-personalisation.html, accessed on 19 May 2011.

206. Neill, M., Allen, J., Woodhead, N., Reid, S., Irwin, L. and Sanderson, H. (2008) 'A positive approach to risk requires person-centred thinking.' *The Tizard Learning Disability Review 14*, 4, 16–23. Hove: Pier Professional.

207. Glendinning, C., Challis, D., Fernandez, J., Jacobs, S. *et al.* (2008) *Evaluation of the Individual Budgets Pilot Programme*. York: Individual Budgets Evaluation Network, Social Policy Research Unit (SPRU), University of York. Available at www.dh.gov.uk/prod_consum_dh/groups/dh_digitalassets/@dh/@en/documents/digitalasset/dh_089506.pdf, accessed on 19 May 2011.

208. Douglas, M. (1992) *Risk and Blame: Essays in Cultural Theory*. London: Routledge.

209. Donnelly, L., Howie, M. and Leach, B. (2010) 'Councils pay for prostitutes for the disabled.' *Daily Telegraph*, 14 August. Available at www.telegraph.co.uk/health/7945785/Councils-pay-for-prostitutes-for-thedisabled. html, accessed on 19 May 2011.

210. Elisabeth, K. (2009) *Community Care Blog*.

211. Power, M. (2004) *The Risk Management of Everything*. London: Demos, p.36.

212. Ibid.

213. Department of Health (2000) *No Secrets: Guidance on Developing and Implementing Multi-Agency Policies and Procedures to Protect Vulnerable Adults from Abuse*. London: DoH.

214. Bates, P. and Silberman, W. (2007) *Modelling Risk Management in Inclusive Settings*. London: National Development Team. Available at www.ndt.org.uk/docsN/ET_SIrisk.pdf, accessed on 19 May 2011. [Site no longer available]

215. Department of Health (2007) *Independence, Choice and Risk: A Guide to Best Practice in Supported Decision Making*. London: DoH.

216. Department of Health (2009) *Report on the Consultation: The Review of No Secrets, Guidance*. London: DoH.

217. Parton, N. (2001) 'Risk and Professional Judgement.' In L.-A. Cull and J. Roche (eds) *The Law and Social Work*. Buckingham: Open University Press.

218. Health and Safety Executive (2006) *Principles of Sensible Risk Management*. Available at www.hse.gov.uk/risk/principlespoints.htm, accessed on 19 May 2011.

219. Ibid., p.2.

220. Better Regulation Commission (2006) *Risk, Responsibility and Regulation – Whose Risk is it Anyway?* Available at www.irr-network.org/document/633/Better_Regulation_Commission_(2006a)_Risk-_Responsibility_and_Regulation_-_Whose_risk_is_it_anyway.html, accessed on 19 May 2011.

221. Bates, P. and Silberman, W. (2007) *Modelling Risk Management in Inclusive Settings*.

222. Department of Health (2009) *Safeguarding Adults Report on the Consultation on the Review of 'No Secrets'*, p.5.

223. Neill, M. *et al.* (2008) *A Positive Approach to Risk*.

224. Ibid., p.311.

225. Department of Health (2009) *Safeguarding Adults Report on the Consultation on the Review of 'No Secrets'*, p.16.

226. Neill, M., Allen, J., Woodhead, N., Reid, S., Irwin, L. and Sanderson, H. (2008) 'A positive approach to risk requires person-centred thinking.' *The Tizard Learning Disability Review 14*, 4, 16–23. Hove: Pier Professional.

227. Bates, P. and Silberman, W. (2007) *Modelling Risk Management in Inclusive Settings*.

228. Ibid., p.7.

229. Neill, M. *et al.* (2008) *A Positive Approach to Risk*.

230. Ibid., p.8.

231. Ibid., p.8.

232. Ibid., p.8.

233. Department of Health (2007) *Independence, Choice and Risk*, p.4.

234. Social Care Institute for Excellence (2010) *Personalisation for Older People: Living at Home*. SCIE TV. Available at www.scie.org.uk/socialcaretv/video-player.asp?guid=957c57f1-8e4a-4651-a9c1-8efe43c3c514, accessed on 10 May 2011.

235. Department of Health (2010) *Capable Communities and Active Citizens*.

236. Robertson, J. *et al.* (2005) *The Impact of Person Centred Planning*.

237. Routledge, M. and Wilton, C. (2010) *Improving the Lives of Disabled and Older People Through Building Stronger Communities*.

238. Online discussion by G. Bailey. 2 April 2011. Available at www.facebook.com/#!/permalink.php?story-fbid=10150153504408815&id=749413763.

239. Neill, M. (2011) Blog entry comment. 4 April. Available at www.helensandersonassociates.co.uk/blogs/helen/2011/4/1/is-person-centred-planning-a-luxury-we-can't-afford.aspx#comments.

About the Authors

Helen Sanderson was the Department of Health's expert adviser on person-centred approaches to the 'Valuing People' Support Team and 'Putting People First' Team. She co-authored the first Department of Health guidance on person-centred planning, and the 2010 guidance *Personalisation Through Person-Centred Planning*. Helen has worked in health, as an occupational therapist, and then in social care, for over 25 years.

Helen is the primary author of *People, Plans and Possibilities: Exploring Person Centred Planning* (1997), the first book on person-centred planning in the UK, which emerged from three years' research. Her PhD was on person-centred planning and organisational change. Helen has written extensively on person-centred thinking, planning, support planning and community building.

Helen leads Helen Sanderson Associates (HSA), an award-winning international development agency passionate about how person-centred thinking and planning can create person-centred change and contribute to changing people's lives, organisations and communities. She is vice chair of the Learning Community for Person-Centred Practices.

Helen lives in Heaton Moor, with Andy and her three daughters, Ellie, Laura and Kate, together with a dog, cats and hens. She is trying to spend more time doing yoga, and is learning mindfulness.

Jaimee Lewis was the Department of Health's strategic communications adviser for its Individual Budgets Pilot programme between 2006–08 and then later for the 'Putting people first' programme until March 2011. She was a contributing writer to the *Think Local, Act Personal* sector-wide agreement, launched in November 2010, and which is now supported by over 30 leading health and social care organisations pushing ahead on personalisation with community-based support. She leads on communications for the Think Local, Act Personal Partnership.

Born in Australia, Jaimee moved to England in 2004 and lives in London, with her husband Damian. They share a passion for travel, which they try to squeeze in between regular visits to their families in Manchester and Brisbane.

Index